HOW TO DRAW MANGA

volume 4

DRESSING YOUR CHARACTERS IN CASUAL WEAR

HOW TO DRAW MANGA Volume 4:
Dressing Your Characters in Casual Wear
by The Society for the Study of Manga Techniques

Copyright © 2000 The Society for The Study of Manga Techniques
Copyright © 2000 Graphic-sha Publishing Co., Ltd.

First published in 2000 by Graphic-sha Publishing Co., Ltd.
This English edition was published in 2001 by
Graphic-sha Publishing Co., Ltd.
1-9-12 Kudan-kita, Chiyoda-ku, Tokyo 102-0073 Japan

Cover Art: Tatsuhiro Ozaki
Original Cover Design: Hideyuki Amemura
Photography: Yasuo Imai
Japanese edition Editor: Morofumi Nakanishi (Graphic-sha Publishing Co., Ltd.)
English edition cover and text layout: Shinichi Ishioka
English translation: Christian Storms
English translation management: Língua fránca, Inc. (an3y-skmt@asahi-net.or.jp)
Foreign language edition project coordinator: Kumiko Sakamoto (Graphic-sha Publishing Co., Ltd.)

All rights reserved. No part of this publication may be reproduced,
stored in a retrieval system, or transmitted in any form or by any means,
electronic, mechanical, photocopying, recording, or otherwise,
without the prior written permission of the publisher.

Distributor:
Japan Publications Trading Co., Ltd.
1-2-1 Sarugaku-cho, Chiyoda-ku, Tokyo, 101-0064
Telephone: 03-3292-3751 Fax: 03-3292-0410
E-mail: jpt@jptco.co.jp
URL: http://www.jptco.co.jp/

First printing: May 2001
Second printing: June 2001
Third printing: November 2001

ISBN: 4-88996-046-5
Printed and bound in China by Everbest Printing Co., Ltd.

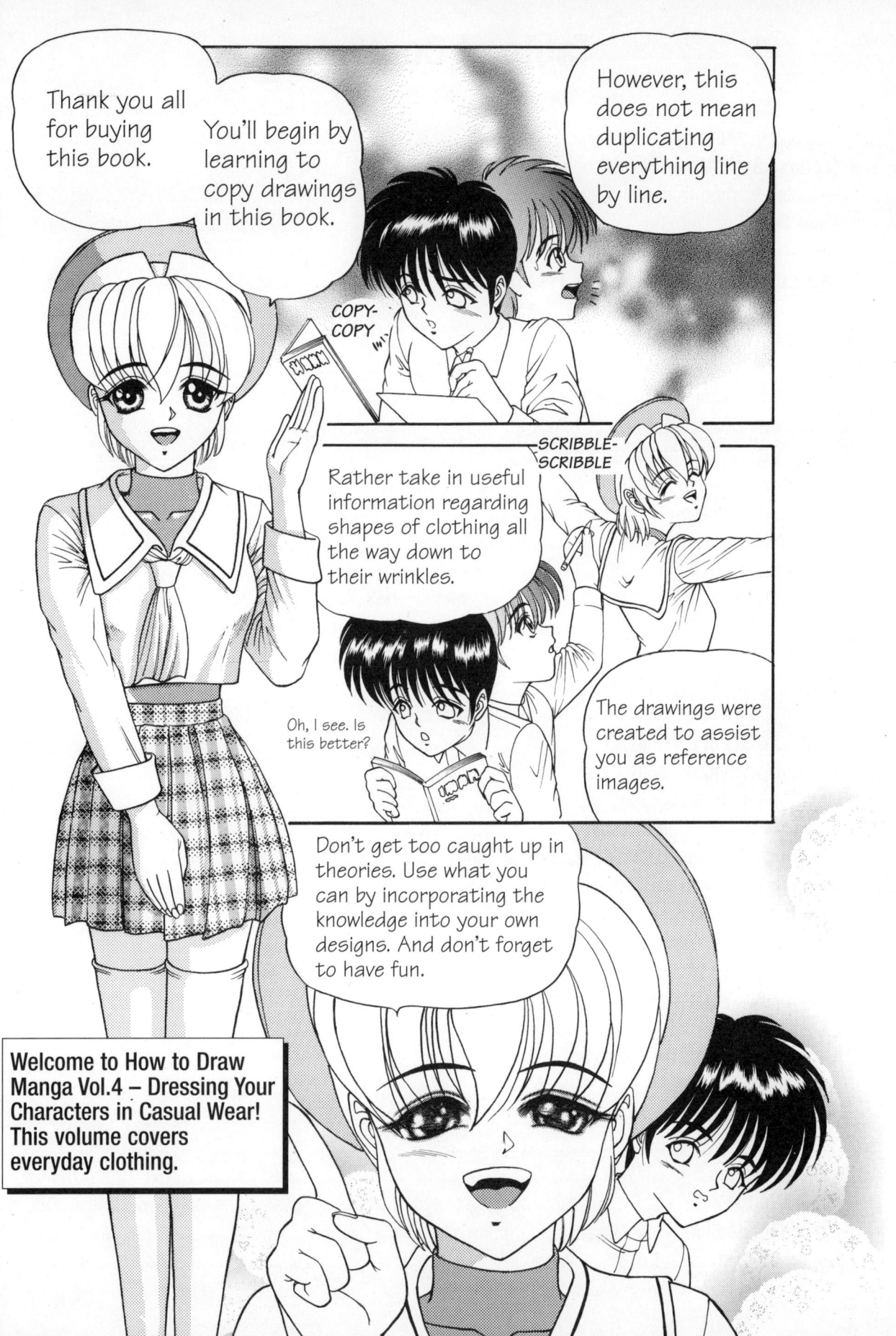

Table of Contents

1. Giving Shape to Characters 6
2. Visualizing Wrinkles 7
3. Creating Basic Three-Dimensionality 8
4. Wrinkles Formed from Gravity 9
5. Lines Found in Clothing 10

Chapter 1 – Underwear and T-shirts 11
Male Underwear – Undershirts 12
Male Underwear – Underpants 14
Female Underwear – Bras 16
Female Underwear – Underpants 19
Quarter Cup Bras (Pattern A) 20
Quarter Cup Bras (Pattern B) 21
More Quarter Cup Bras (Pattern B) 22
Semi-bikini Underpants 23
Bikini Underpants 24
Quarter Cup Bras (Pattern A) with Bikini Underpants – Low Angle 25
Quarter Cup Bras (Pattern A) with Bikini Underpants – High Angle 26
More Quarter Cup Bras (Pattern B) with Semi-bikini Underpants – Low Angle 28
More Quarter Cup Bras (Pattern B) with Semi-bikini Underpants – High Angle 29
Sportswear Undergarments 30
Lingerie 31
Standing Wearing a T-shirt 39
Standing Wearing a T-shirt – Low Angle 40
Sitting on the Knees Wearing a T-shirt 41
Sitting at Ease Wearing a T-shirt 42
Sitting with the Legs Extended Wearing a T-shirt 44
Sitting Cross-legged Wearing a T-shirt 46
Standing on One Knee Wearing a T-shirt – Part 1 47
Standing on One Knee Wearing a T-shirt – Part 2 48
Sitting in a Chair Wearing a T-shirt 49
Crossing the Legs Wearing a T-shirt 50

Chapter 2 – Tops and Skirts 51
Sweatshirts and Skirts 52
Crewnecks 54
Crewnecks – High Angle 55
Folding the Arms 56
Bending to the Side 58
Bending to the Side – High Angle 61
Turning the Body 62

Turning the Body – High Angle 63
Picking Something Up – Part 1 64
Picking Something Up – Part 2 65
Picking Something Up – Part 3 66
Picking Something Up – Part 4 67
Bending Back 68
Bending Back – High Angle 69
Sitting on the Knees 70
Sitting at Ease 71
Sitting with the Legs Extended 73
Sitting with the Legs Bent 74
Standing on One Knee 75
Putting On and Taking Off Sweatshirts – Front Angle 77
Putting On and Taking Off Sweatshirts – Side Angle 79
Putting On and Taking Off Sweatshirts – Rear Angle 81
Sitting in a Chair 83
Crossing the Legs 84
Standing on All Fours 86

Chapter 3 – Jackets and Jeans 87
Jackets 88
Quality and Feel 94
Jeans 96
Standing – Zipped 98
Standing – Zipped, Low Angle 100
One Arm Raised – Zipped, Slight Side Angle 102
One Arm Raised to the Side – Zipped, Front Angle 104
One Arm Raised to the Side – Unzipped, Rear Angle 106
One Arm Raised to the Side – Unzipped, Right Side Front Angle 108
Both Arms Raised – Unzipped 110
Turning the Body – Zipped 112
Turning the Body – Zipped, Low Angle 114
Bending to the Side – Zipped 116
Bending Back – Zipped 118
Sitting in a Chair 120
Legs Crossed 121
Sitting Cross-legged 122
Falling on One's Buttocks 123
Looking Back on All Fours – Unzipped 124
Putting On and Taking Off Jackets – Part 1 126
Putting On and Taking Off Jackets – Part 2 128

1 Giving Shape to Characters

When drawing clothing, roughly sketch the character's entire body. Give shape to the character and adjust the balance of the drawing.

Picture the shape as your character naked. Think of drawing clothing as dressing your character.

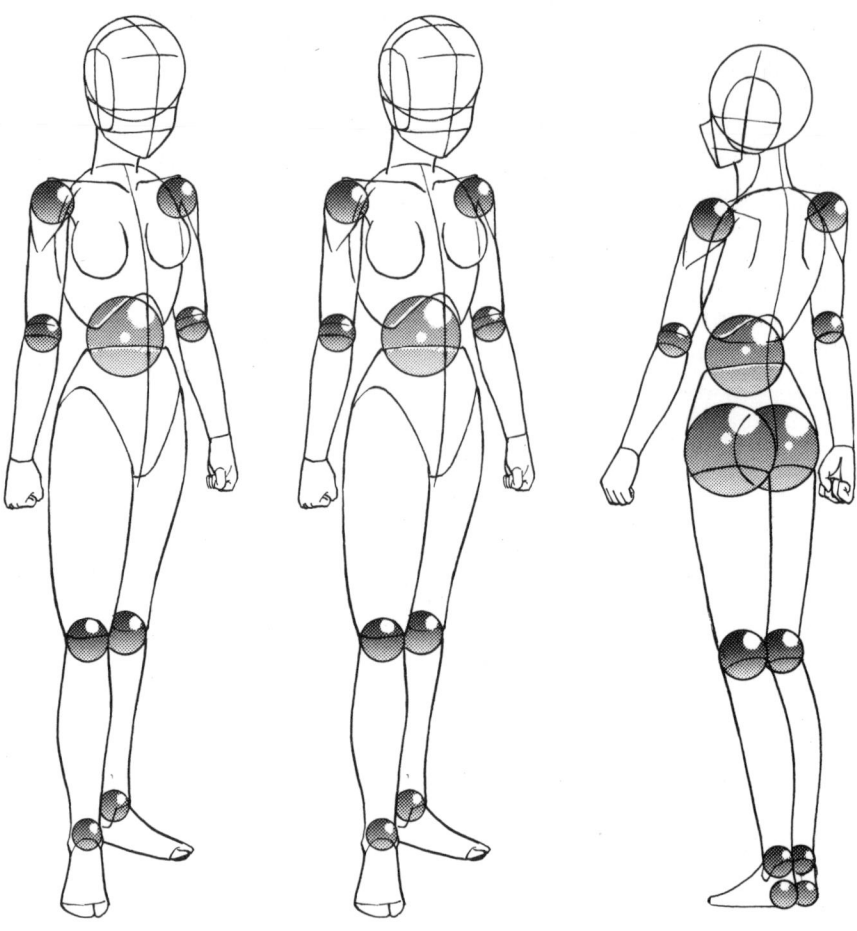

These drawings represent the shape of the characters. Visualize the joint areas as spheres in your mind when drawing.

Draw the clothing on top of the shape as if you were dressing the character. At this point, take into consideration the size of the clothing.

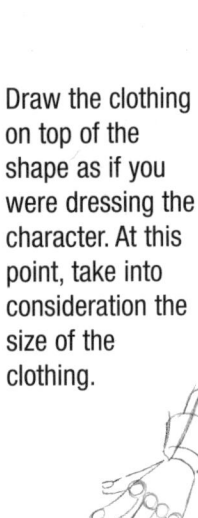

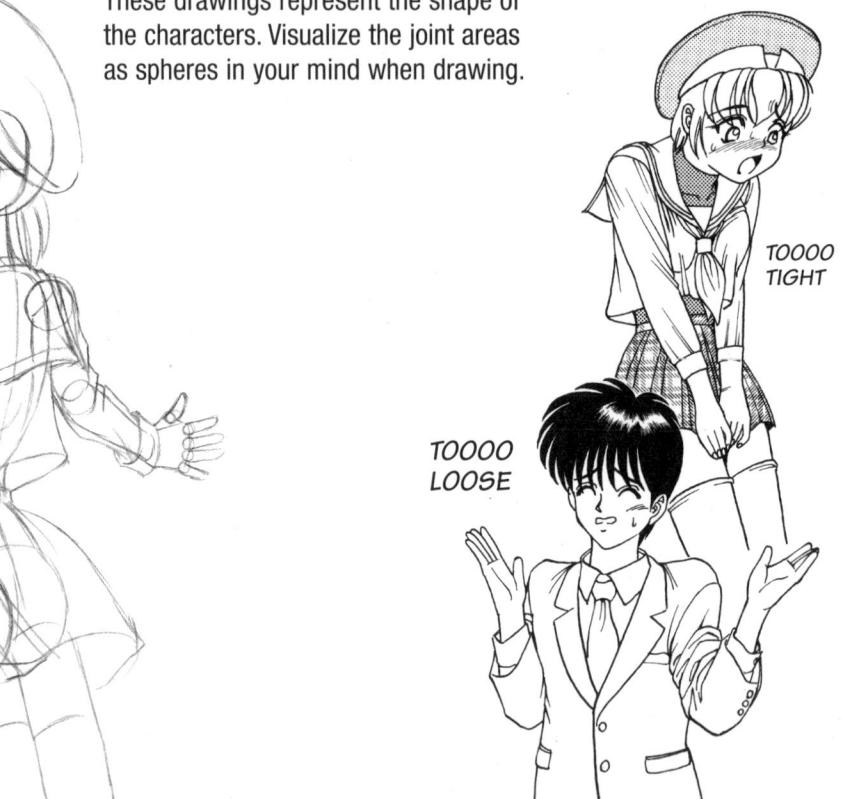

TOOOO TIGHT

TOOOO LOOSE

2 | Visualizing Wrinkles

Wrinkles always come with clothing. So, where do wrinkles form anyway? View wrinkles as a basic means to express three-dimensionality.

The basic theory involves drawing curved lines for uneven parts of material depending on the expansion and contraction of the clothing in places where the body bends. Most wrinkles tend to appear in these places.

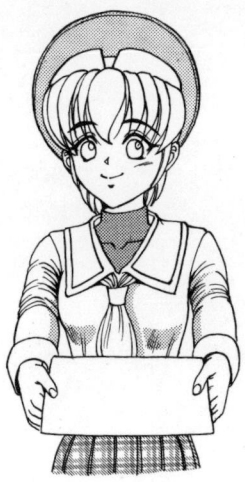

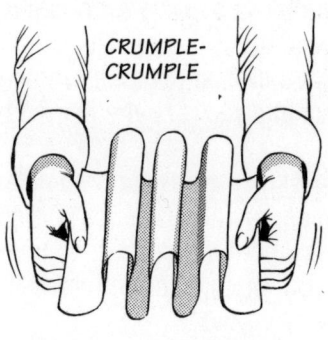

From a drawing standpoint, wrinkles can be defined as uneven areas formed from expansion and contraction.

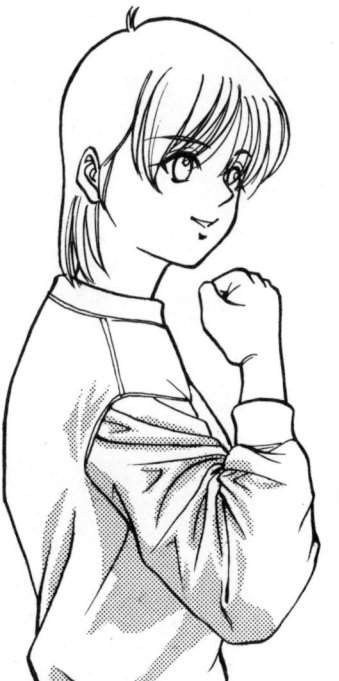

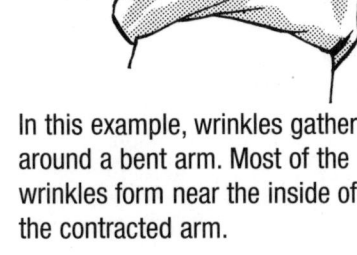

In this example, wrinkles gather around a bent arm. Most of the wrinkles form near the inside of the contracted arm.

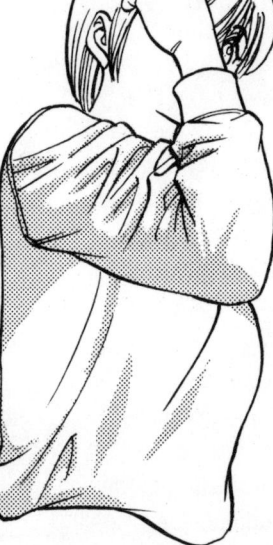

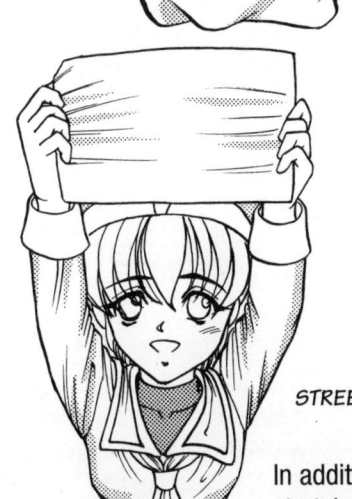

STREEETCH

In addition, when material is stretched as illustrated, small wrinkles are formed.

3 Creating Basic Three-Dimensionality

Attaching a tone to the side of a box is the basic method for bringing out three-dimensionality. The same method can be used for wrinkles by attaching a tone to the bulged parts.

However, wrinkles form complex shapes for various reasons. Don't worry about the details too much. Fill your head with the basics and draw from there.

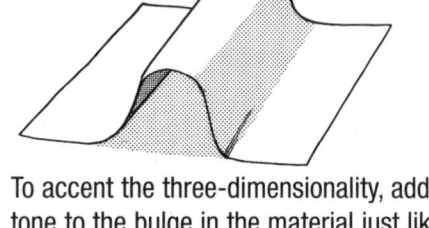

To accent the three-dimensionality, add a tone to the bulge in the material just like with the side of the box.

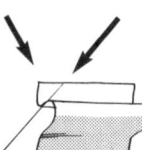

Light source

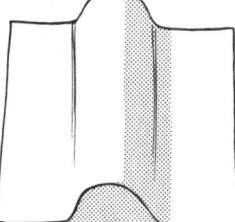

Eye-level (horizon line)

The shape of the bulges varies depending on the angle in which they are viewed. Consider the angle and the direction of the light source when attaching tones to the shaded areas of the material.

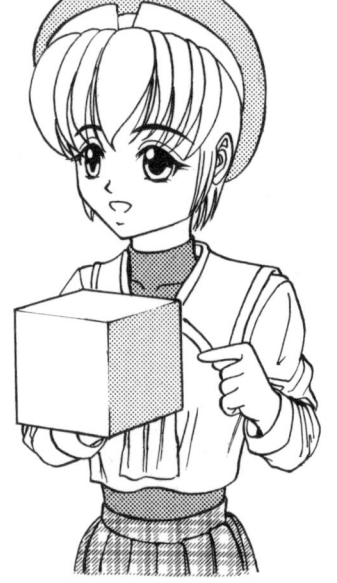

Attach a tone to the side of box to accent the three-dimensionality.

A big part of drawing is visualizing the image in your mind. The same logic can be applied to drawing wrinkles. While there is no better way to hone your imaginative skills then practice, possessing an understanding of the fundamentals and taking these into consideration when drawing is the fastest way to improve your skills.

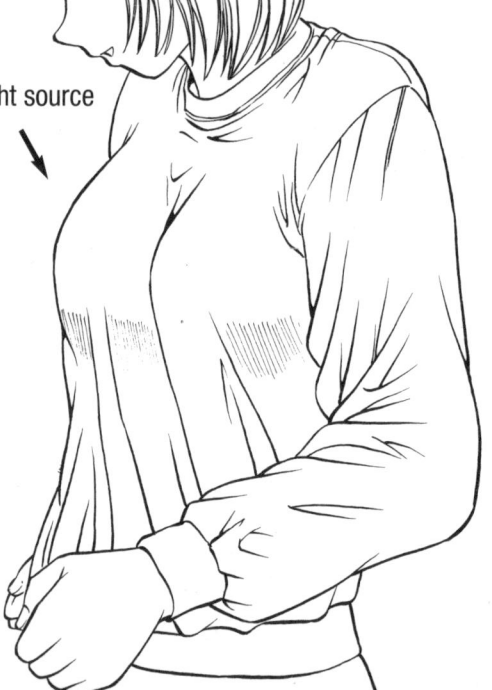

Light source

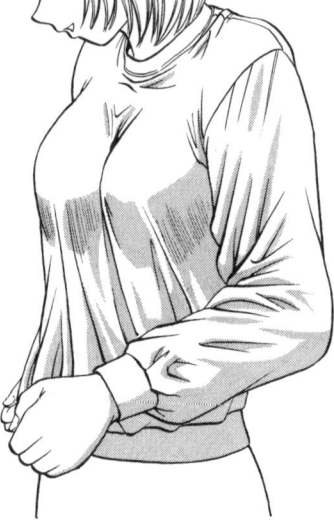

First, consider the light source and imagine where the bulges in the wrinkles will appear. Then, attach tones to accent the three-dimensionality.

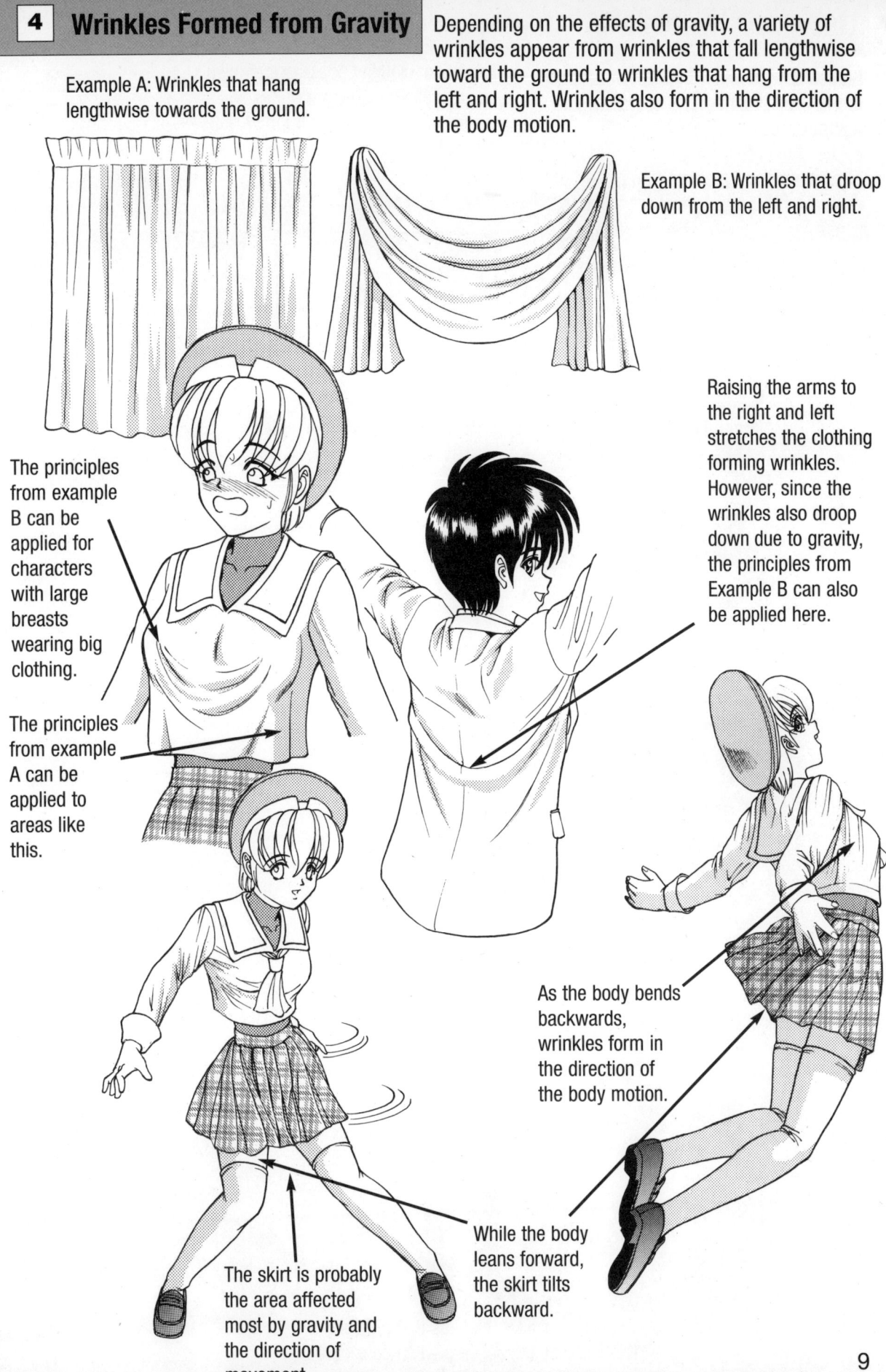

4 Wrinkles Formed from Gravity

Depending on the effects of gravity, a variety of wrinkles appear from wrinkles that fall lengthwise toward the ground to wrinkles that hang from the left and right. Wrinkles also form in the direction of the body motion.

Example A: Wrinkles that hang lengthwise towards the ground.

Example B: Wrinkles that droop down from the left and right.

The principles from example B can be applied for characters with large breasts wearing big clothing.

The principles from example A can be applied to areas like this.

Raising the arms to the right and left stretches the clothing forming wrinkles. However, since the wrinkles also droop down due to gravity, the principles from Example B can also be applied here.

As the body bends backwards, wrinkles form in the direction of the body motion.

While the body leans forward, the skirt tilts backward.

The skirt is probably the area affected most by gravity and the direction of movement.

5 | Lines Found in Clothing

Skilled artists place high emphasis on the overall balance of the drawing as a silhouette.

The same principle can be applied to drawing the bodies of your character.

Clothing Silhouettes

All forms of clothing possess their own unique lines. Being aware of this and visualizing them can help improve your design skills.

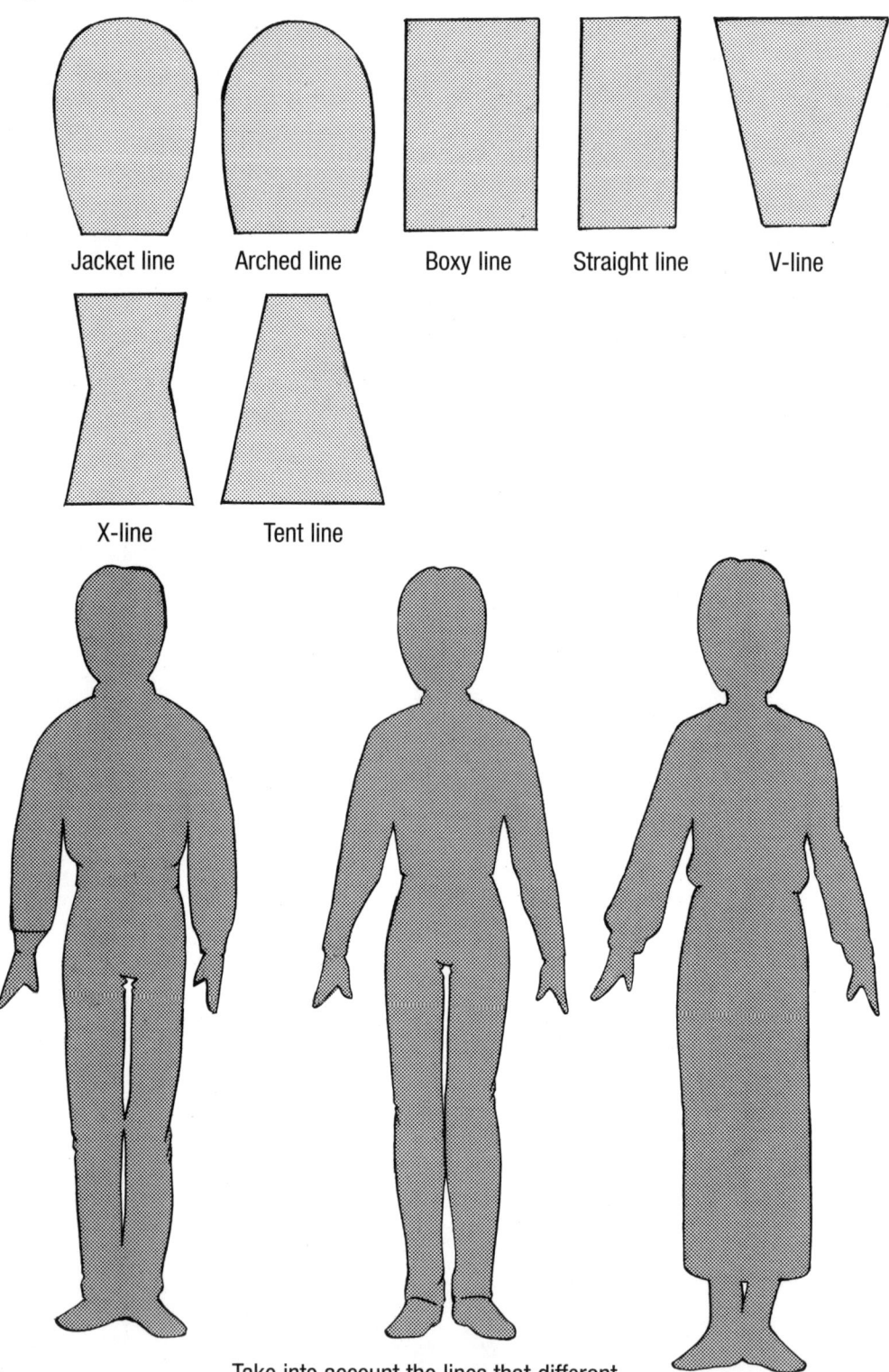

Jacket line Arched line Boxy line Straight line V-line

X-line Tent line

Take into account the lines that different types of clothing possess when considering the overall balance of the character.

Chapter 1
Underwear and T-shirts

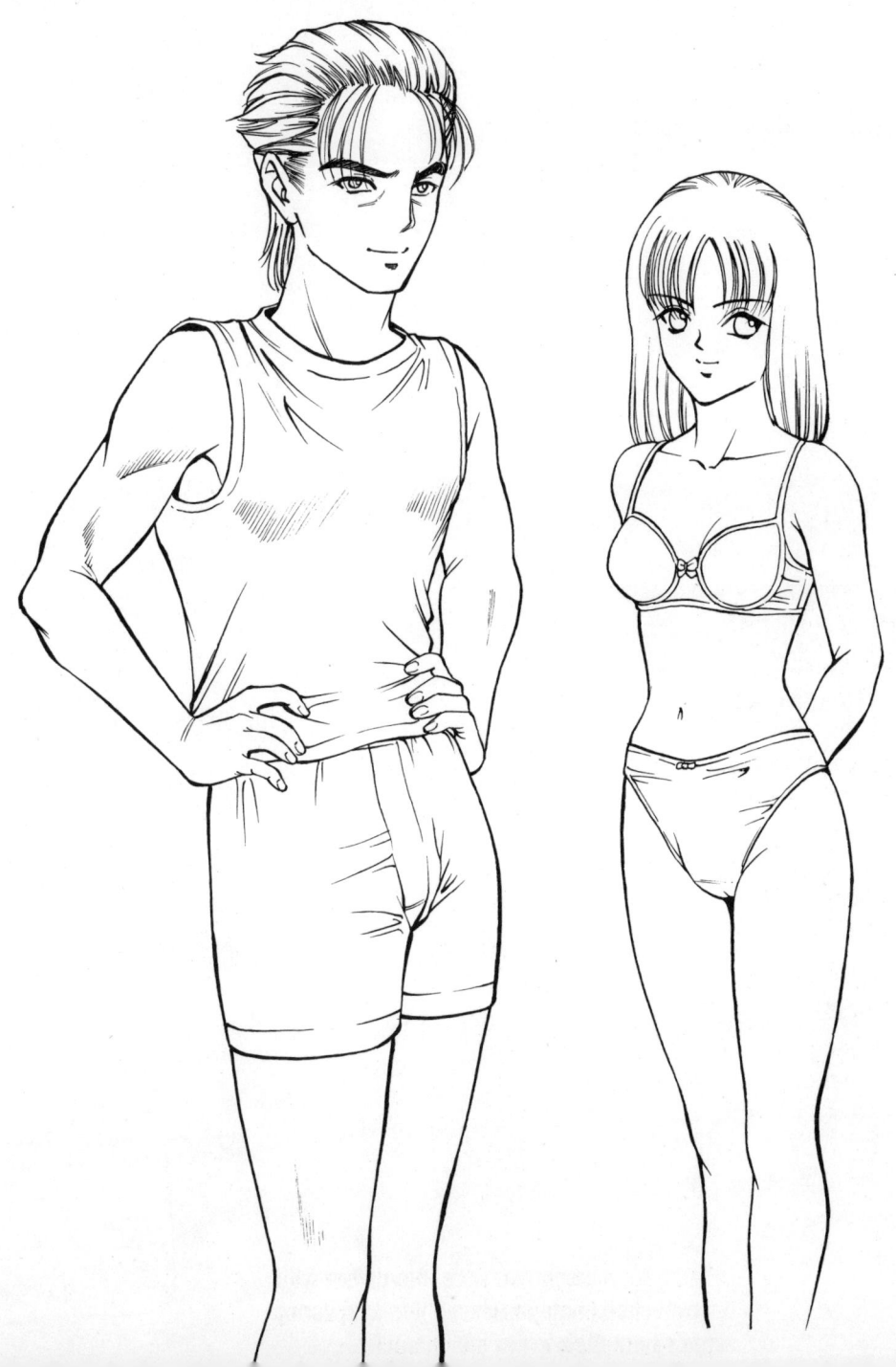

Underwear

Underwear is something that is generally not shown to other people. Since you simply can't go around asking the opposite sex to show you their underwear, this section has been designed for your learning.

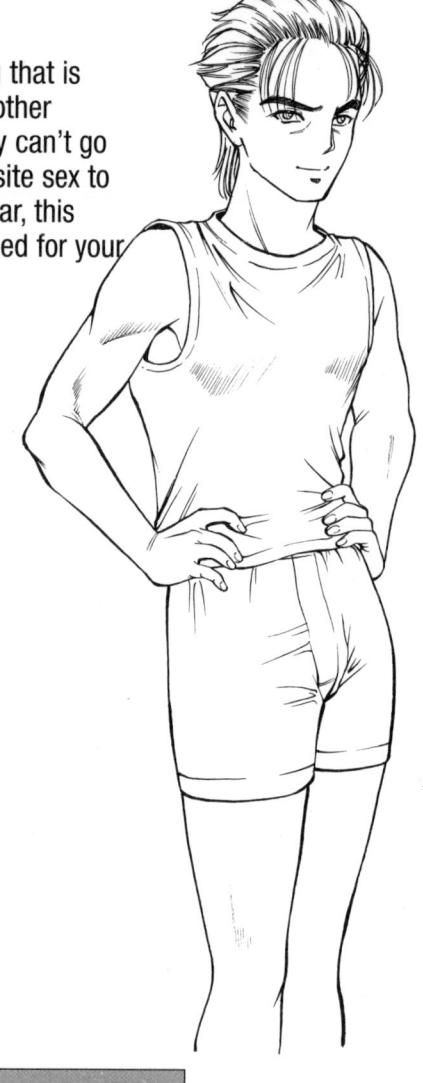
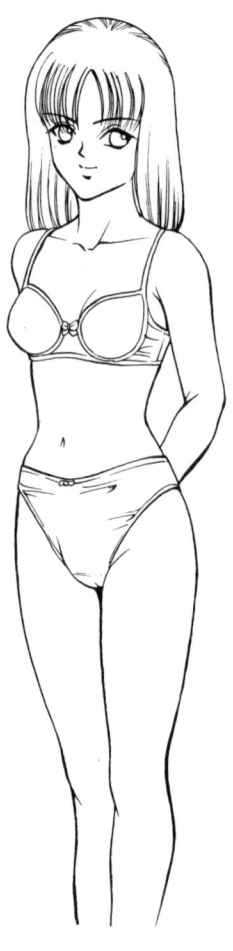

Male Underwear - Undershirts

Undershirts are male underwear designed to cover the upper body with the most basic type being the T-shirt. Other general types include: running shirts, non-sleeved shirts and surfer shirts. The three basic necklines are illustrated here.

T-shirts

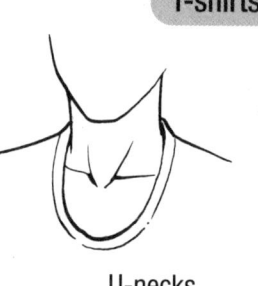

U-necks

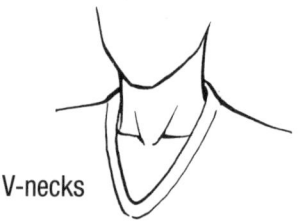

V-necks

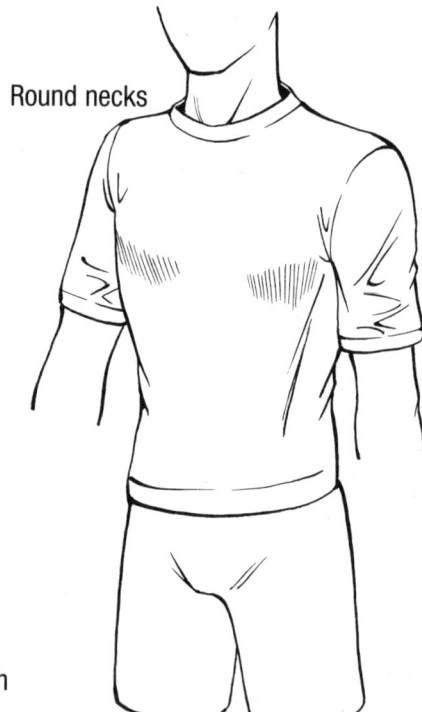

Round necks

U-neck and V-neck types are often worn with open-necked shirts or when shirts are worn slightly unbuttoned.

Non-sleeved Shirts

As the name suggests, this shirt has no sleeves. These are usually worn in the summer. Unlike the running shirt, the lines of these shirts don't show up.

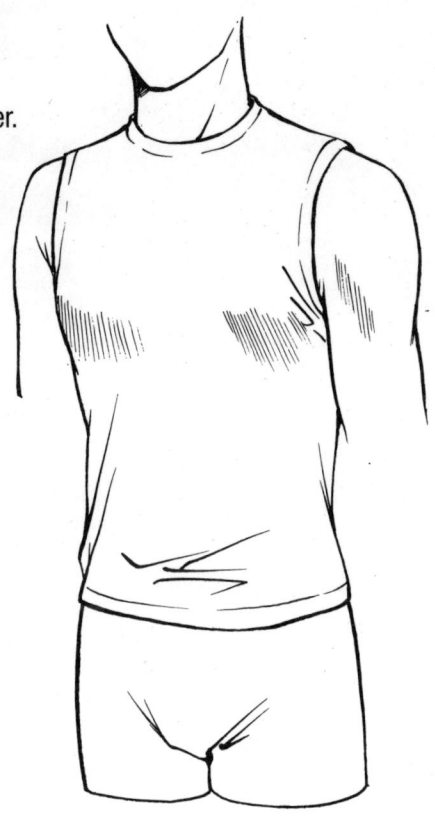

Running Shirts

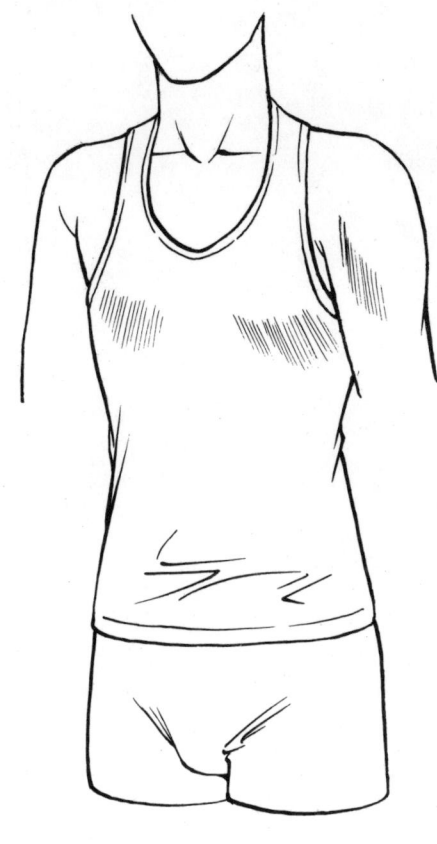

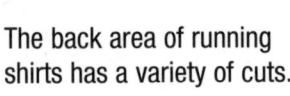

The back area of running shirts has a variety of cuts.

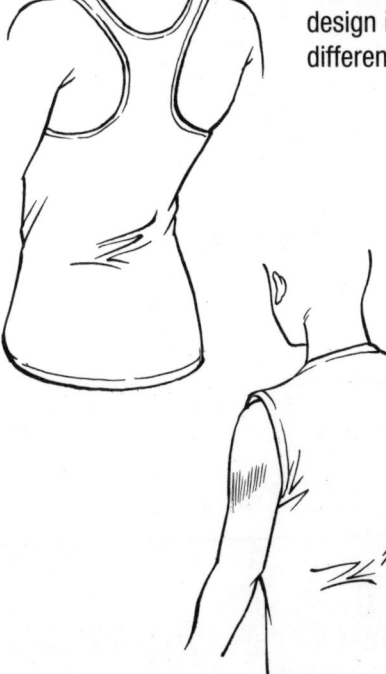

Surfer Shirts

While this is a non-sleeved shirt, the design is slightly different.

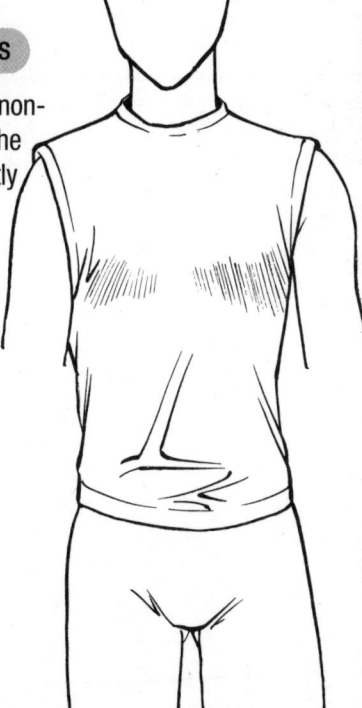

Male Underwear - Underpants

Underpants are designed to cover the lower body. There are three basic types: briefs, boxers and trunks.

Briefs

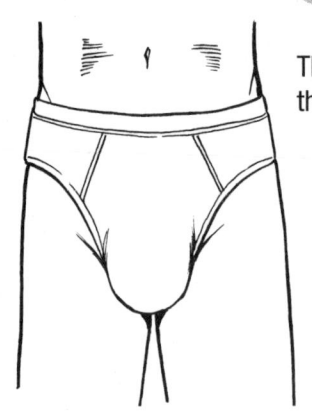

This part is the opening.

Briefs with a high cut design are called bikini briefs.

This illustration shows the basic brief design. There is an opening in the front.

Boxers

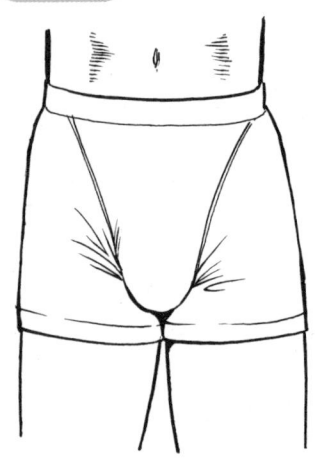

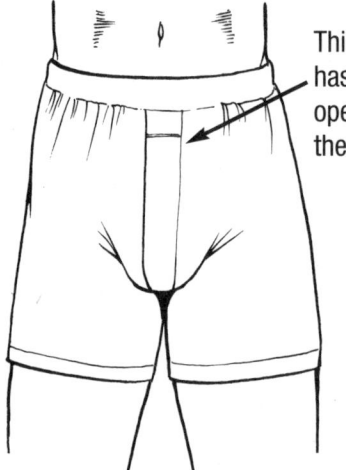

This design has an opening in the front.

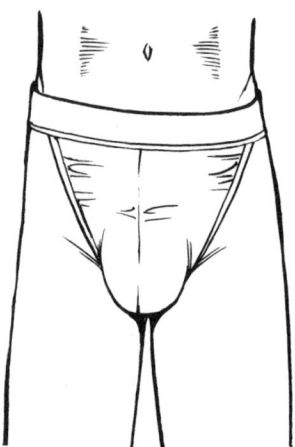

The shape of these briefs looks a lot like trunks. They are sometimes called boxer briefs and have the same short, tight fit as briefs.

Briefs with an extremely high cut design are called super bikini briefs.

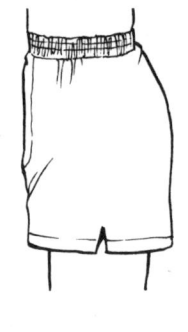

Boxers vary in their design and whether or not they have an opening.

Trunks

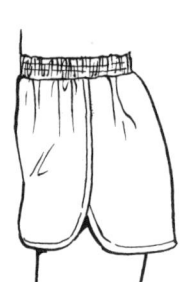

Trunks, which are sometimes called boxers, have a straight look with plenty of room to move around in.

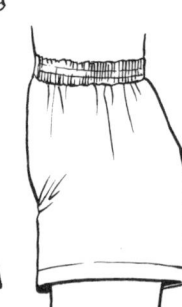

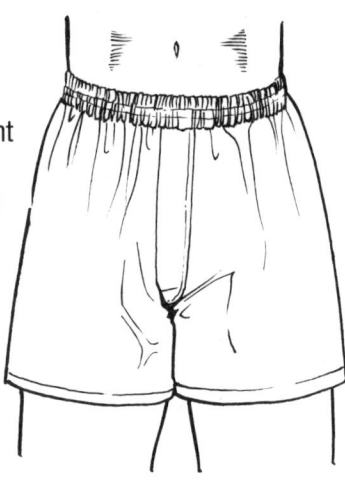

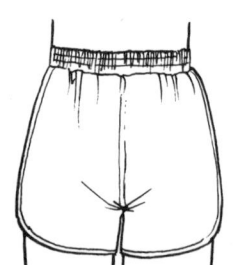

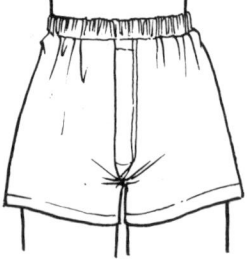

This type does not have an opening.

A wide variety of designs can be created by varying things like the cut. Here are just a few of the many possibilities.

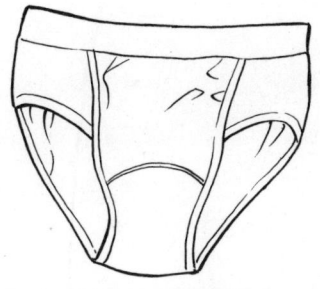 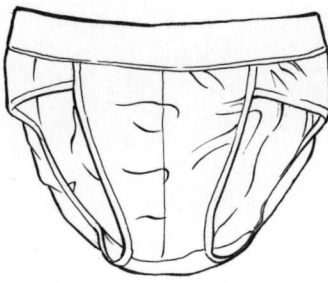 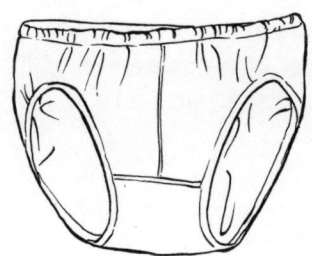

In general, men's briefs have an opening in the front but a few types do not.

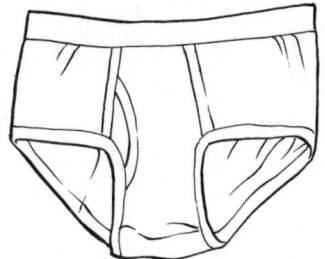 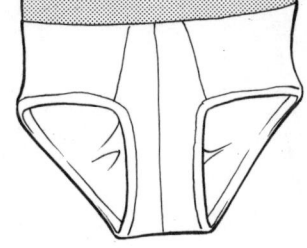 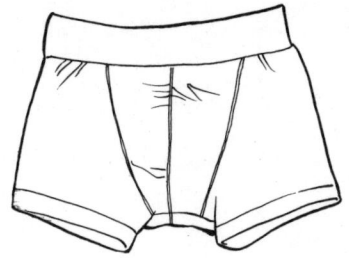

Briefs with an opening in the front.

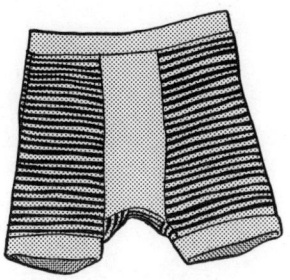 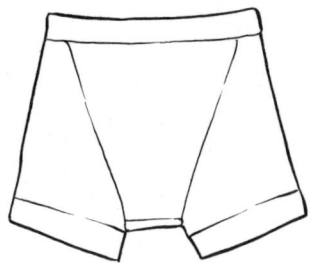 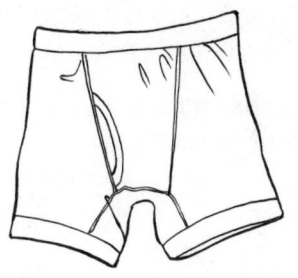

Designer briefs with an opening in the front.

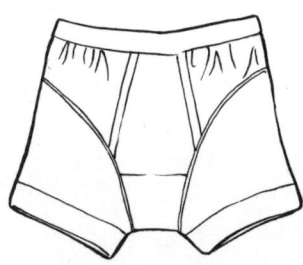 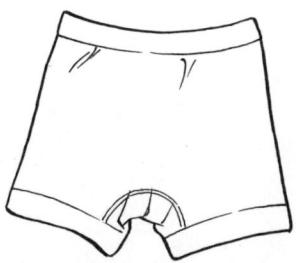 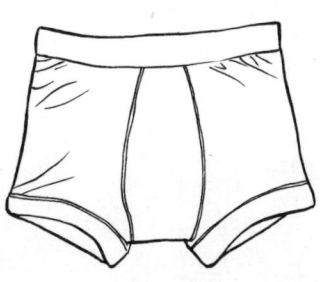

Female Underwear - Bras

Female underwear is also known as innerwear. Female lingerie comes in a wealth of designs with a much wider variety than male underwear.

Bras come in a wide variety of cups, designs and functions to meet the size of their users and to complement other clothing. Consider which bra works best for the body shape and silhouette of your character.

Half Cups

Most of these are geared for characters that wear A or B cupped bras.

Full Cups

This bra wraps the entire breast area and is well suited for characters with large breasts.

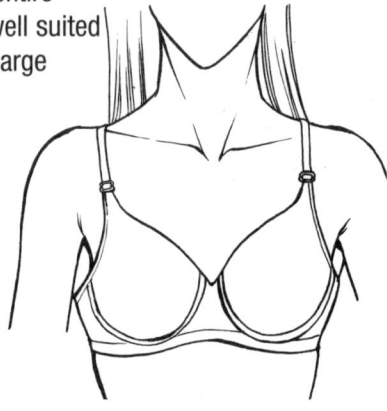

Quarter Cups

This type usually has a wire attached to the lower area that can be used with a wide range of cup sizes.

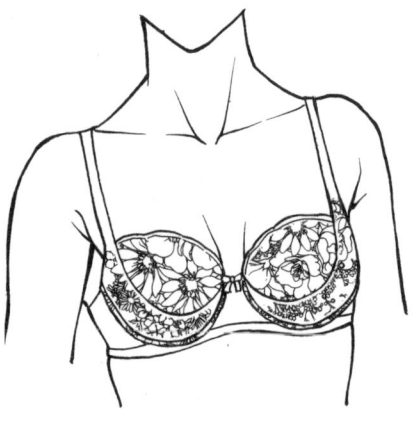

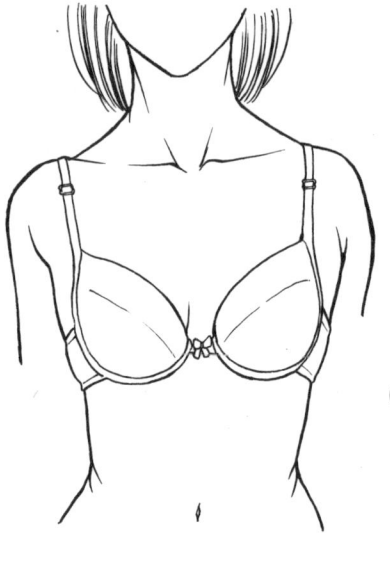

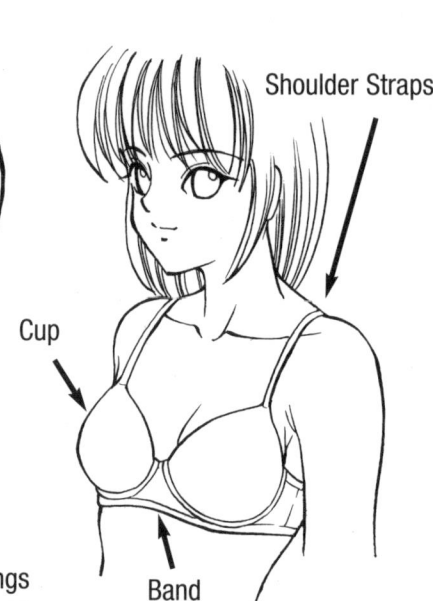

Shoulder Straps

Cup

Band

Lift Up

The material that makes up the cup is divided into two layers. Straps on the sides and the bottom push the breasts together adding volume and making the breasts rounder.

Push Up Bras

The construction of this bra brings together the breasts from both sides creating a cleavage line.

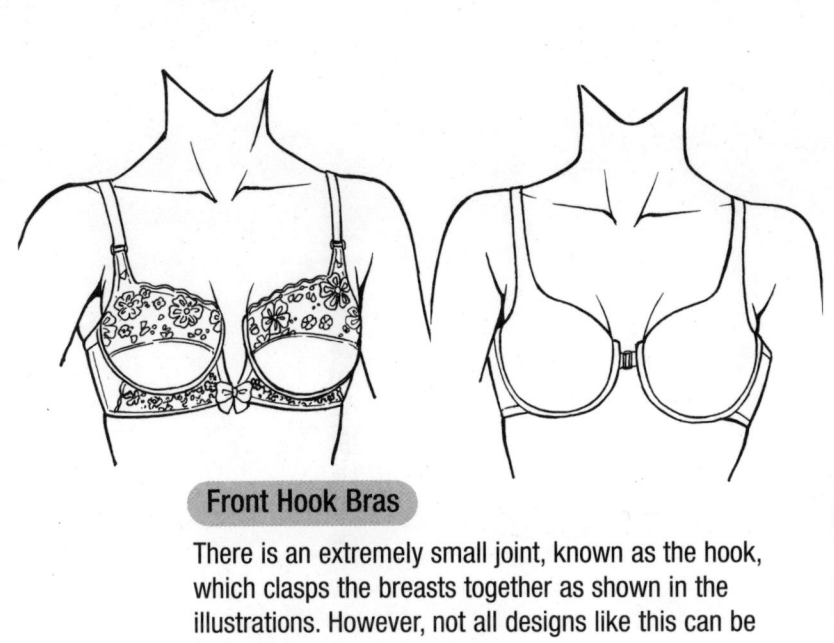

Front Hook Bras

There is an extremely small joint, known as the hook, which clasps the breasts together as shown in the illustrations. However, not all designs like this can be classified as front hook bras.

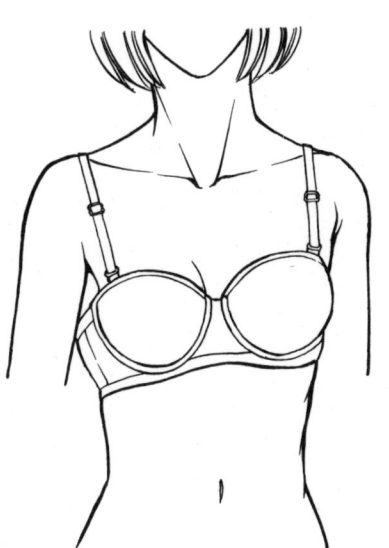
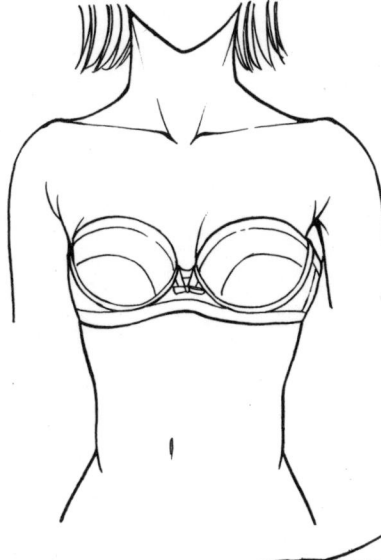
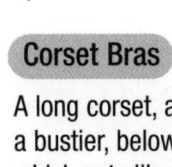

Corset Bras

A long corset, also known as a bustier, below the cups, which acts like a belt gives this bra its name. The fit and boning has an effect of tidying up the waistline. This is an interesting bra from a design standpoint.

Strapless Bras

The straps on this bra are removable making it easy to wear with clothing that shows the shoulders or cleavage.

An under-wire is often attached under the cup area to aid in the lifting function. Since this is the case, be sure and consider the wire along the cup and avoid getting off the track of the ellipse.

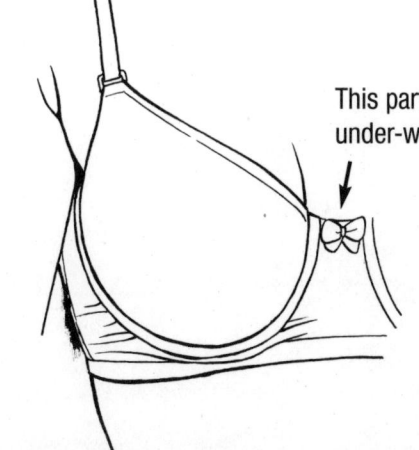

This part has an under-wire inside of it.

Various other designs exist in addition to the previous examples. Please compare the differences.

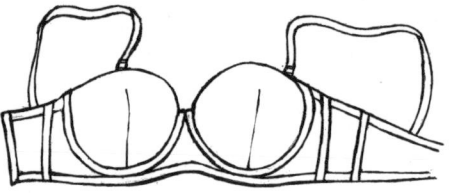
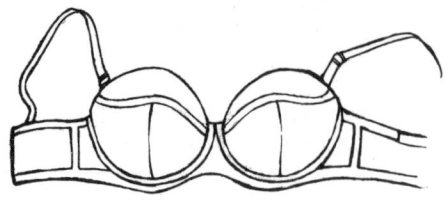

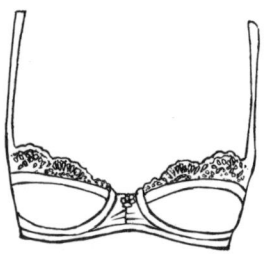
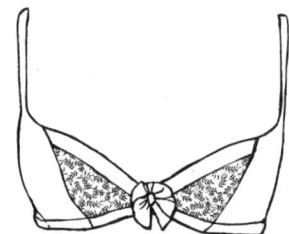
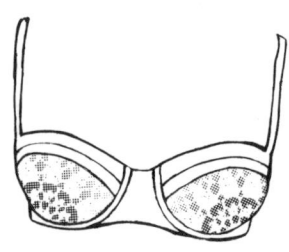

There are also a variety of cuts for the cup area.

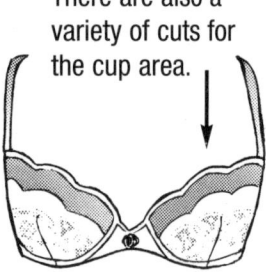
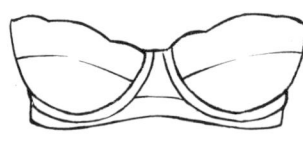
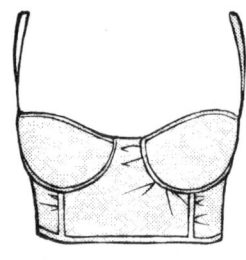

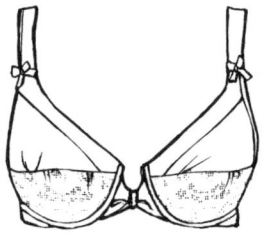
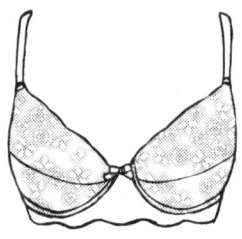
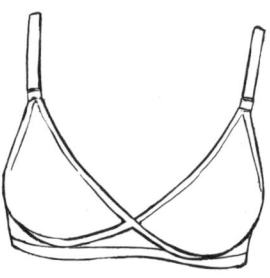

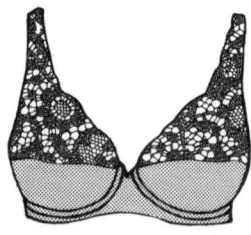
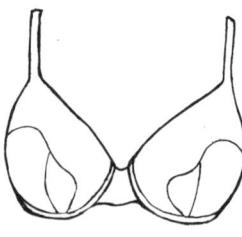
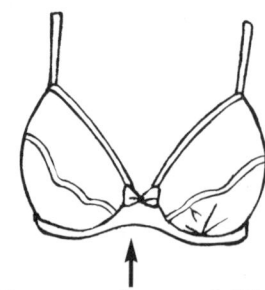

This is a full cup bra where the cup and strap are joined as one piece of material.

There are all sorts of different designs for the band below the cup area.

Female Underwear - Underpants

Since a wide variety of designs and patterns exist, we will examine the basic categories here.

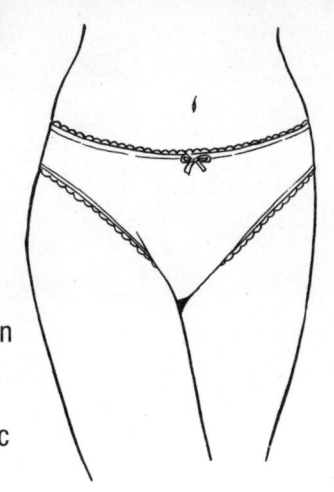
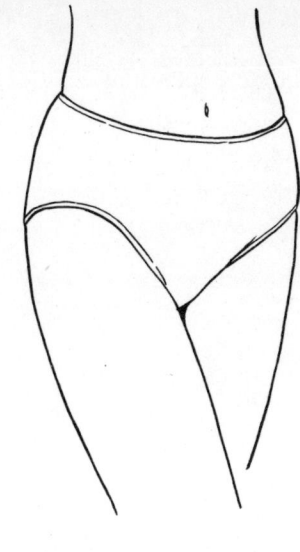

Semi-bikini Underpants

While some differences are seen with the cut around the leg depending on the kind, the illustrations here show the basic design of female underpants.

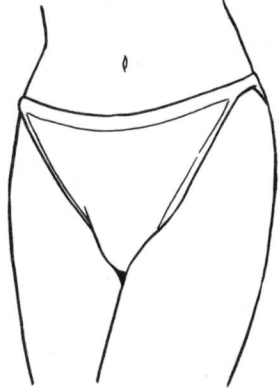
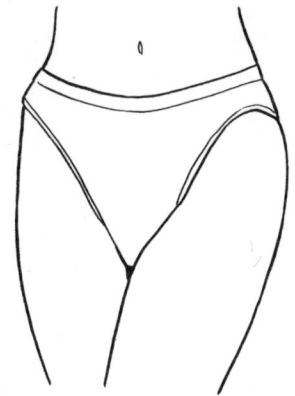

Bikini Underpants

This kind emphasizes design over function. If your character is wearing this type of underpants, she may be trying to appeal to some other character.

Standard Underpants

The image usually associated with this type is that of little girl. The basic functions of these are insulation to heat and absorption of sweat. The most basic design covers the bellybutton.

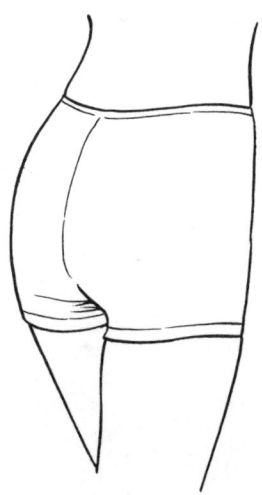
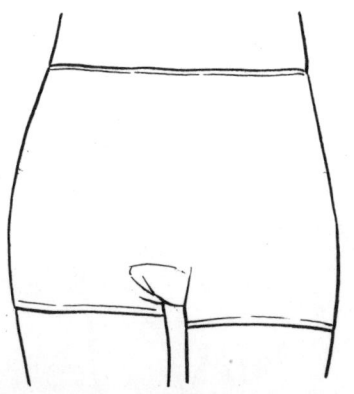
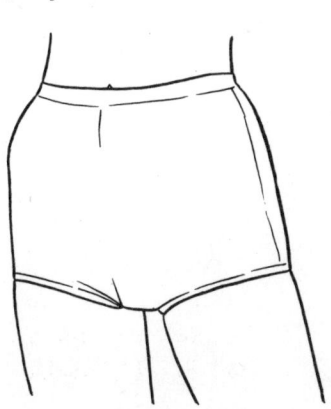

Boxer-style Underpants

Women often wear this type with jeans or trousers to avoid showing a panty line.

Quarter Cup Bras (Pattern A)

Let's take a look from various angles.

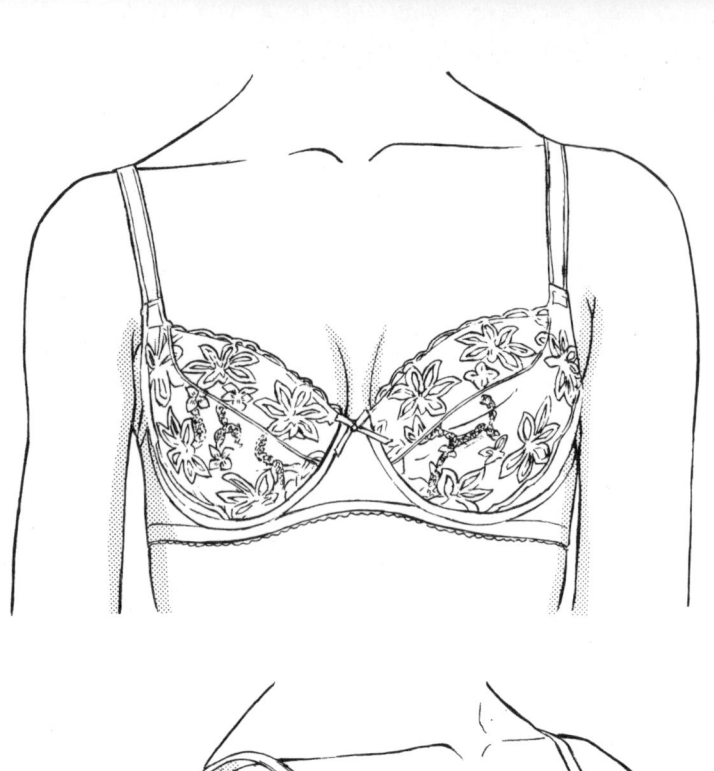

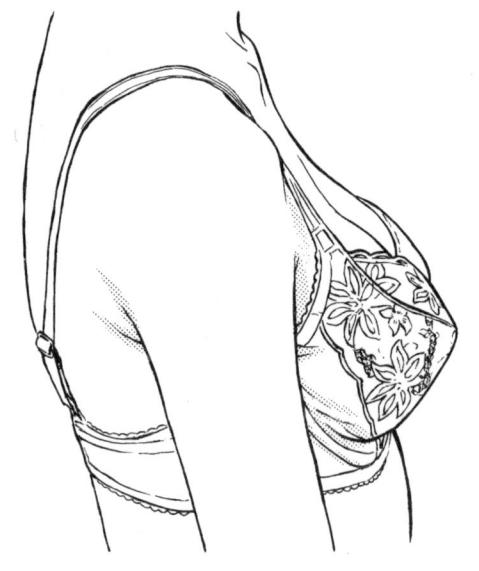

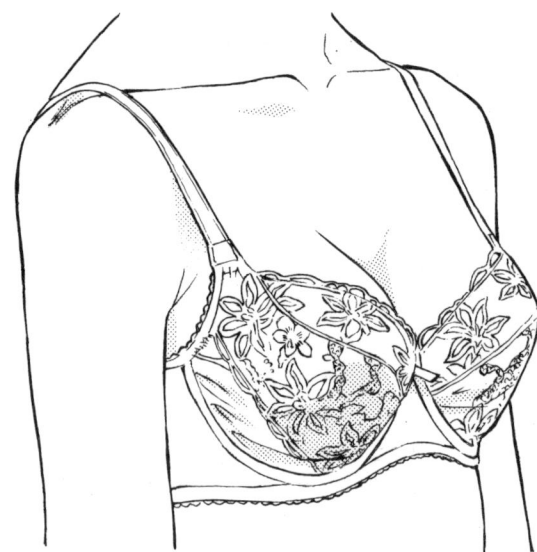

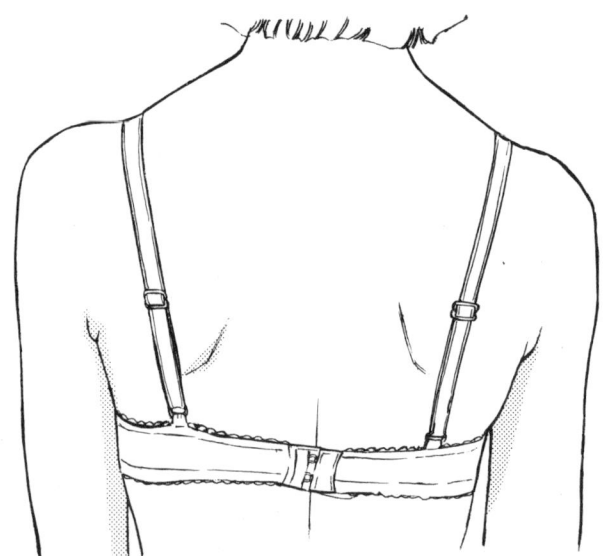

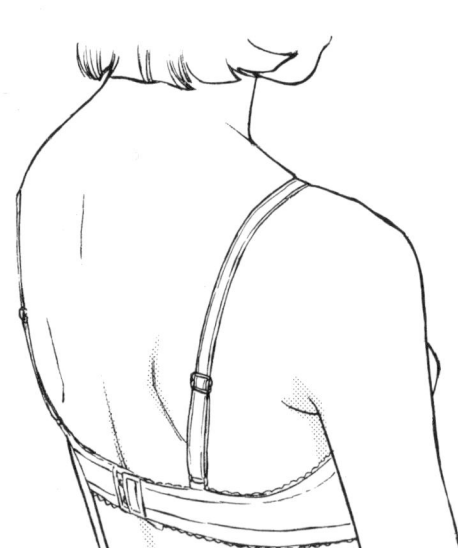

Quarter Cup Bras (Pattern B)

Let's take a look at the difference in the design of the bands and cut of the cup.

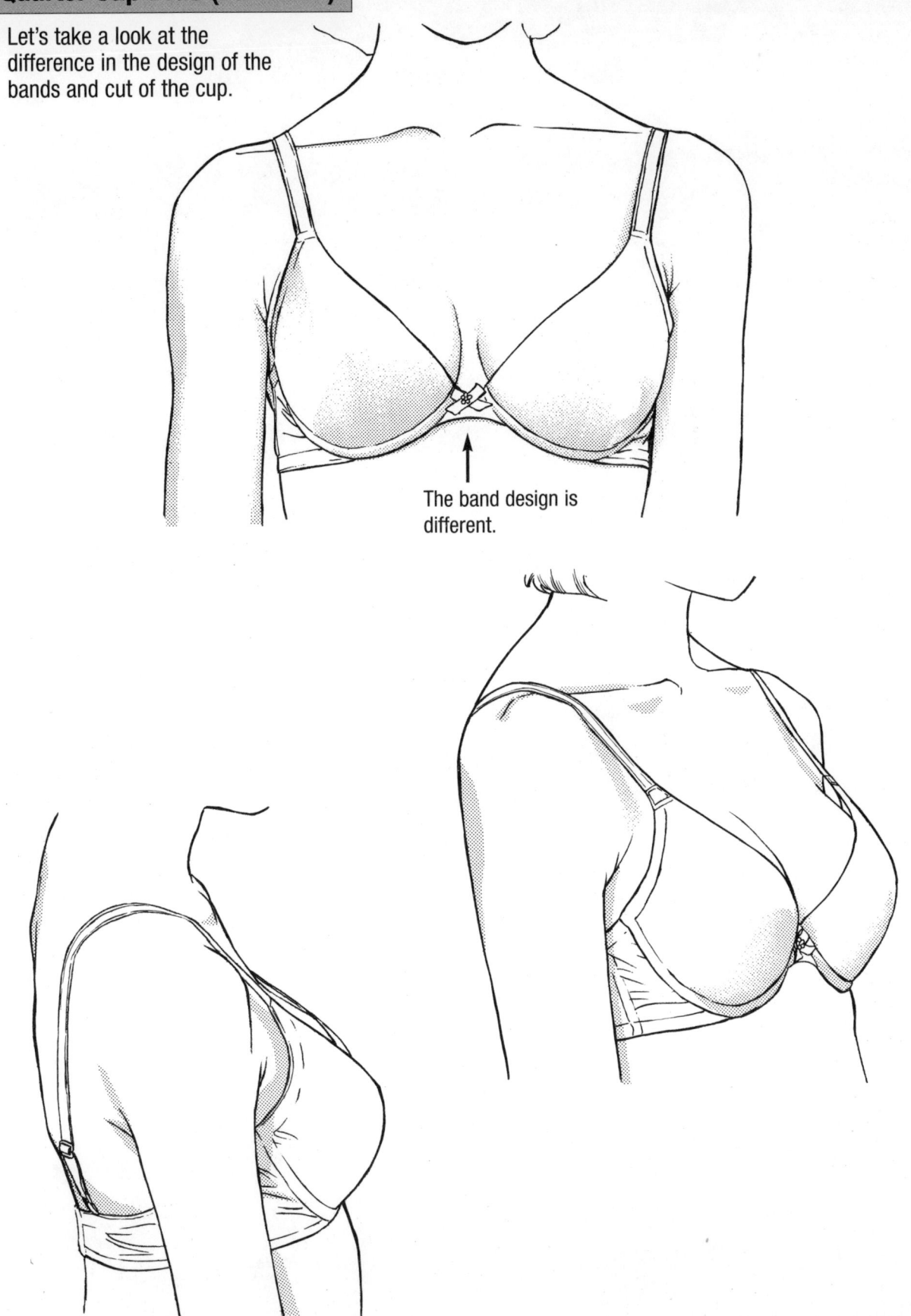

The band design is different.

More Quarter Cup Bras (Pattern B)

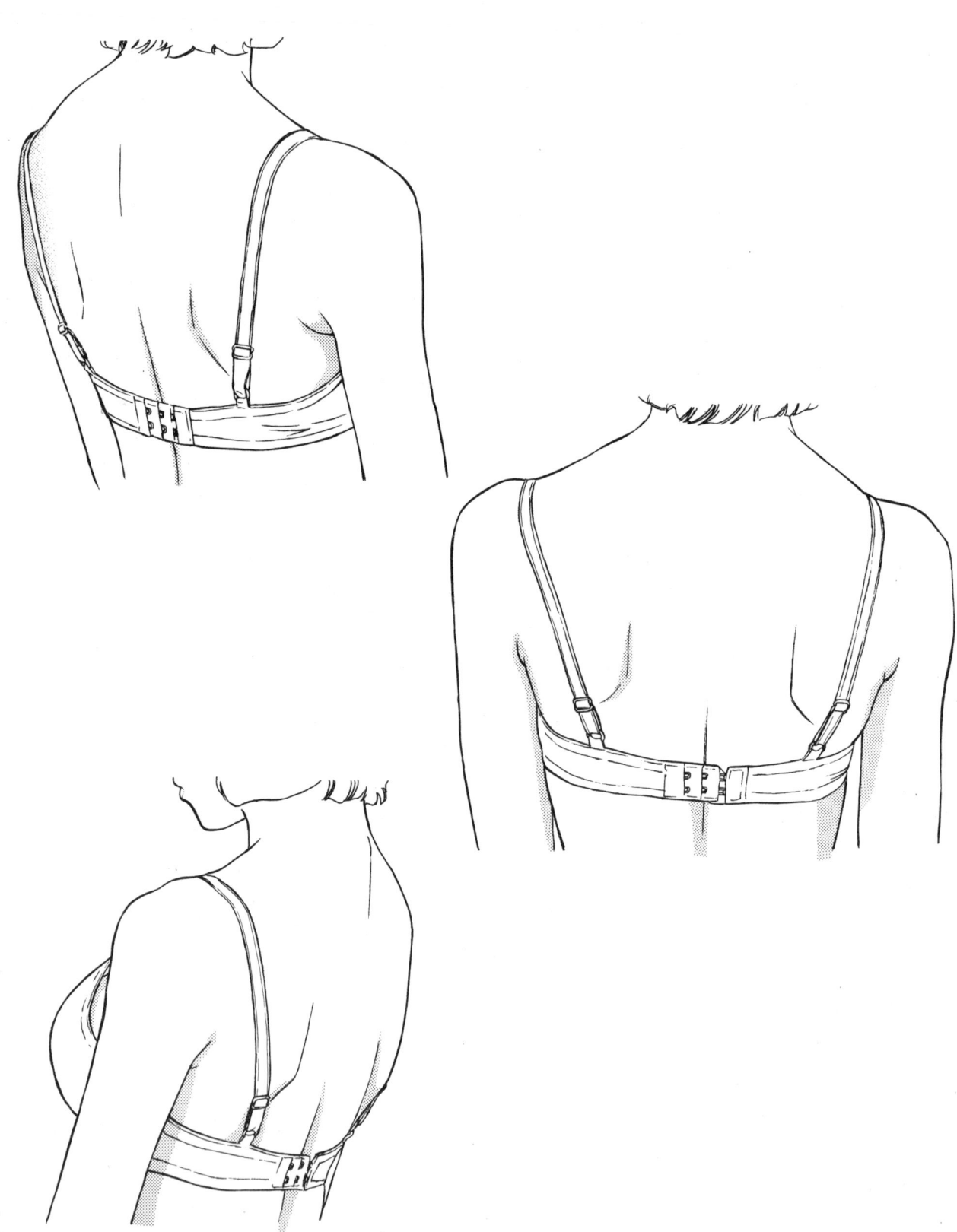

Semi-bikini Underpants

The angle of the leg cut shown here is a standard type. Let's take a look at the pants from a variety of angles.

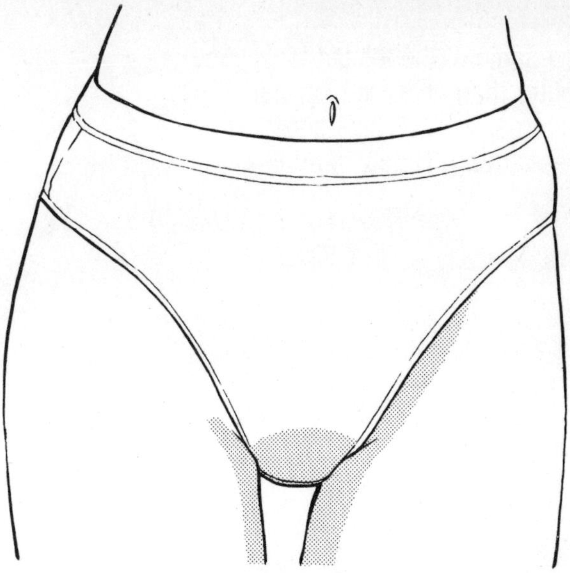

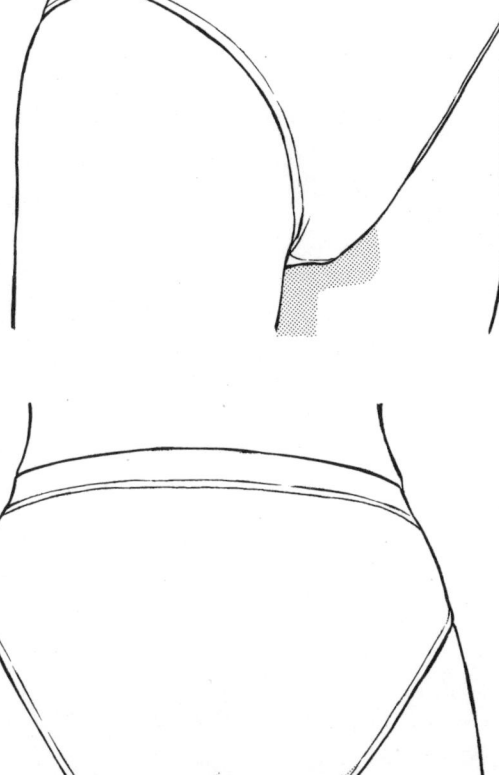

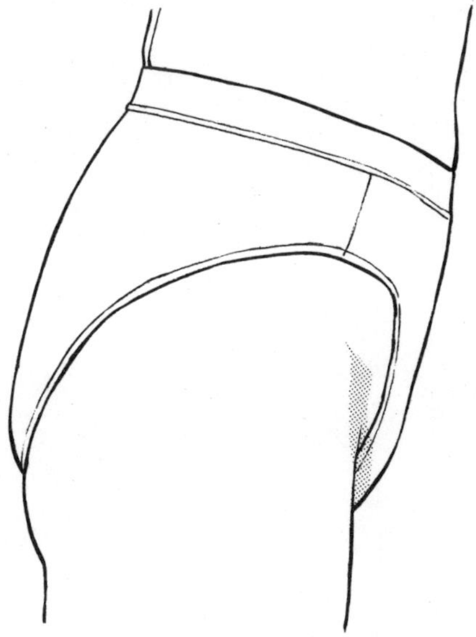

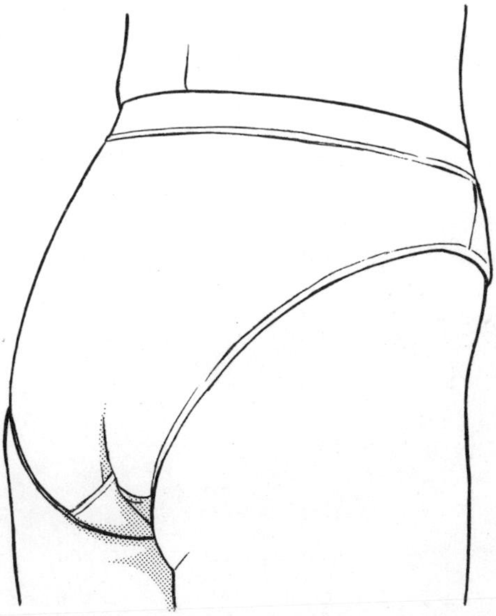

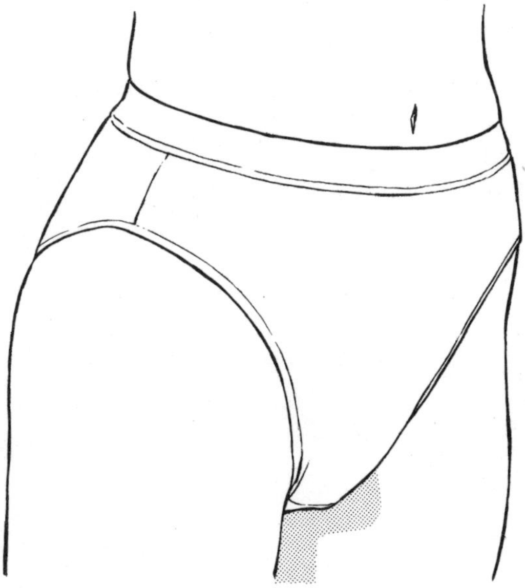

Bikini Underpants

The angle of the leg cut is tighter than with the high-cut underpants. Let's take a look at these from a variety of angles.

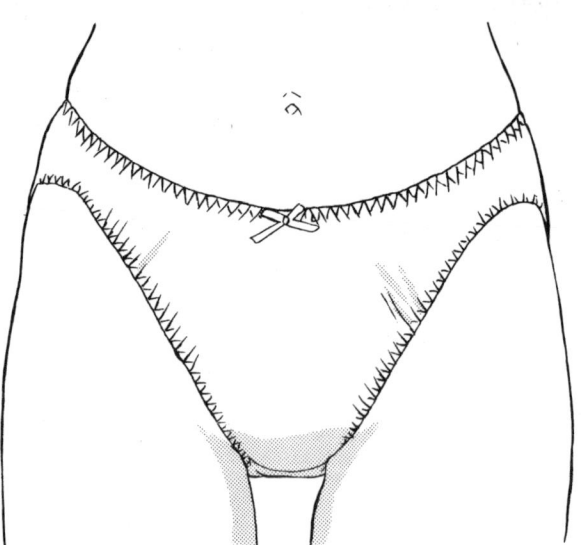

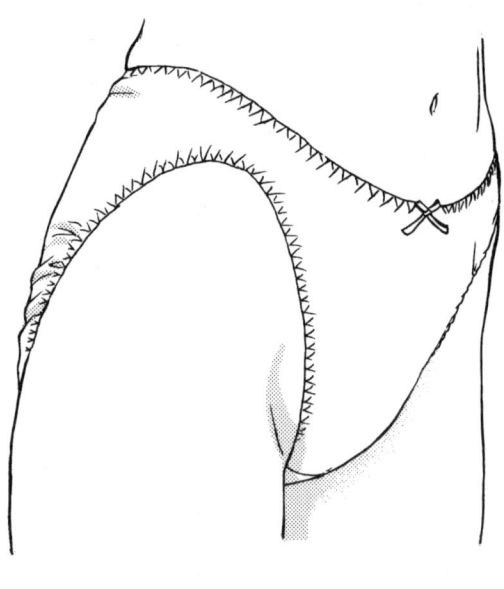

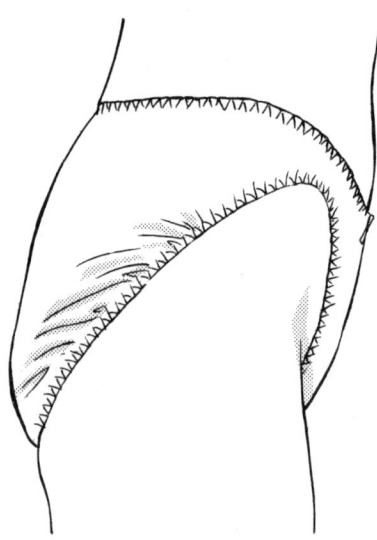

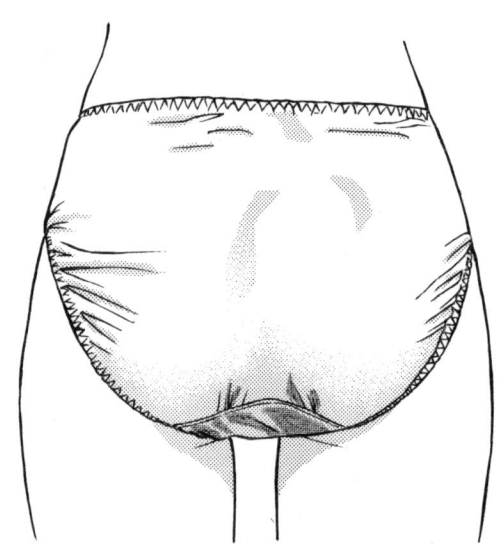

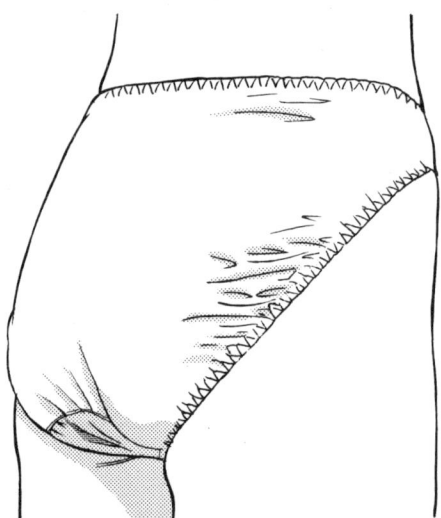

Quarter Cup Bras (Pattern A) with Bikini Underpants — Low Angle

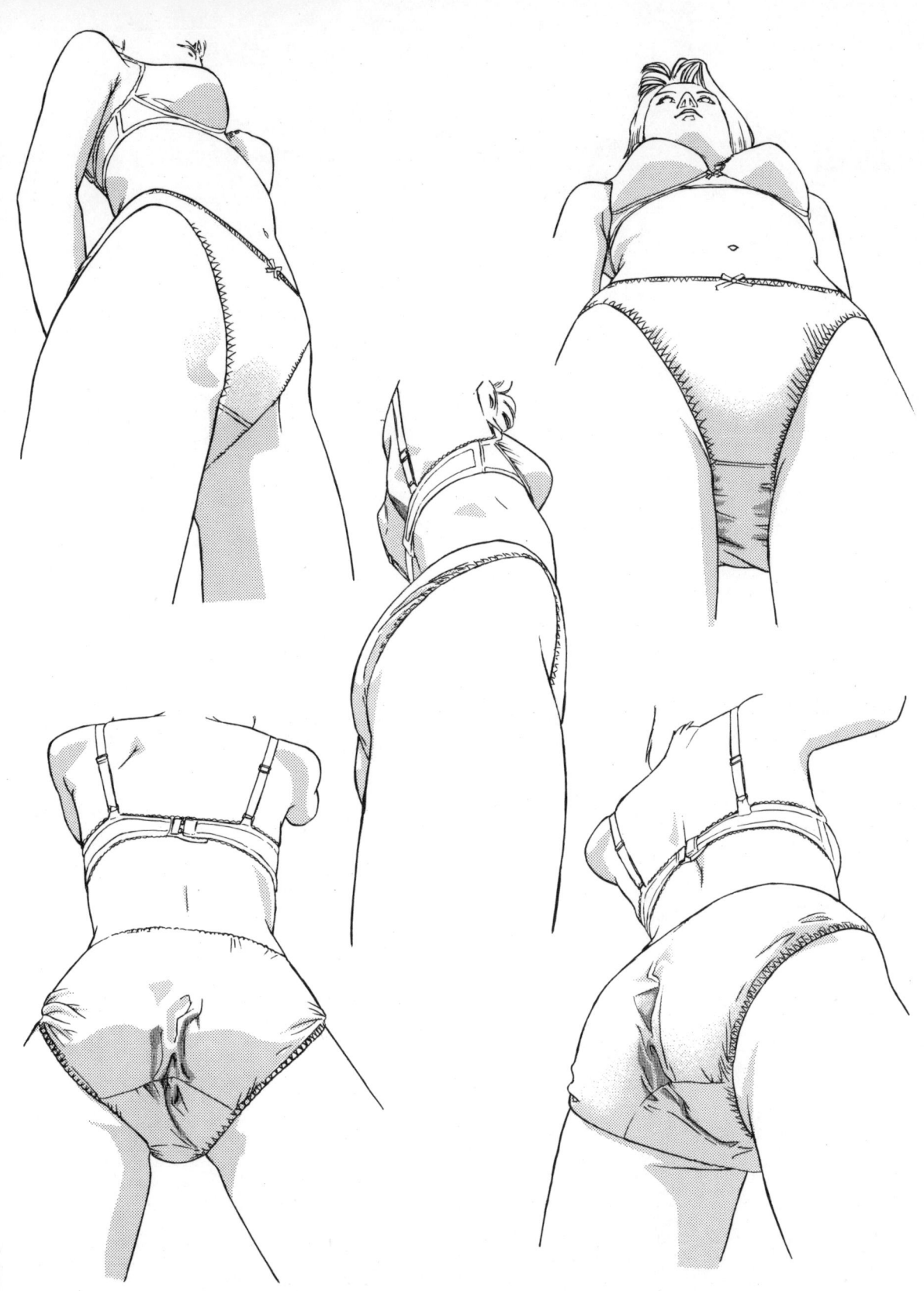

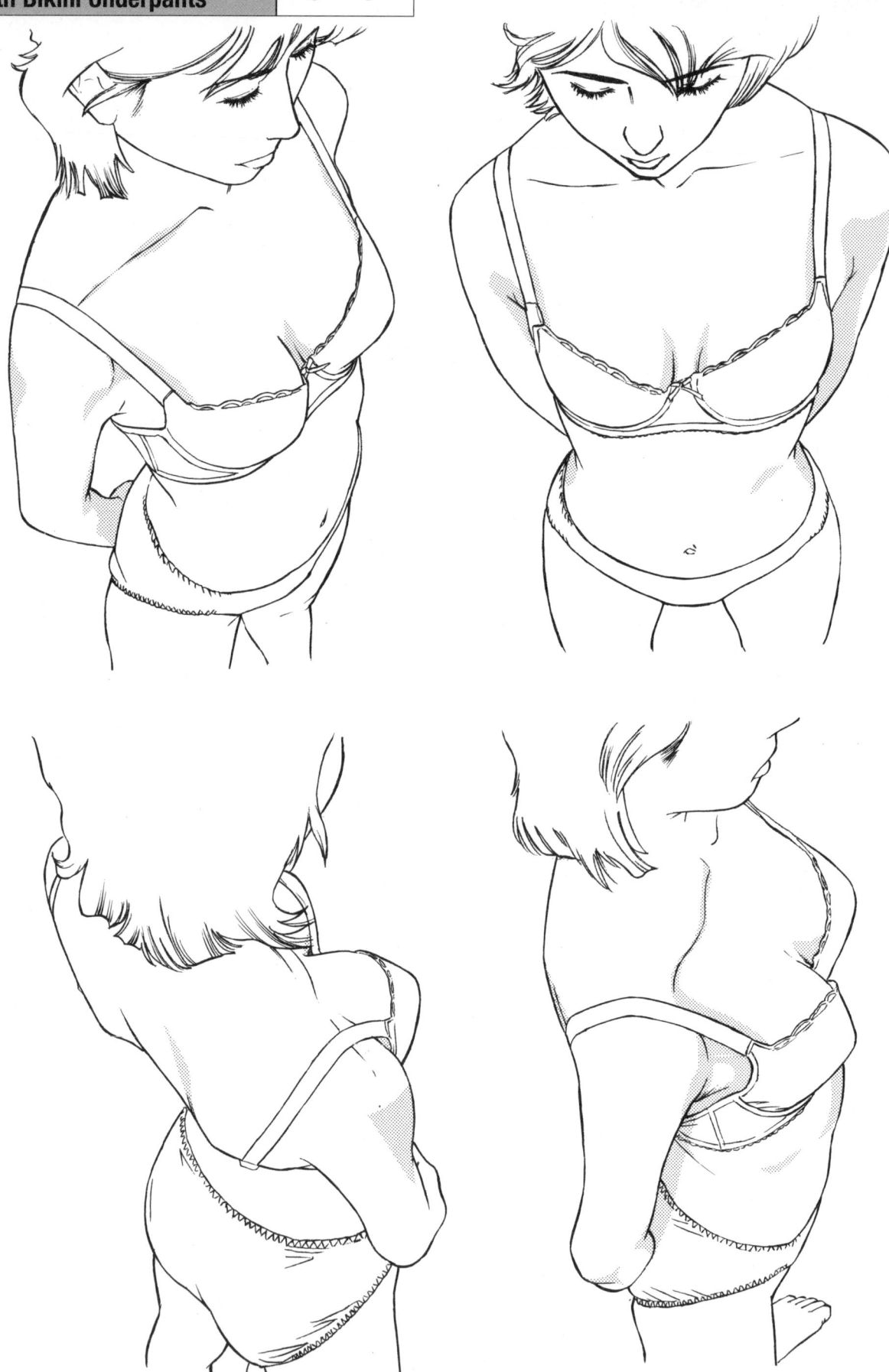

Quarter Cup Bras (Pattern B) with Bikini Underpants — Low Angle

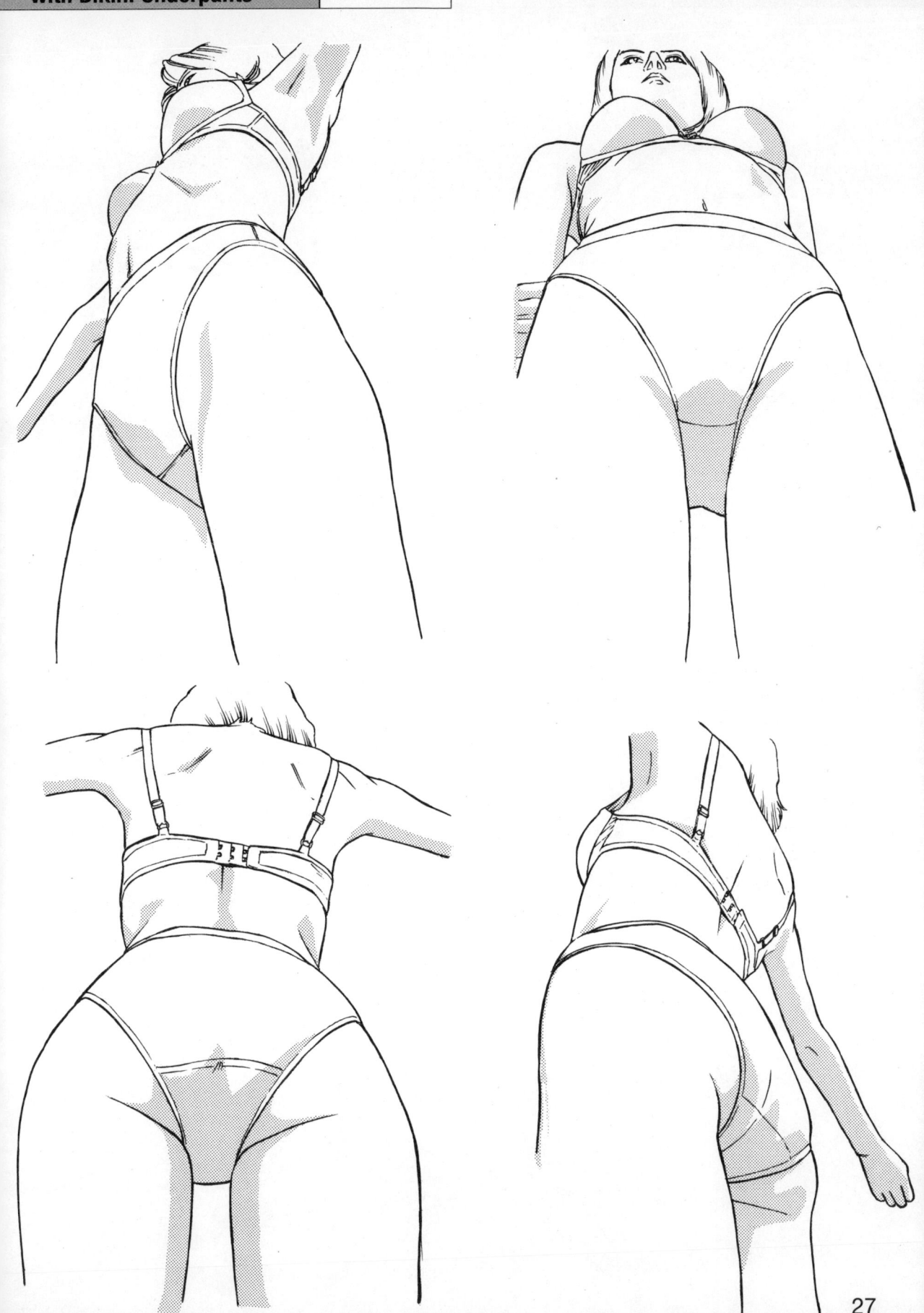

More Quarter Cup Bras (Pattern B) with Semi-bikini Underpants — Low Angle

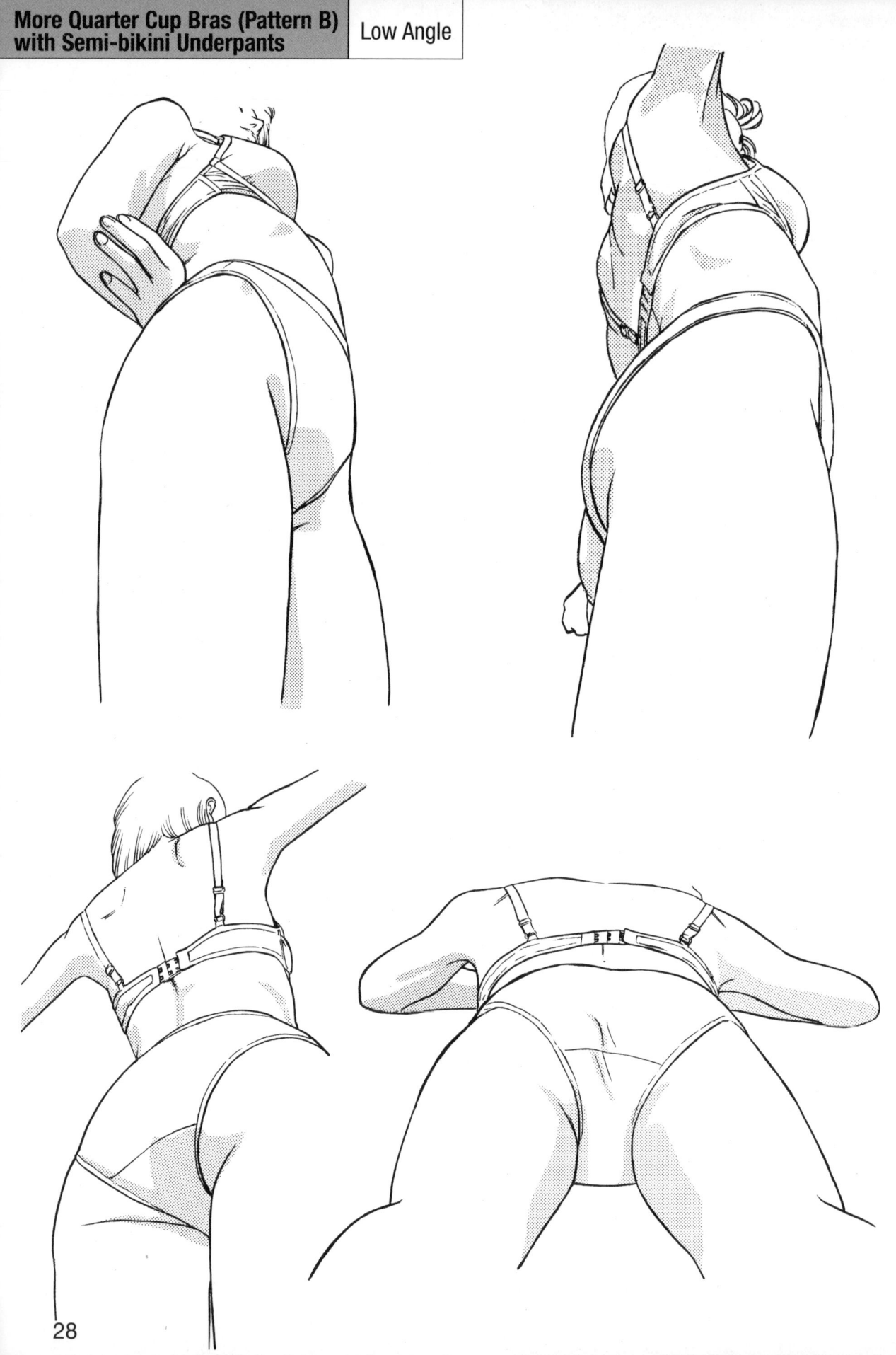

More Quarter Cup Bras (Pattern B) with Semi-bikini Underpants | High Angle

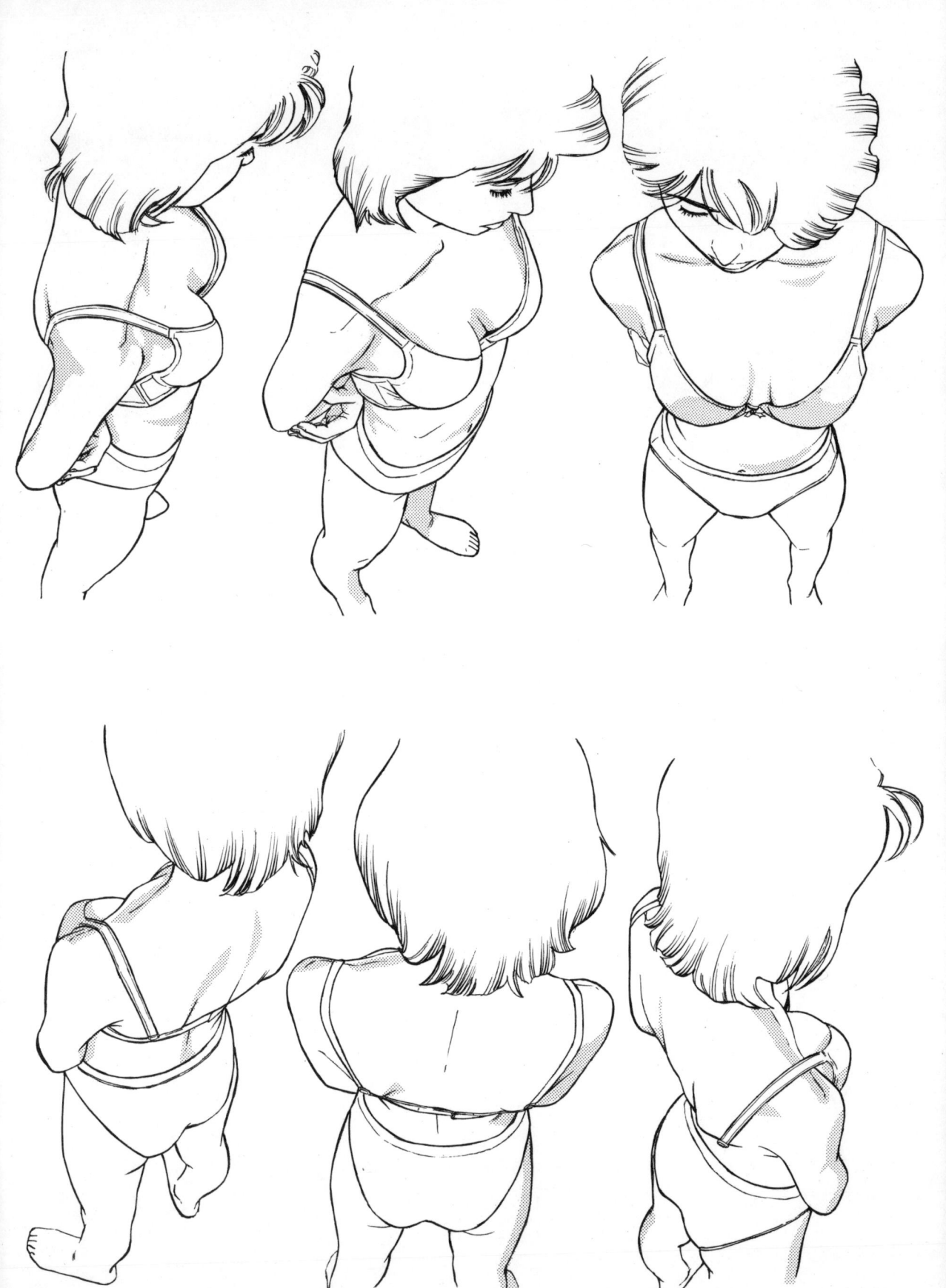

Sportswear Undergarments

While you won't see many people wearing these, this type of undergarment was thought up for people who play sports and exercise.

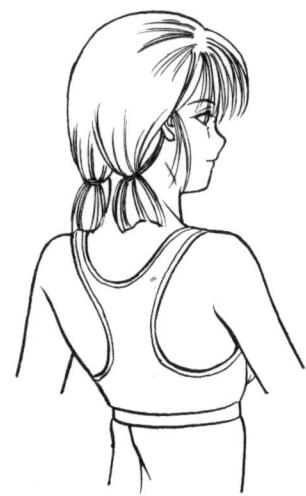

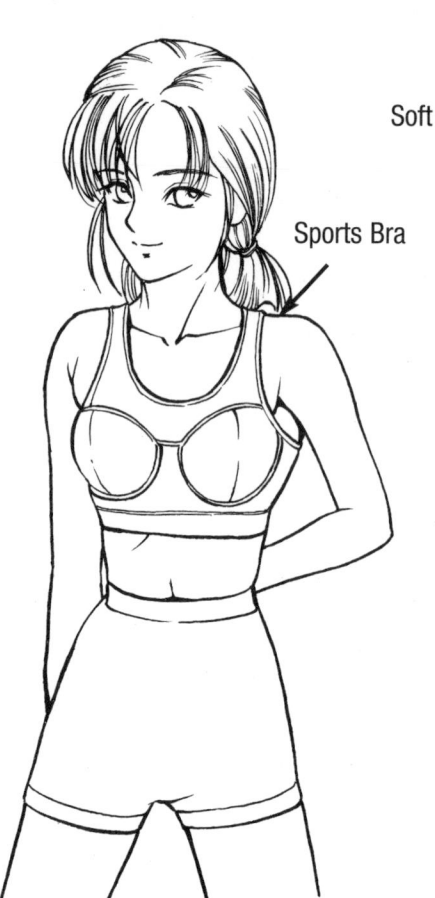

Sports Bra

Soft Bra

Sports Shorts
The design looks like boxers or spats. There should not be any problems when you draw them as long as you decide whether they should resemble underwear or sportswear.

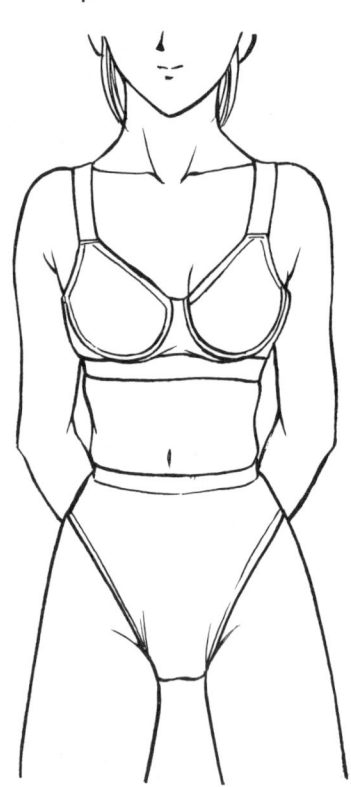

While these bras do resemble sportswear, some of them contain wires under the cup area, which really makes them underwear. However, since the back looks like aerobics wear, it may better to draw them like sportswear.

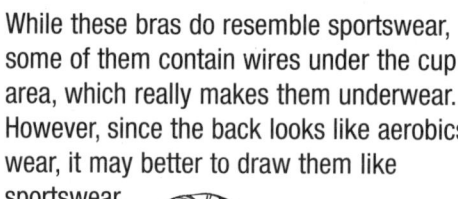

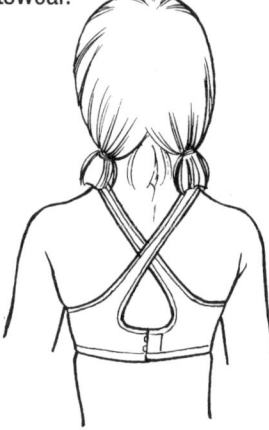

There are also models where the shoulder straps crisscross in the back.

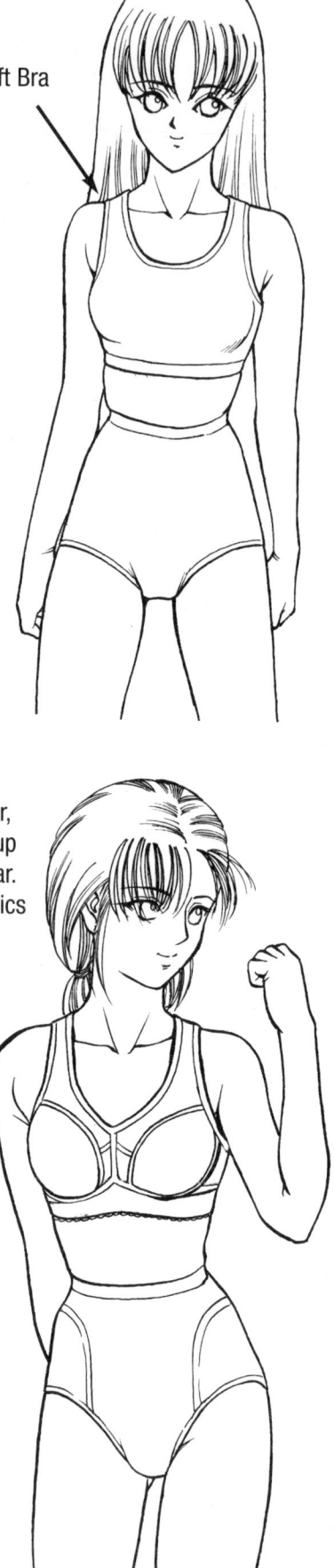

Lingerie

Lingerie seems to have the most sense of fashion of all types of underwear. There is a wealth of types from slips to camisoles.

Camisoles

A camisole is a type of underwear like a slip that has been cut off at the waist.

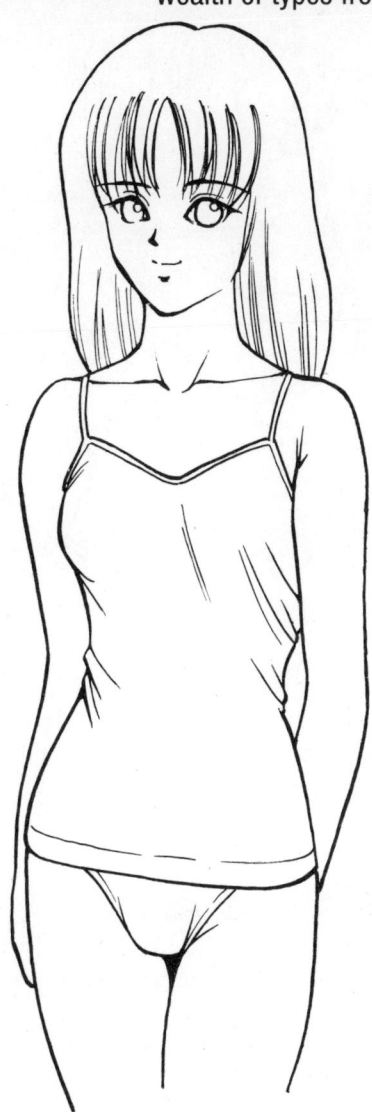

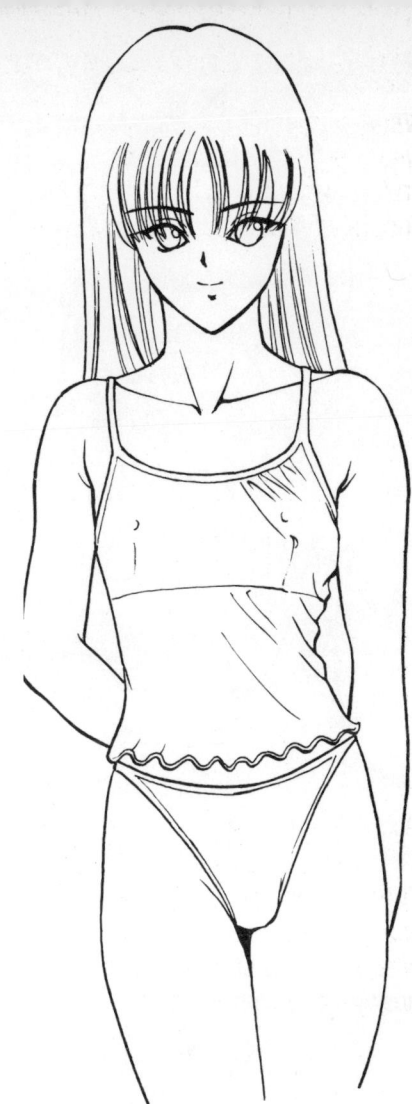

They come in a variety of lengths from ones that cover the bellybutton and ones that don't.

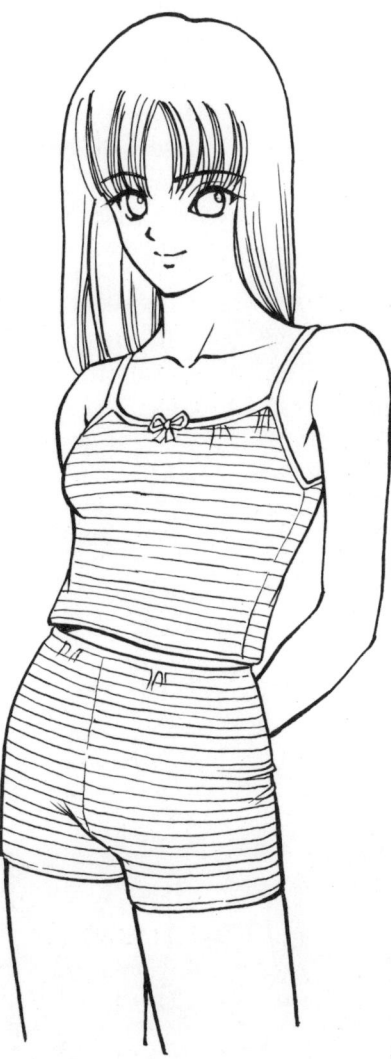

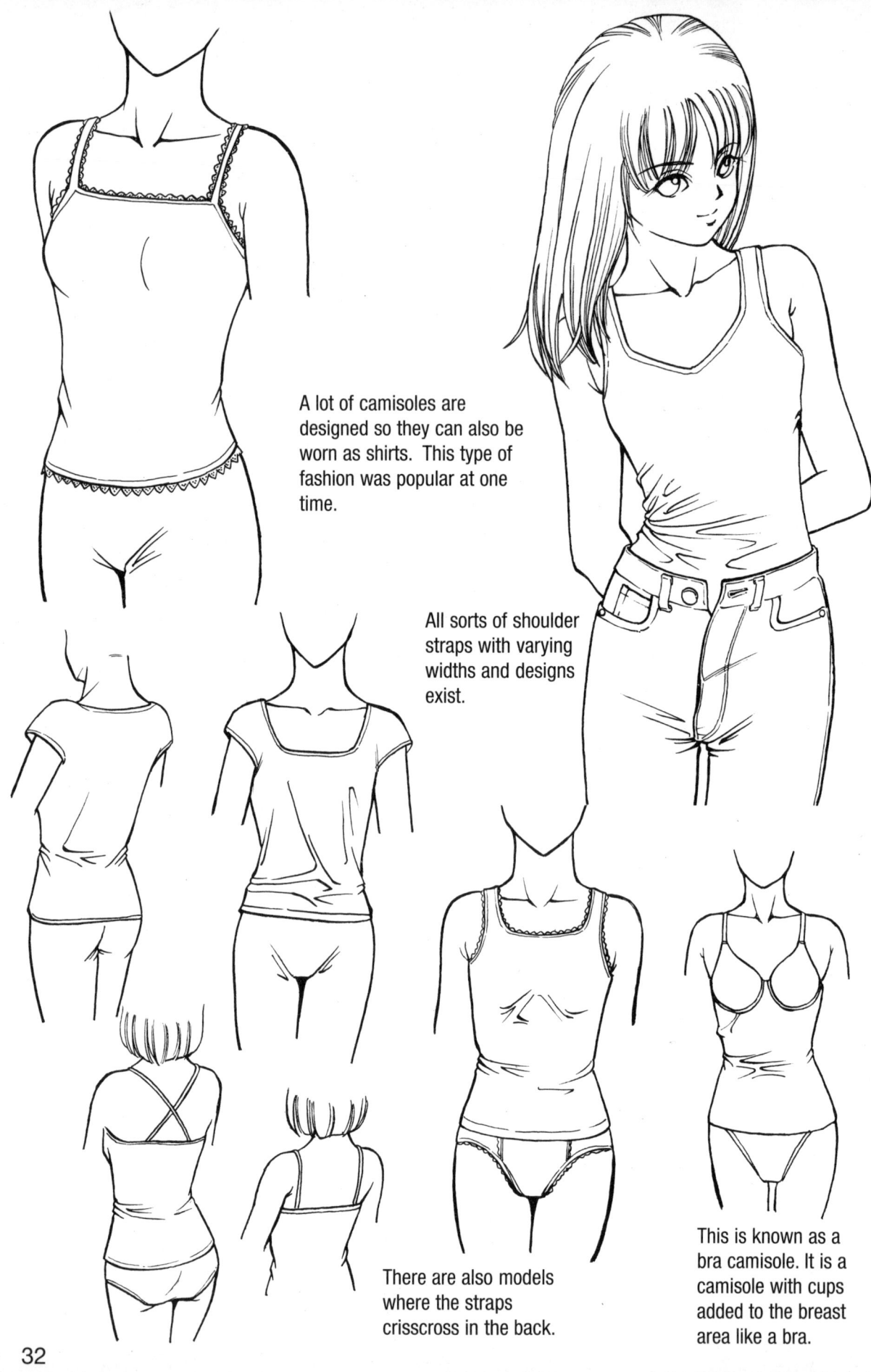

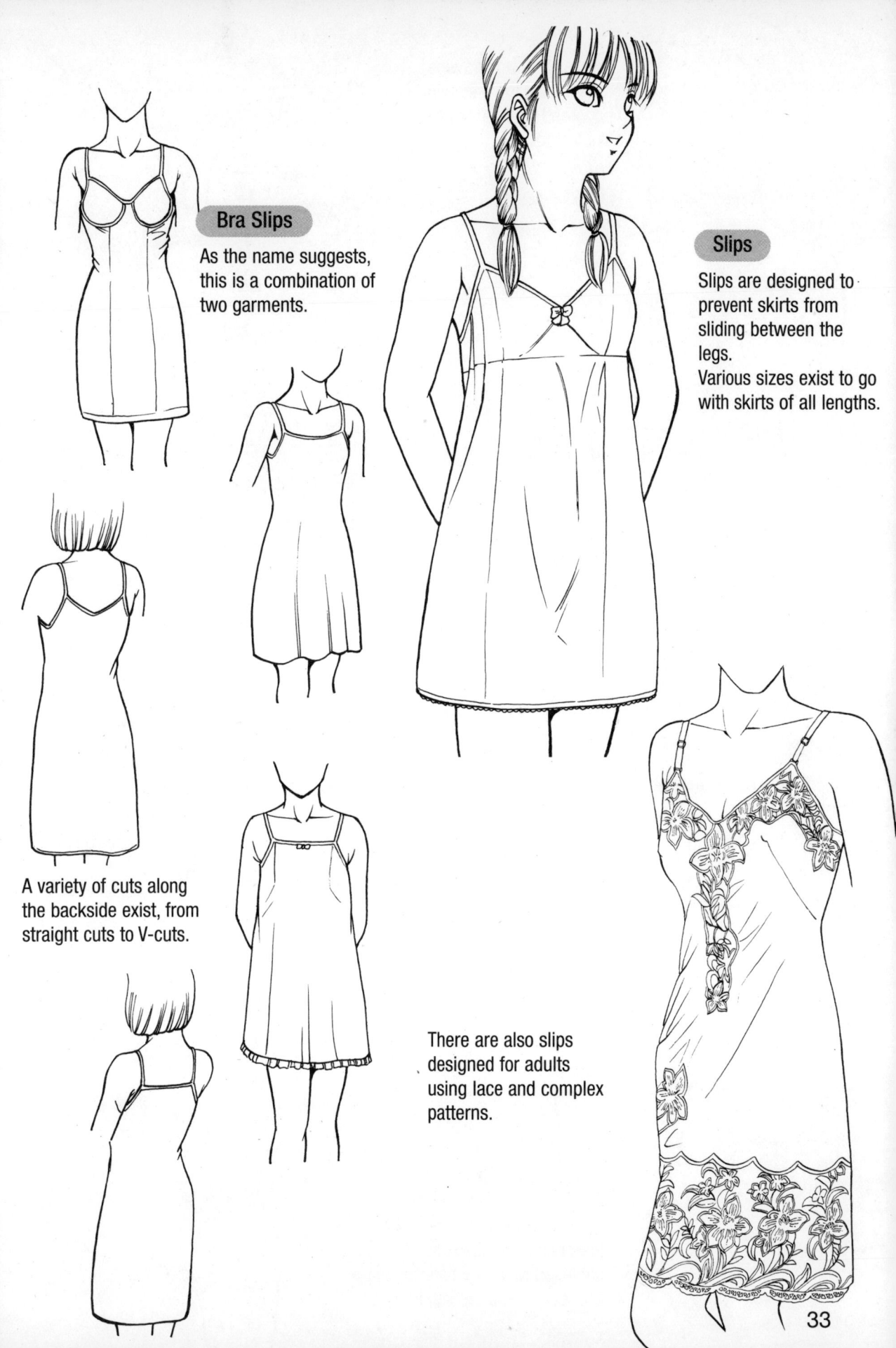

Bra Slips

As the name suggests, this is a combination of two garments.

Slips

Slips are designed to prevent skirts from sliding between the legs.
Various sizes exist to go with skirts of all lengths.

A variety of cuts along the backside exist, from straight cuts to V-cuts.

There are also slips designed for adults using lace and complex patterns.

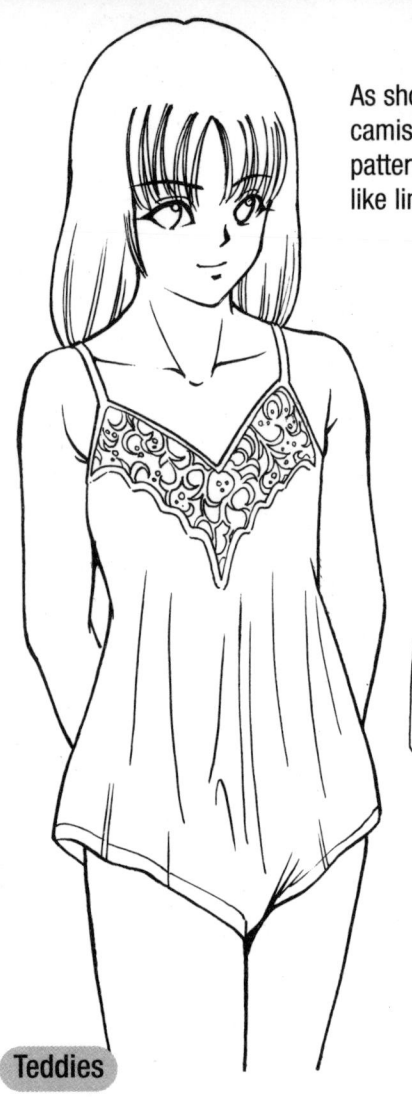

As shown in the drawing, camisoles garnished with patterned lace really look like lingerie.

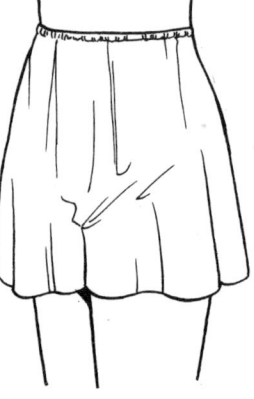

This is an example of flare panties.

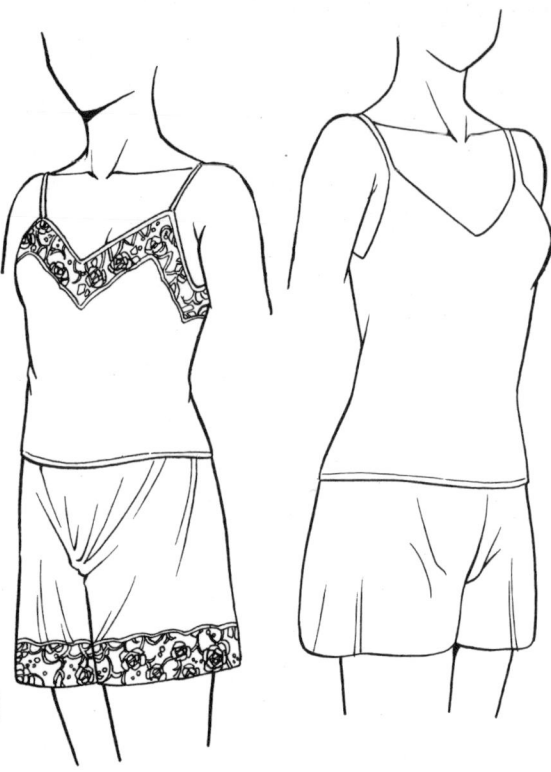

Since a camisole is like the upper part of a slip, flare pants needs to make up for the lower part of the slip. Their design can be coordinated with a petticoat pattern.

Teddies

A teddie is a combination of a slip and flare panties.

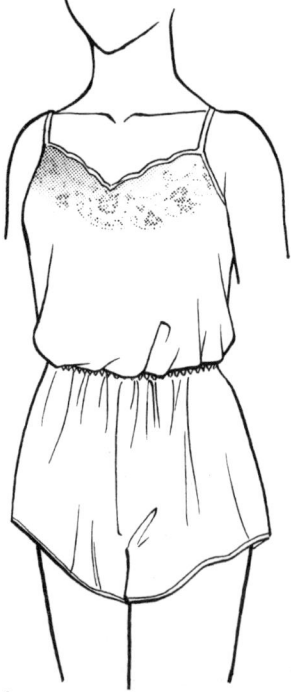
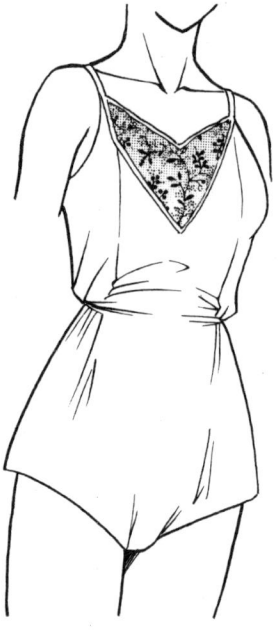
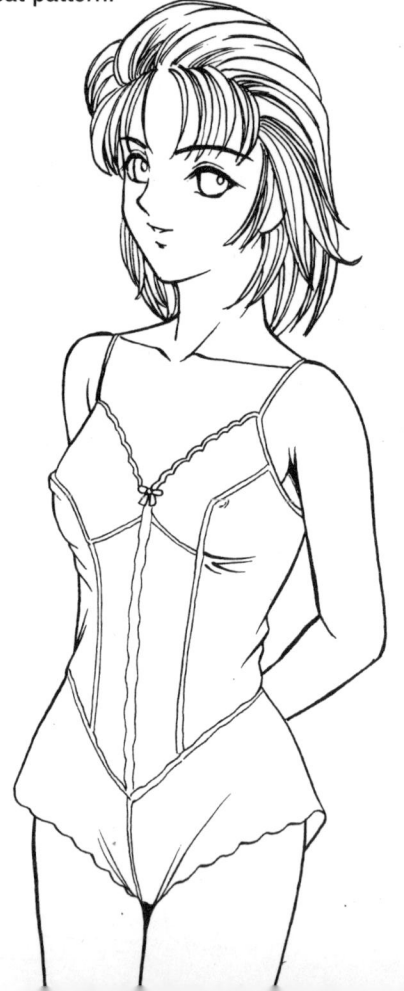

Teddies come in a variety of designs from ones with the waist area tightened to ones where the upper and lower parts are separate.

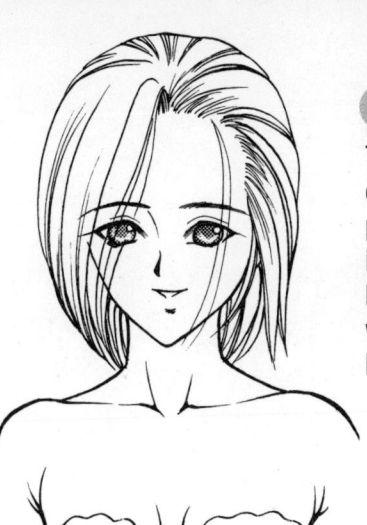

Lingerie Sets

These are a combination of several pieces of lingerie including a bra, a bustier, to slim the waistline, and garter belts.

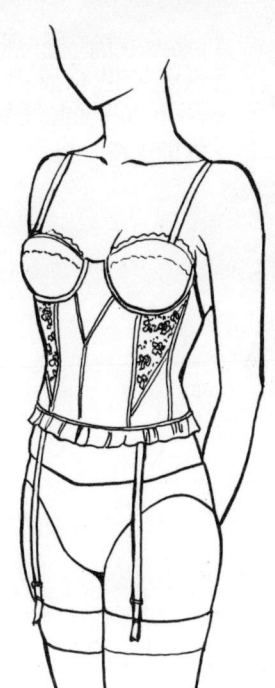 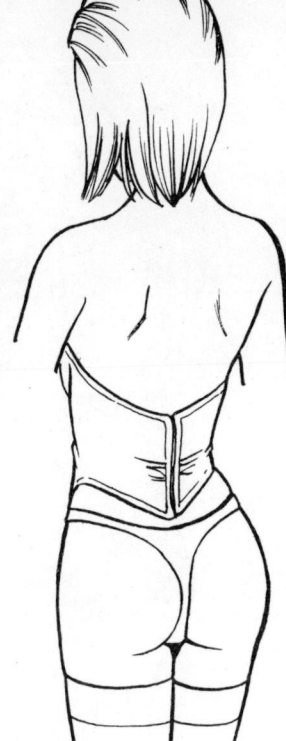

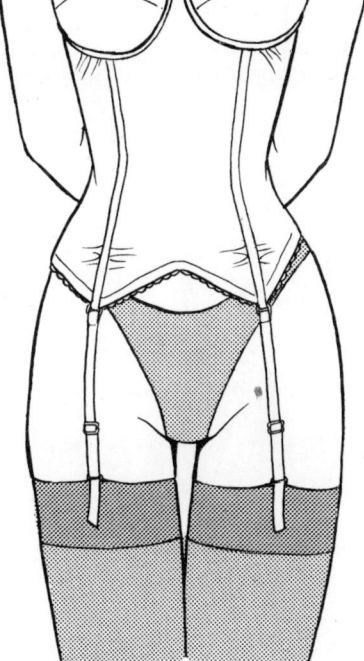
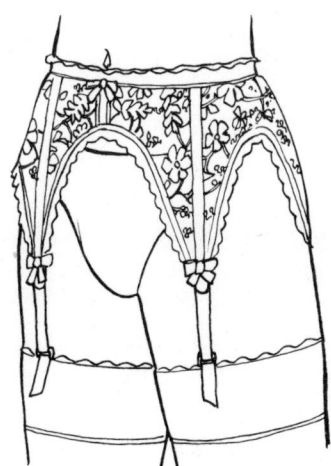

Garter Belts

Garter belts can be worn as part of a lingerie set or independently.

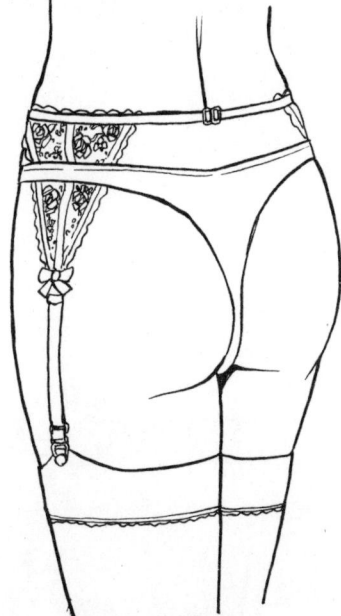

There are all sorts of fasteners to hold up stockings. One commonly seen type is shown here.

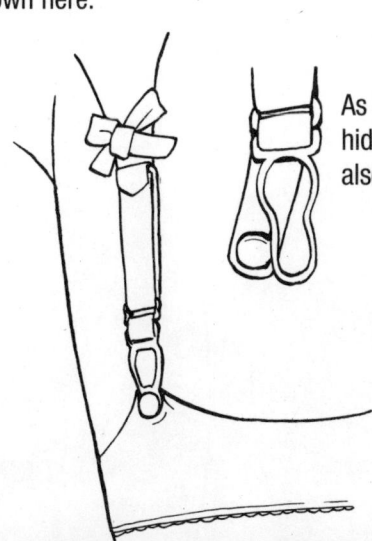

As illustrated, hidden fasteners also exist.

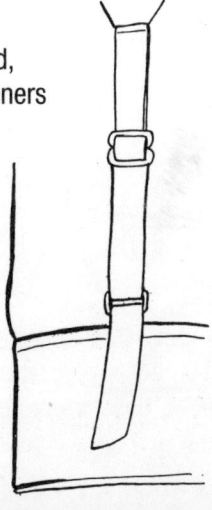

Garter belts can also be worn under the panties.

35

Bodysuits

These are for shaping up the bust, waist and hips. Other types of underwear fashion that shape up the body are bras, girdles, and lingerie sets.

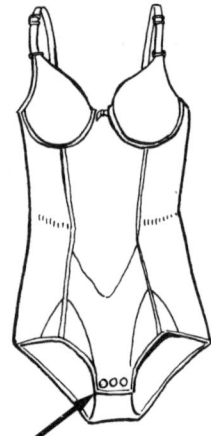

This part has snaps attached making these out on, as well as, take off.

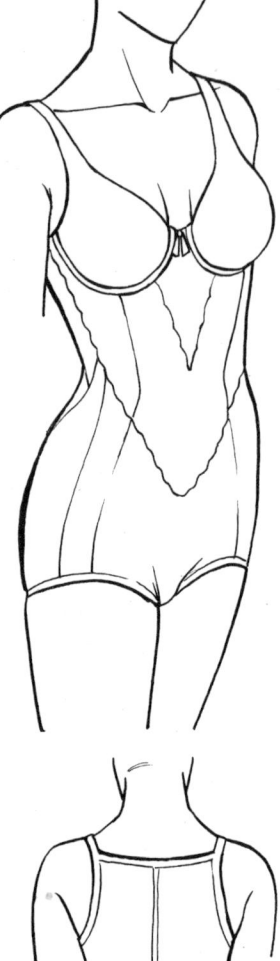

Differences in design manifest in the back area too. The strength of the shaping function ranges from soft to medium to hard and the seams in the materials tend to differ depending on this.

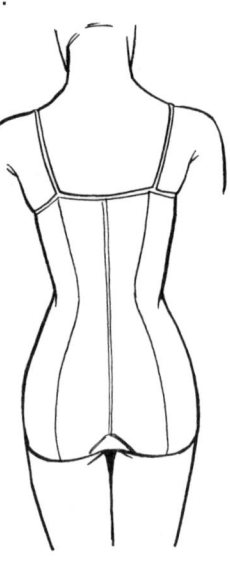

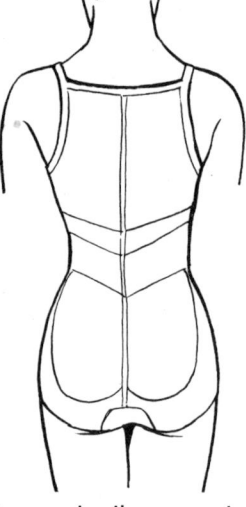

The greater the amount of seams, the better the body suit shapes the body.

Girdles

These help shape the body in the waist and hip areas.

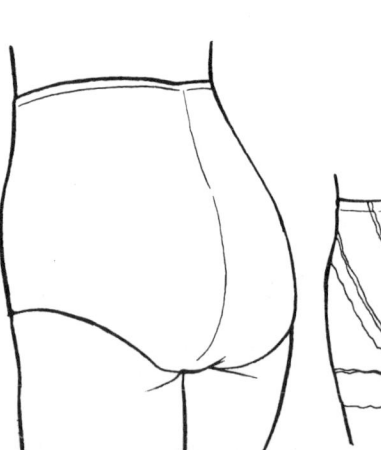

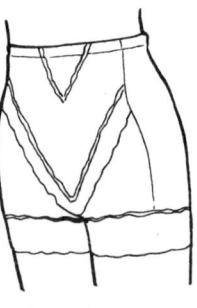

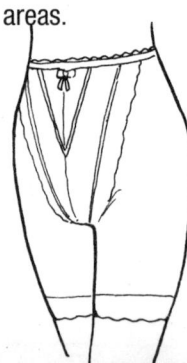

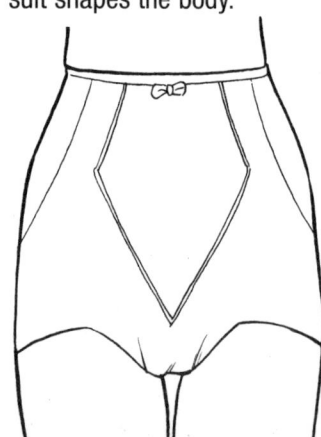

Panty Hose Also called sheer tights, these are worn by women as everyday items. Beige, black and white are commonly seen colors. Other colors such as red and yellow also exist.

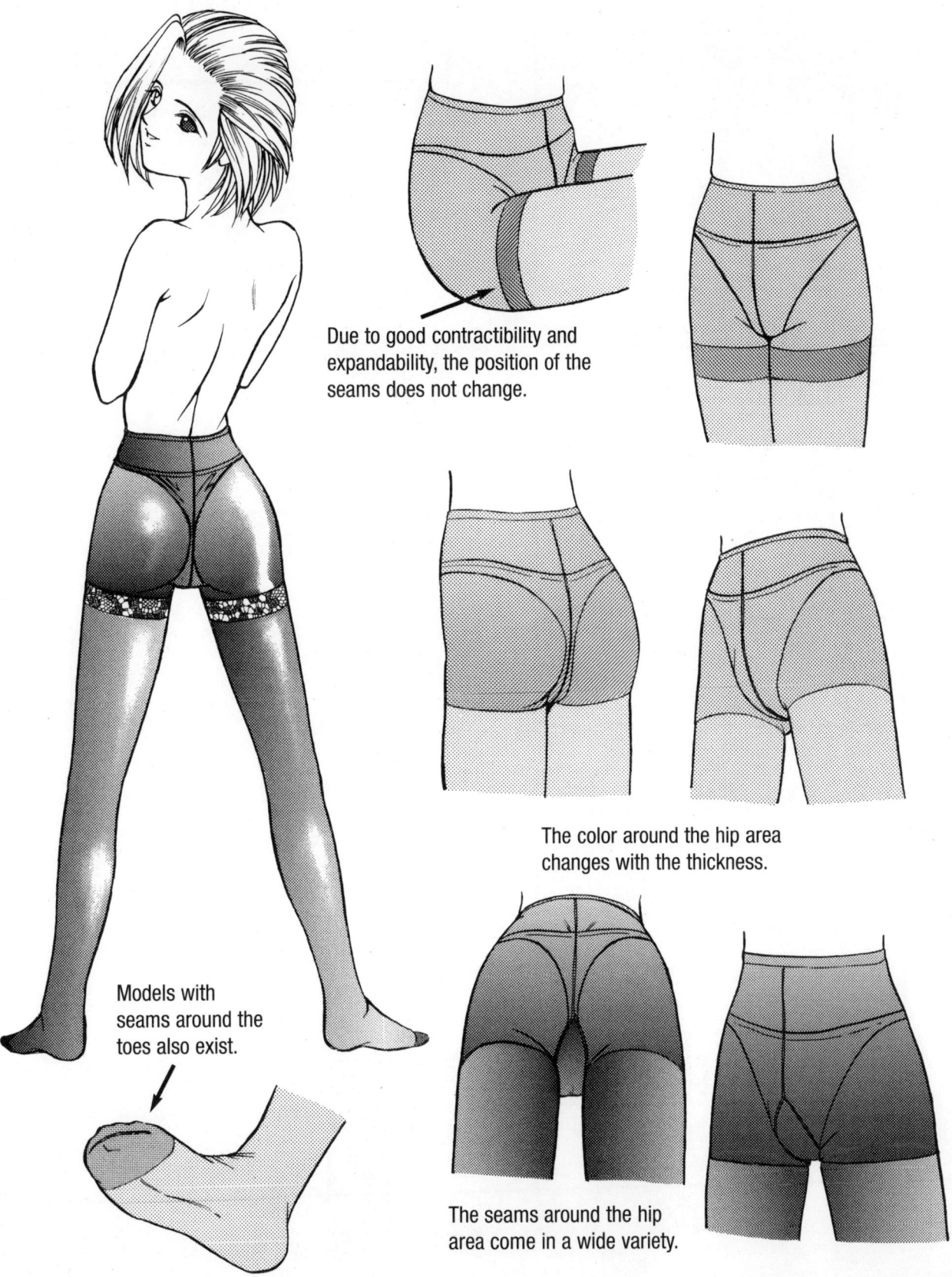

Due to good contractibility and expandability, the position of the seams does not change.

The color around the hip area changes with the thickness.

Models with seams around the toes also exist.

The seams around the hip area come in a wide variety.

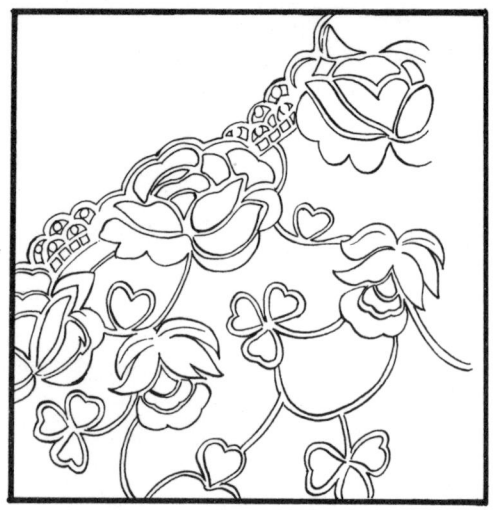

Most of the patterns found in lingerie are floral and leave prints.
How precisely you want to draw the patterns is up to you. It is also okay to gradate them.

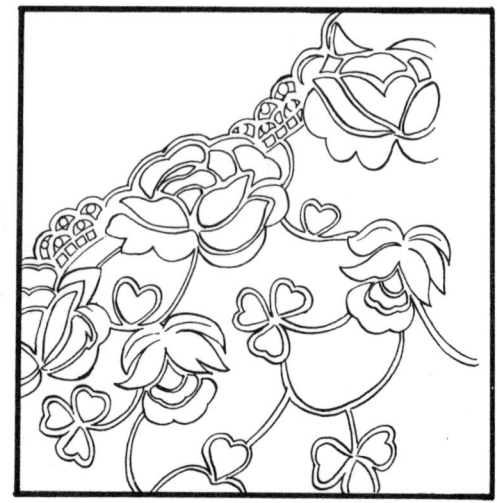

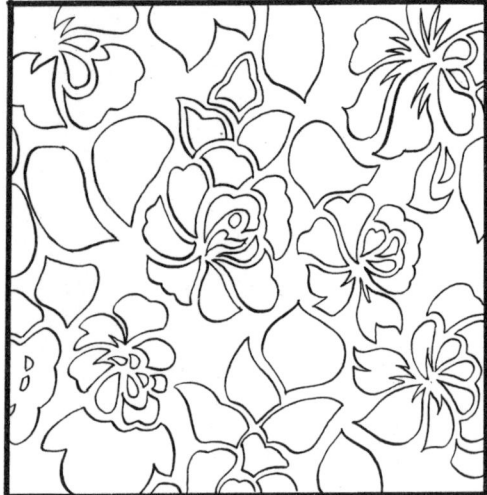

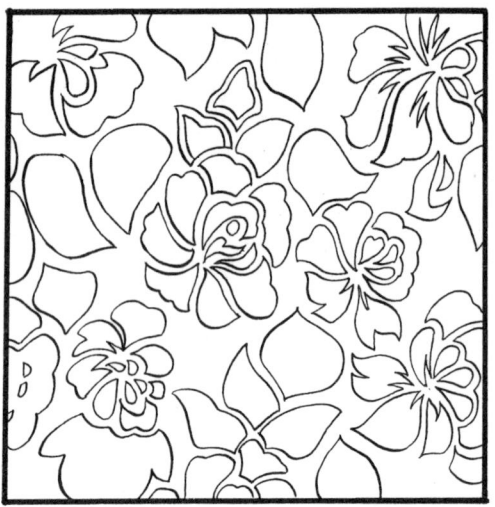

I·C Screen Tones

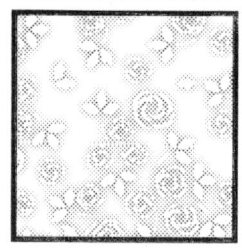

S-982 (over)

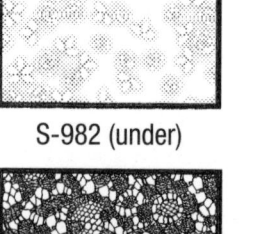

S-982 (under)

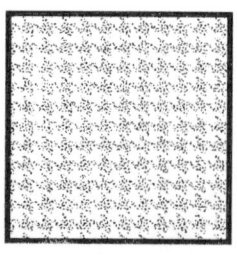

S-758

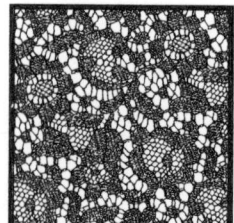

S-917

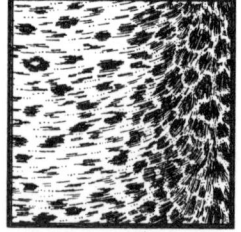

S-911

While tones come in a wide variety, many people tend to use these ones.

Standing Wearing a T-shirt

Let's take a look a model wearing jeans where the hip area is not hidden by a jacket.

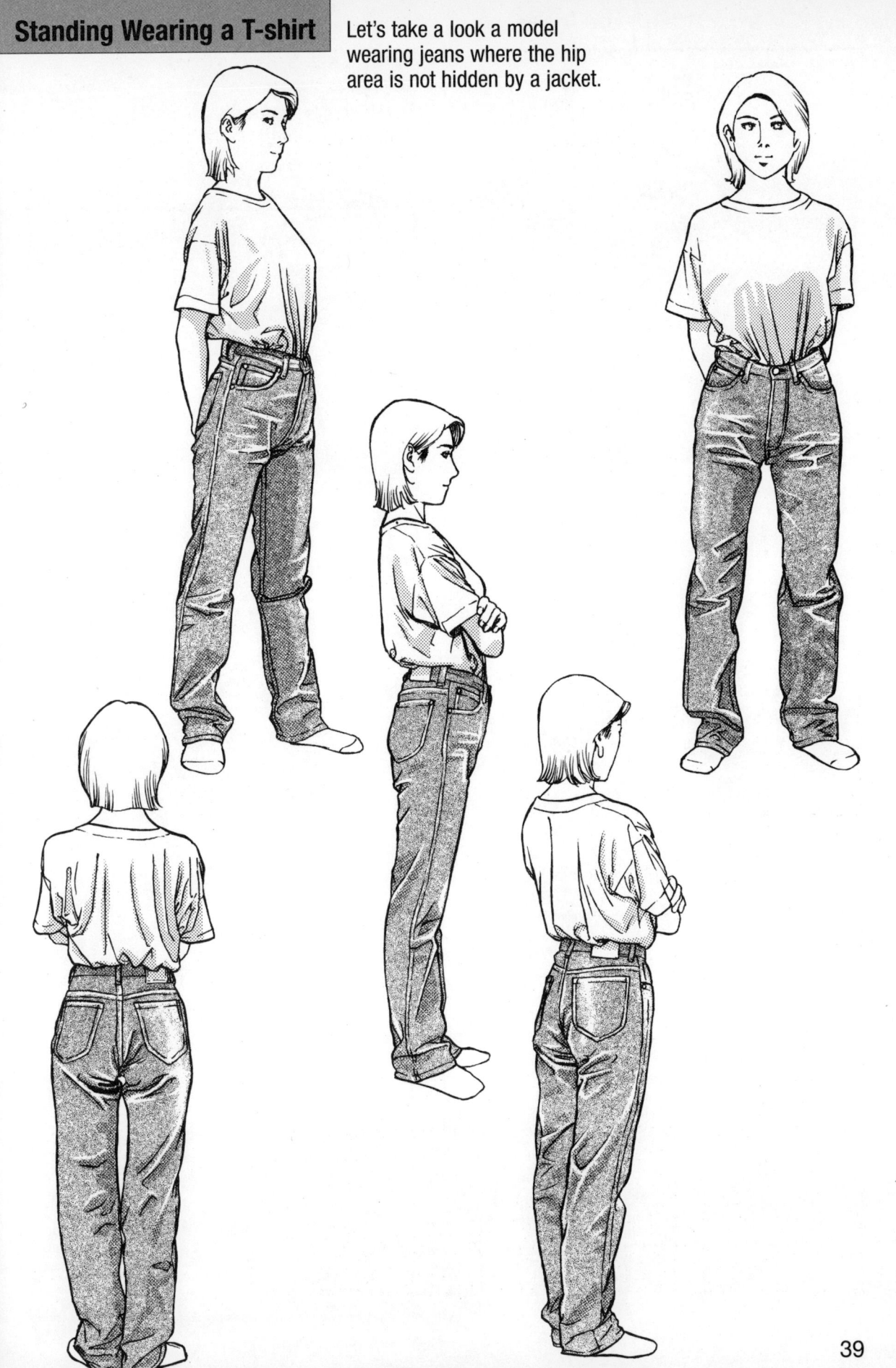

Standing Wearing a T-shirt | Low Angle

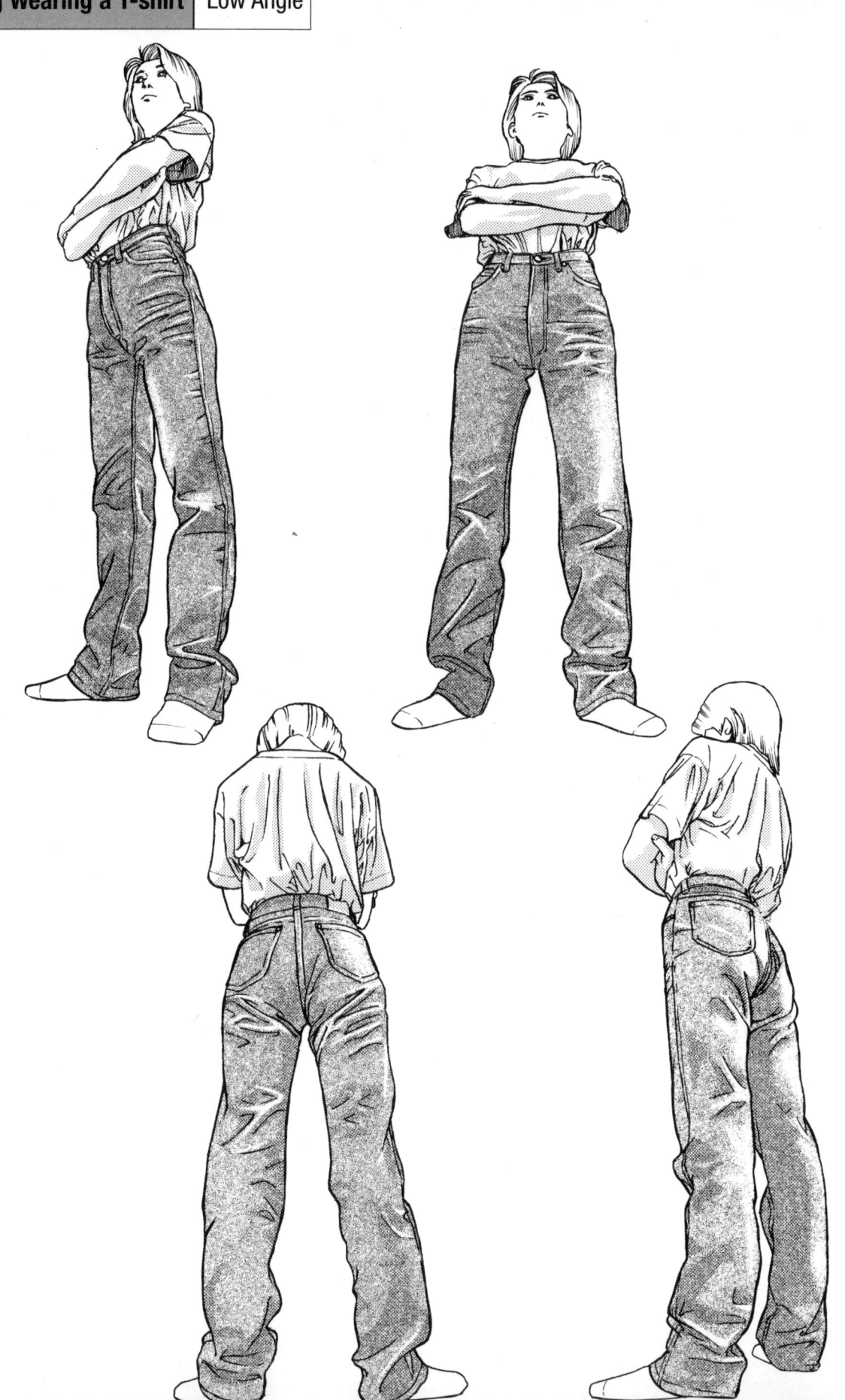

Sitting on the Knees Wearing a T-shirt

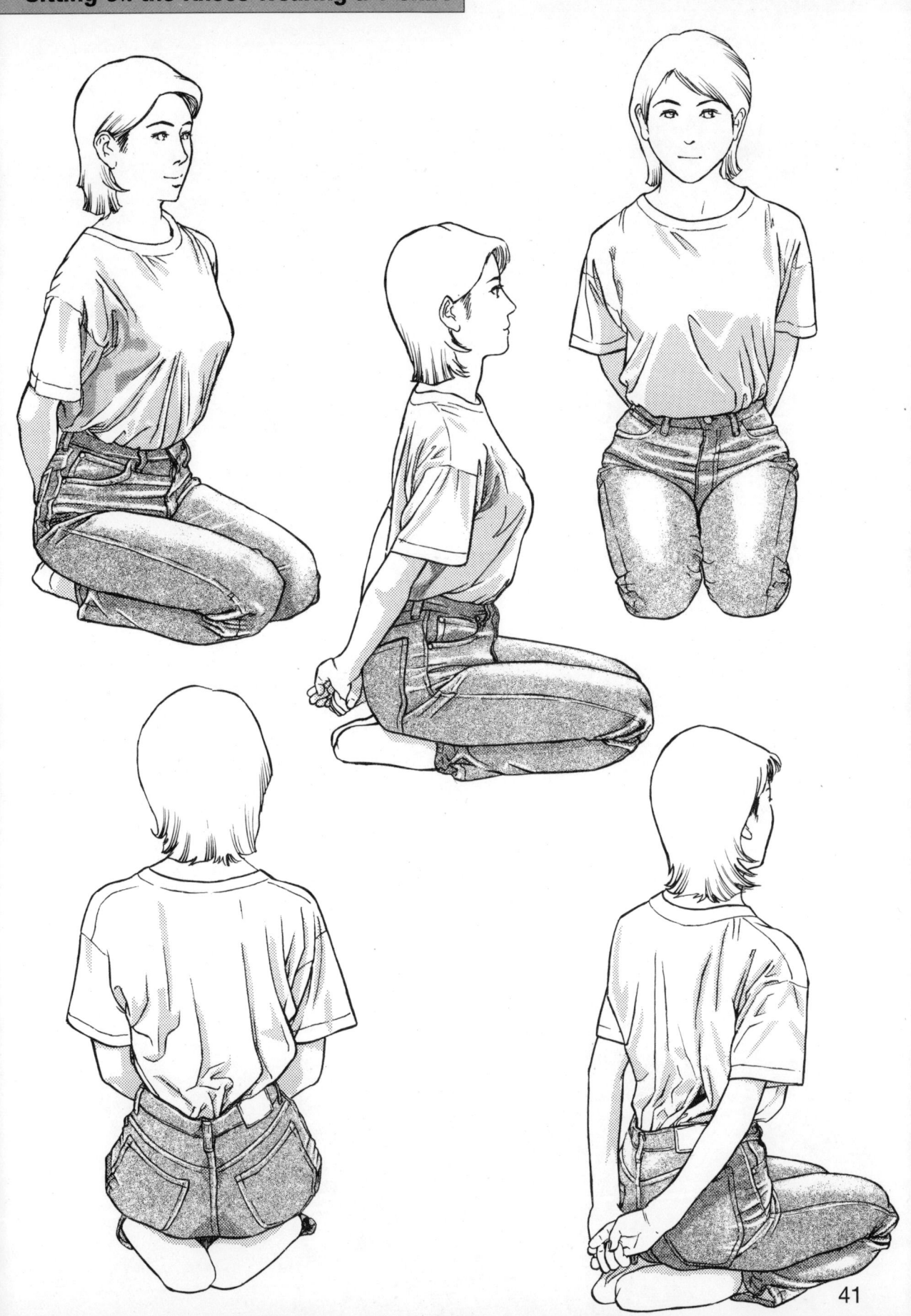

Sitting at Ease Wearing a T-shirt

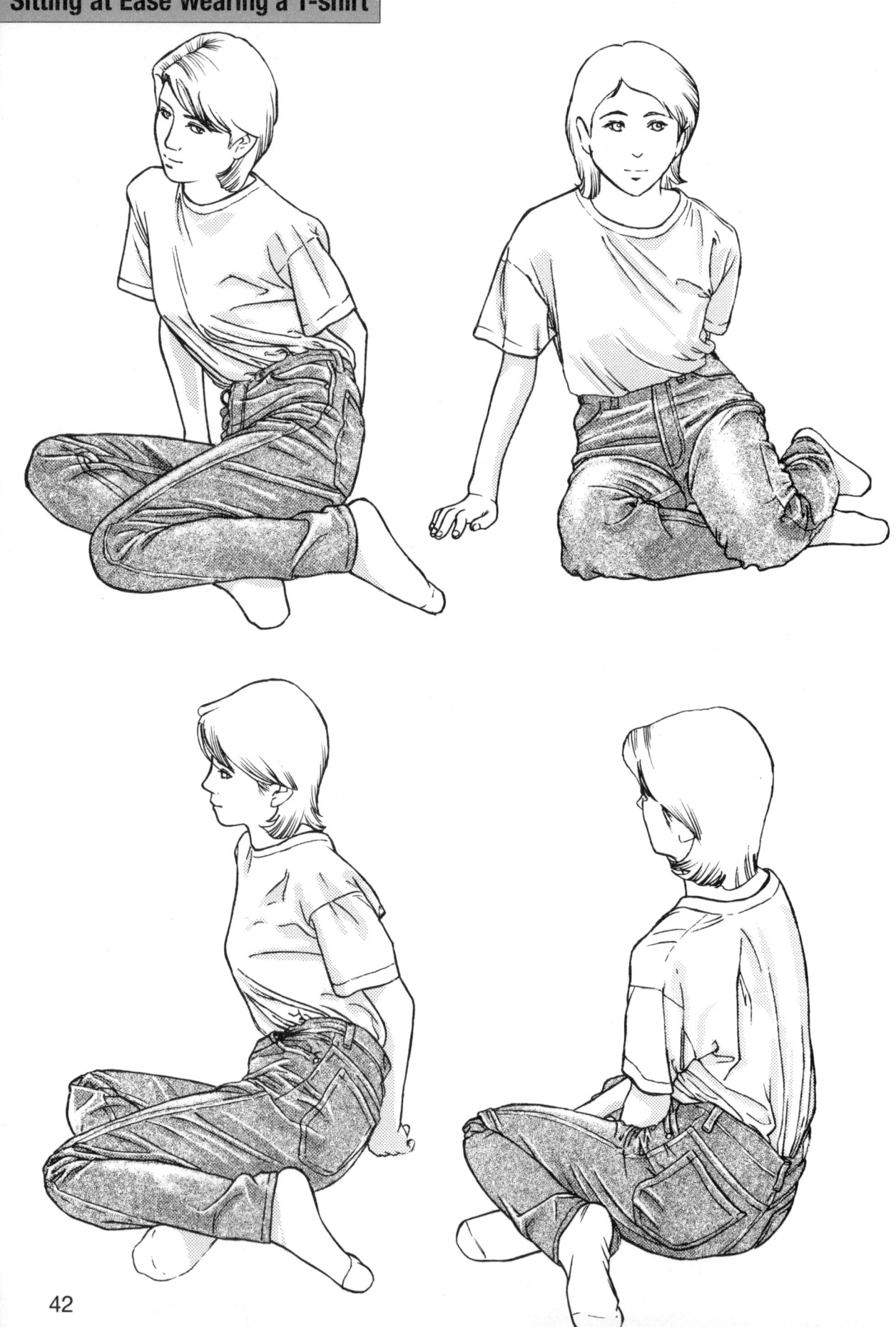

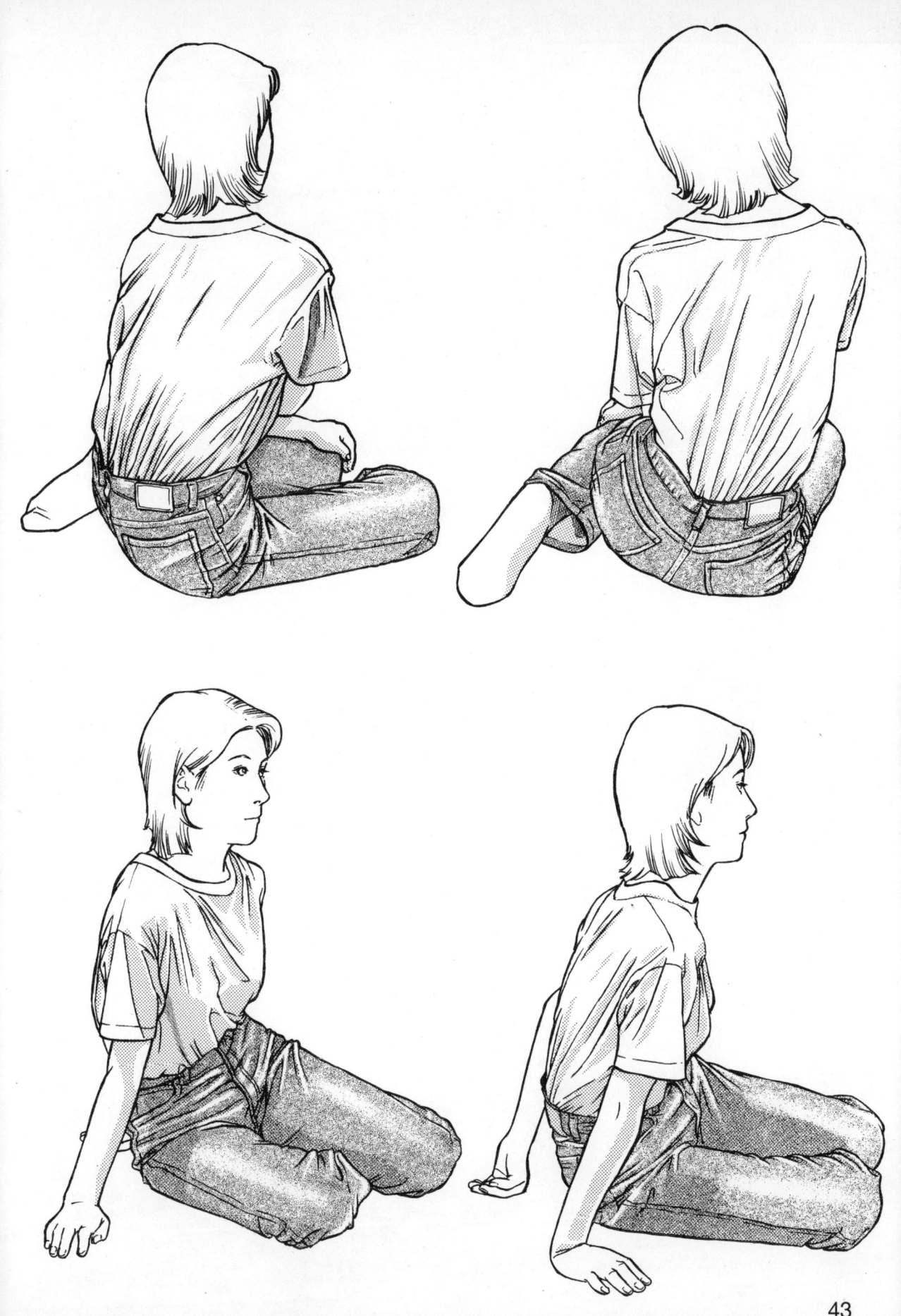

Sitting with the Legs Extended Wearing a T-shirt

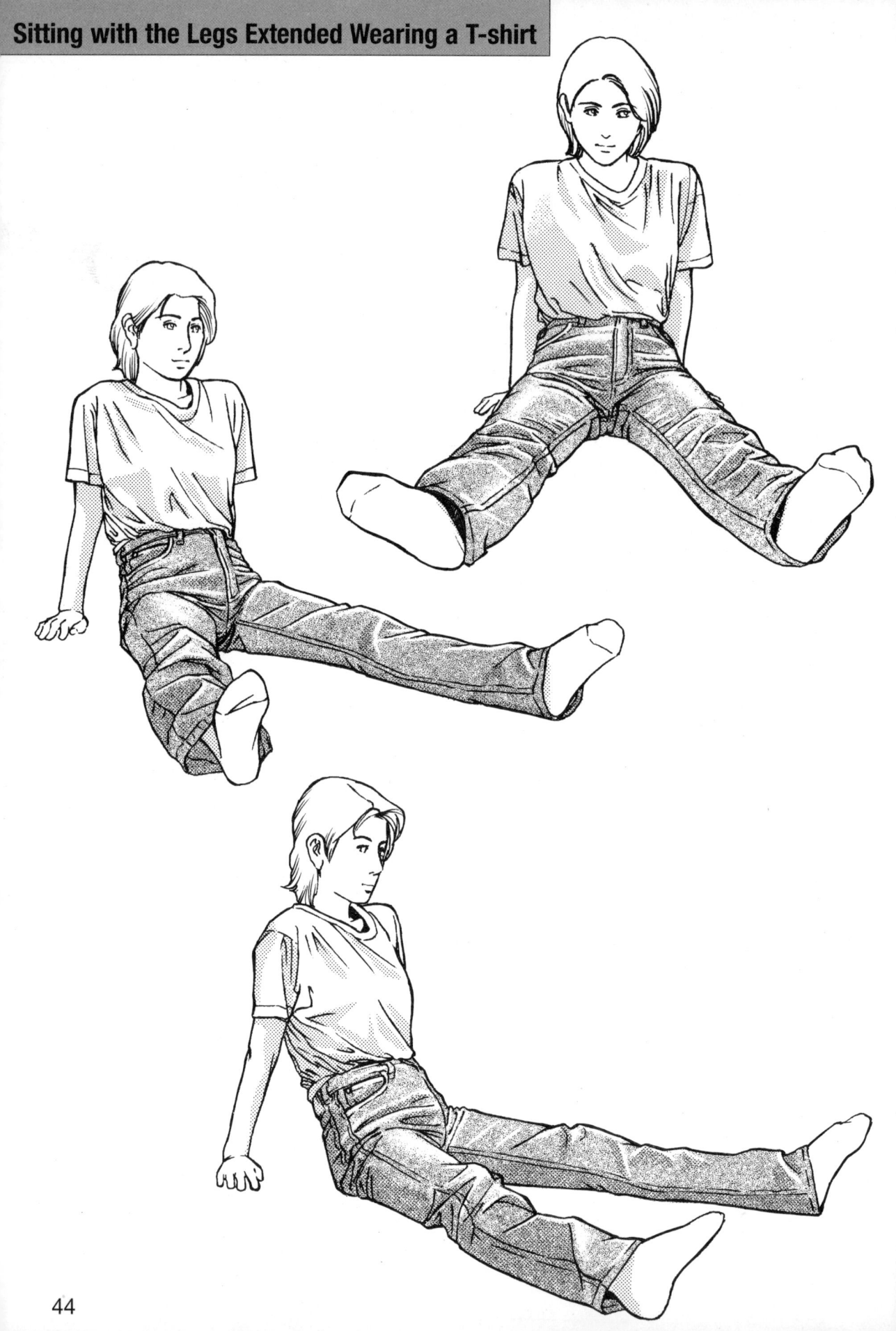

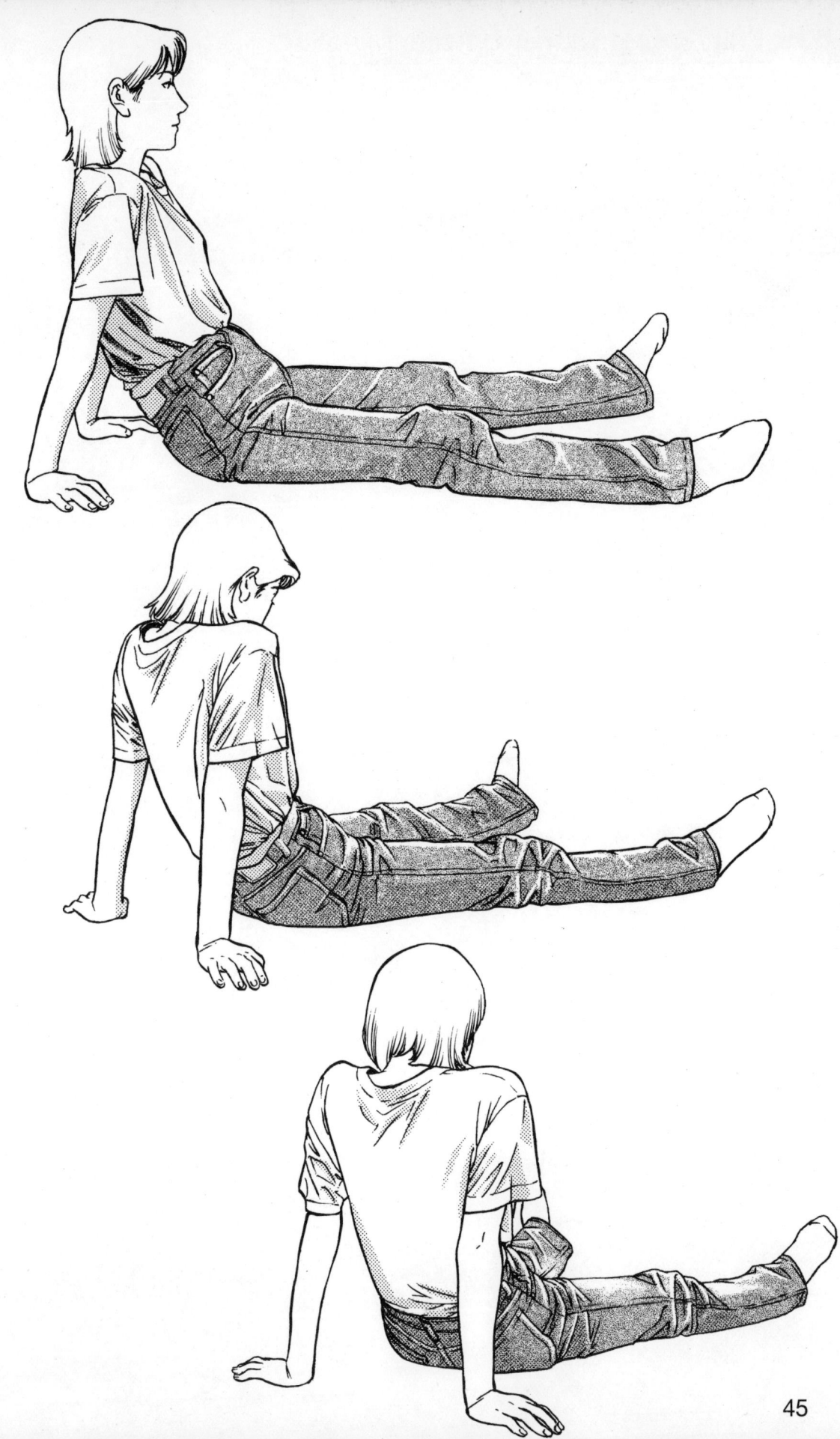

Sitting Cross-legged Wearing a T-shirt

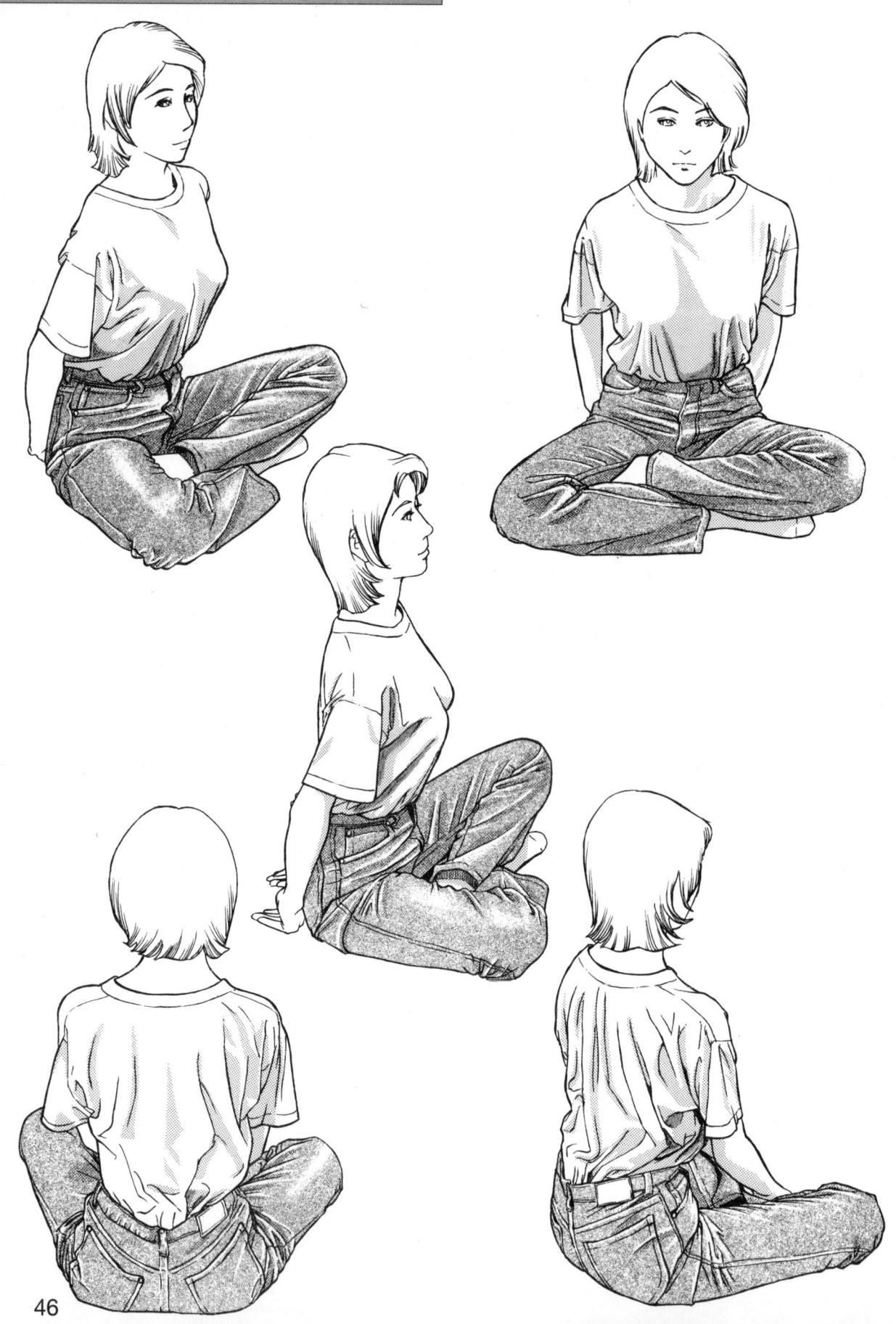

Standing on One Knee Wearing a T-shirt – Part 1

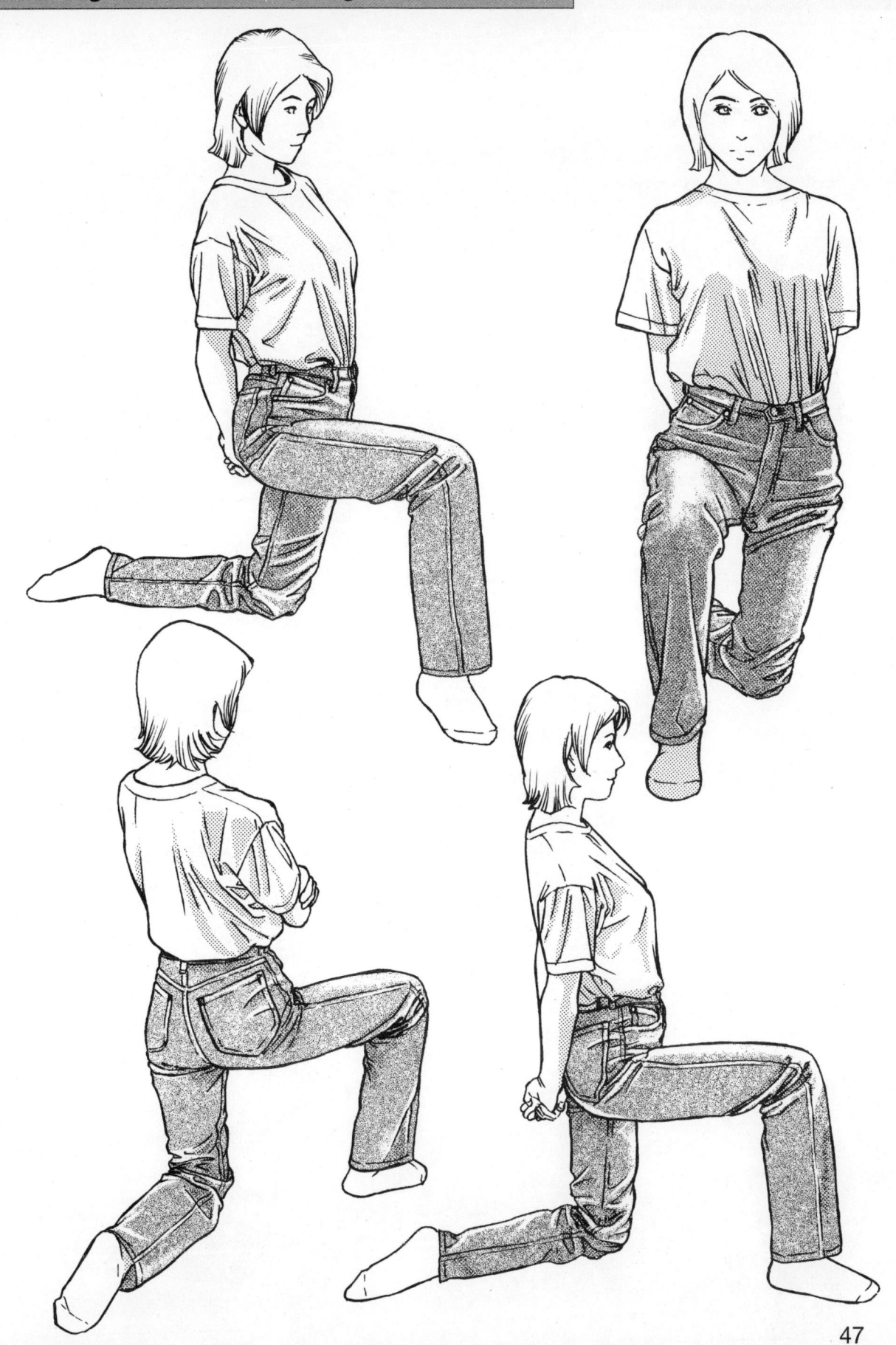

Standing on One Knee Wearing a T-shirt – Part 2

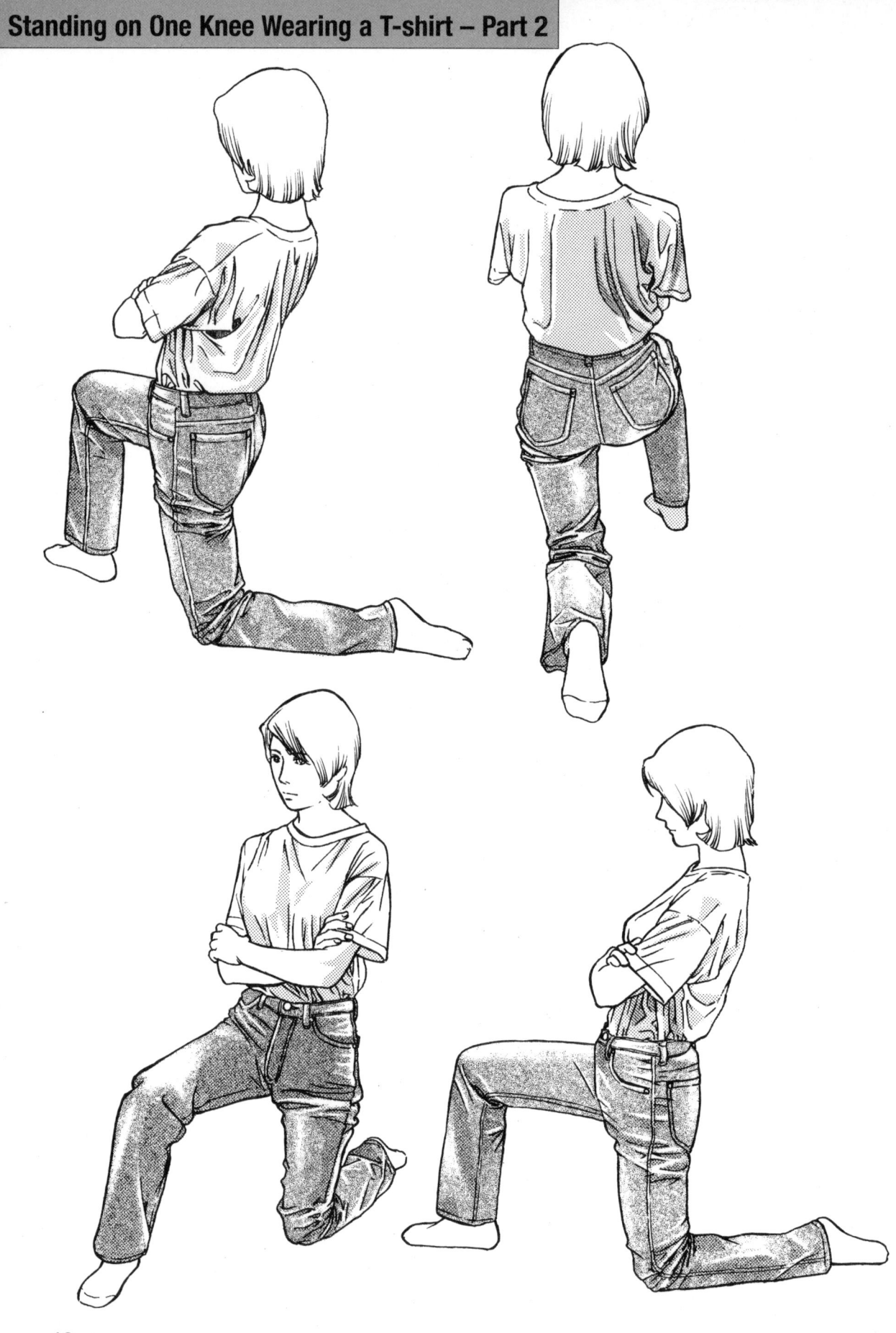

Sitting in a Chair Wearing a T-shirt

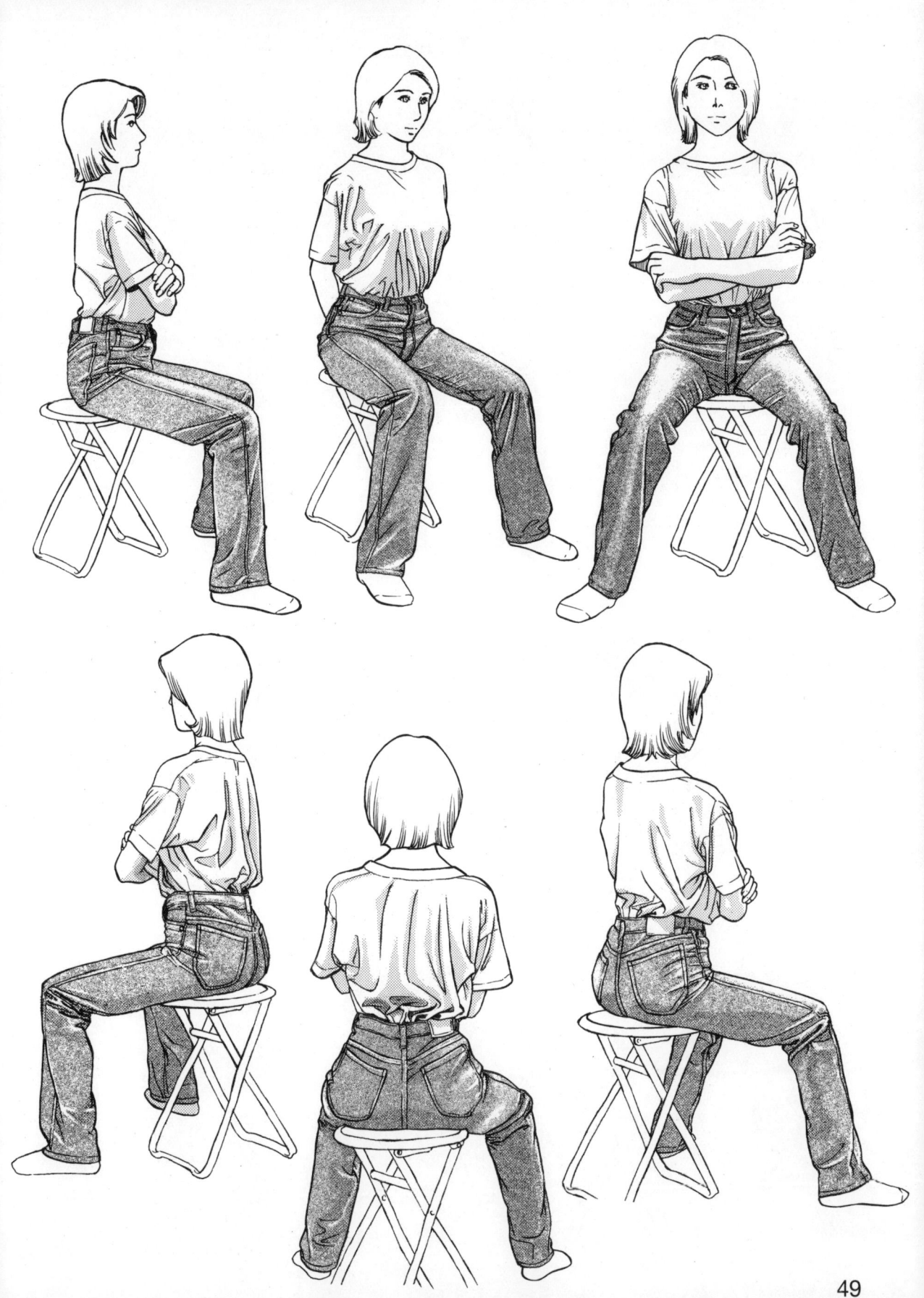

Crossing the Legs Wearing a T-shirt

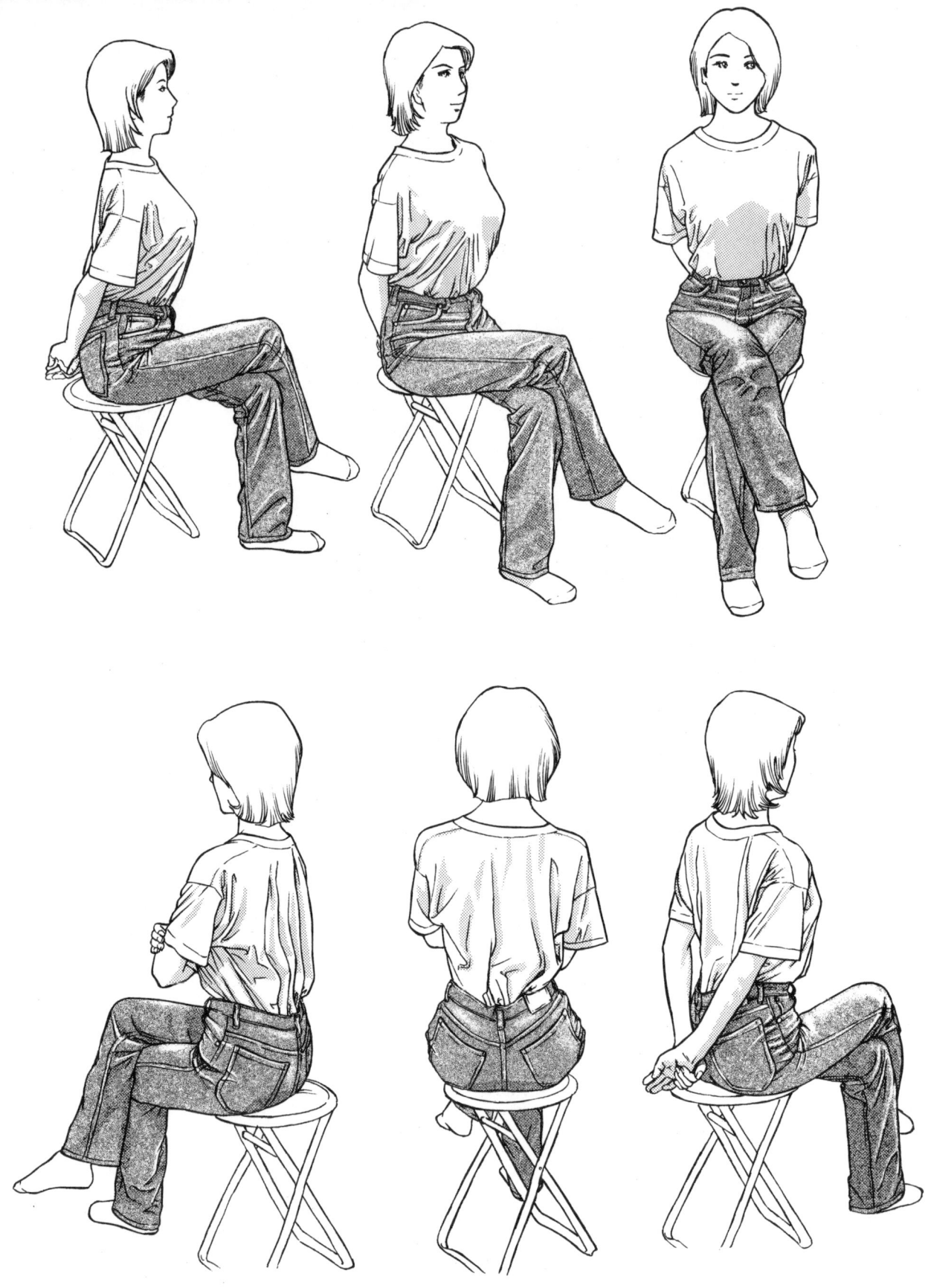

Chapter 2
Sweatshirts and Skirts

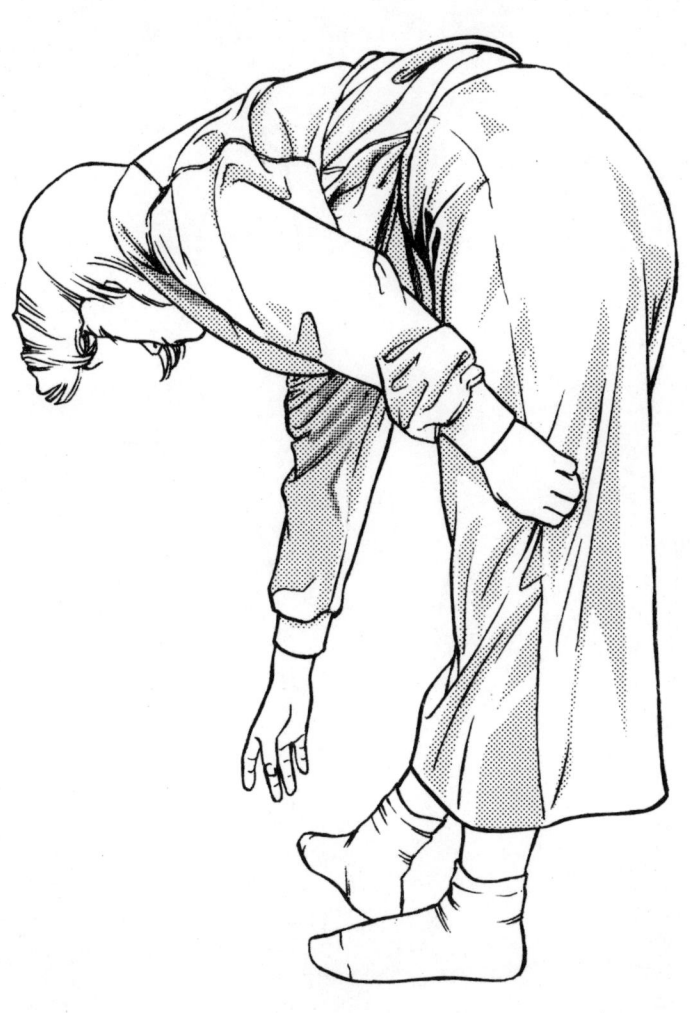

Sweatshirts and Skirts

Here we introduce various skirts and tops that make up ensembles.

Please be aware that any combination of the various kinds is possible. Please take a look each of their differences and make reference to them.

Sweatshirts

In addition to being worn around the house, this type of clothing has a wide range of use in fashion. The biggest difference in the designs is found in the neck area.

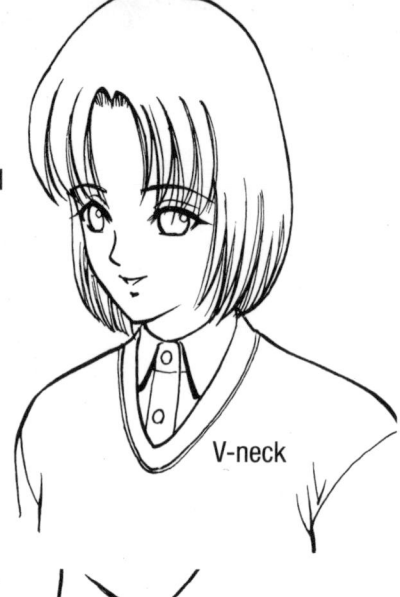

V-neck

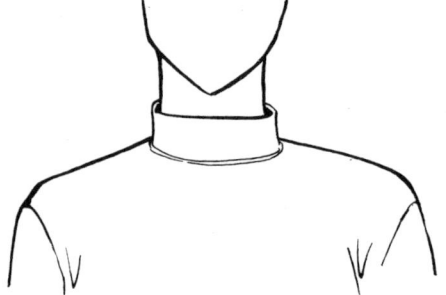

High-neck

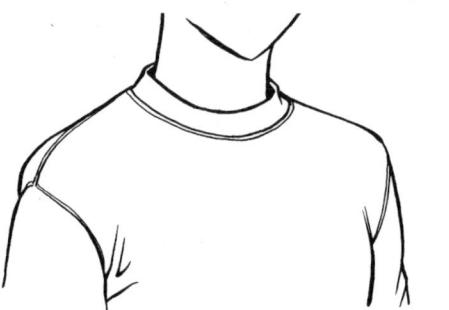

Crewneck

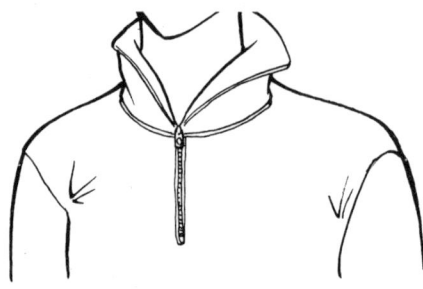

Zip-up Neck

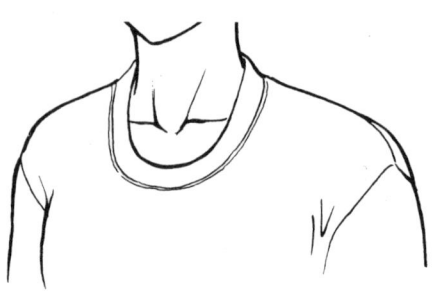

U-neck

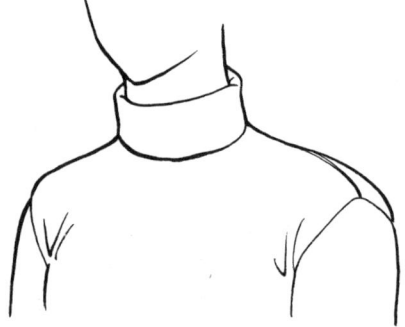

Turtle Neck

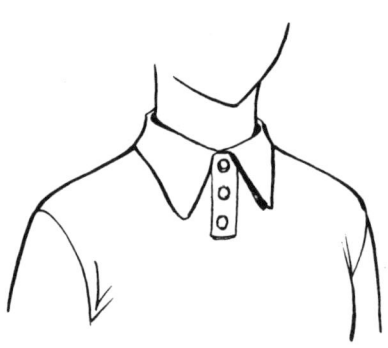

Polo Collar

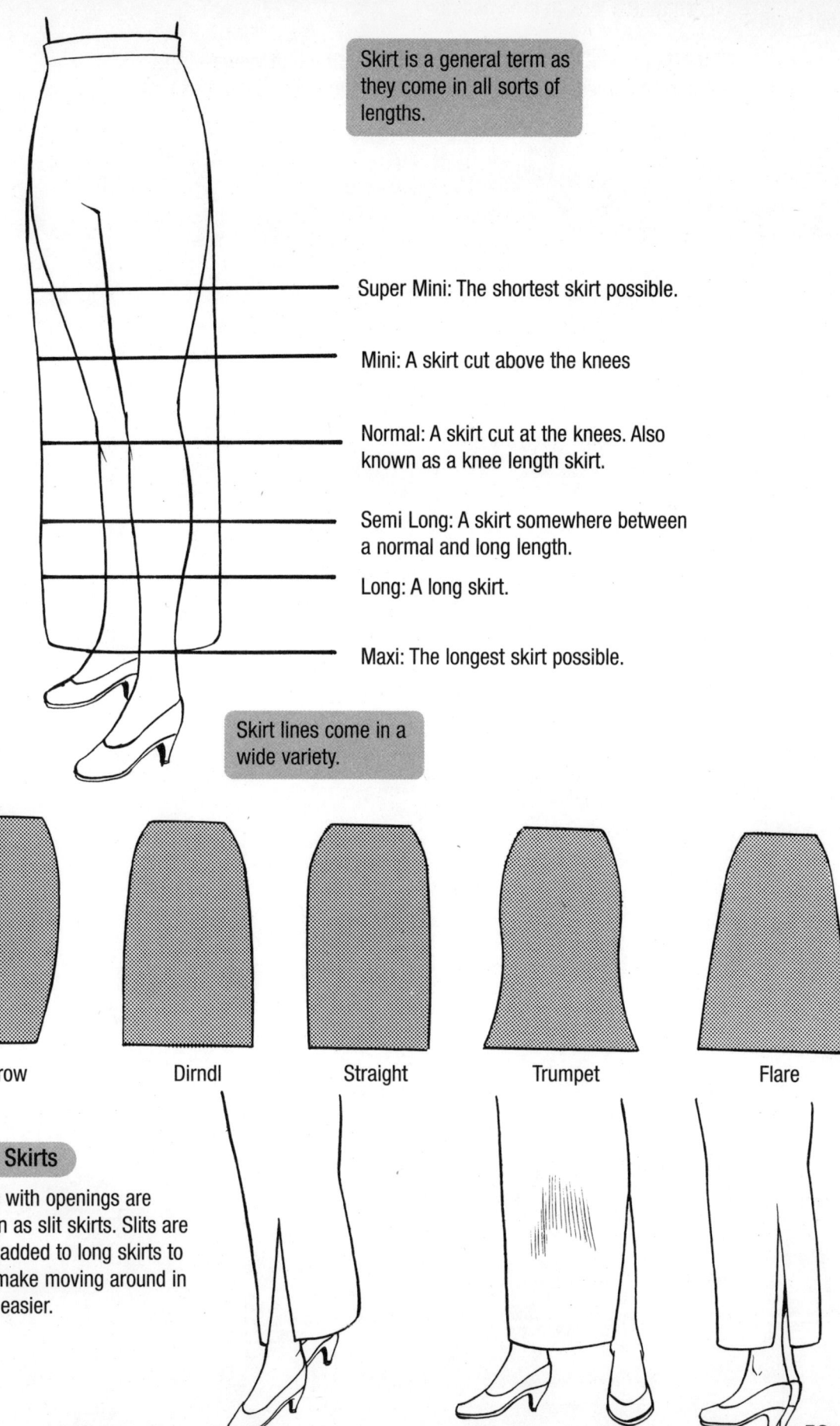

Skirt is a general term as they come in all sorts of lengths.

Super Mini: The shortest skirt possible.

Mini: A skirt cut above the knees

Normal: A skirt cut at the knees. Also known as a knee length skirt.

Semi Long: A skirt somewhere between a normal and long length.

Long: A long skirt.

Maxi: The longest skirt possible.

Skirt lines come in a wide variety.

Narrow   Dirndl   Straight   Trumpet   Flare

Slit Skirts

Skirts with openings are known as slit skirts. Slits are often added to long skirts to help make moving around in them easier.

Crewnecks

Let's take a look at crewnecks.

At first glance, these look easy to draw, but when viewed from different angles, they are harder to draw than you would expect.

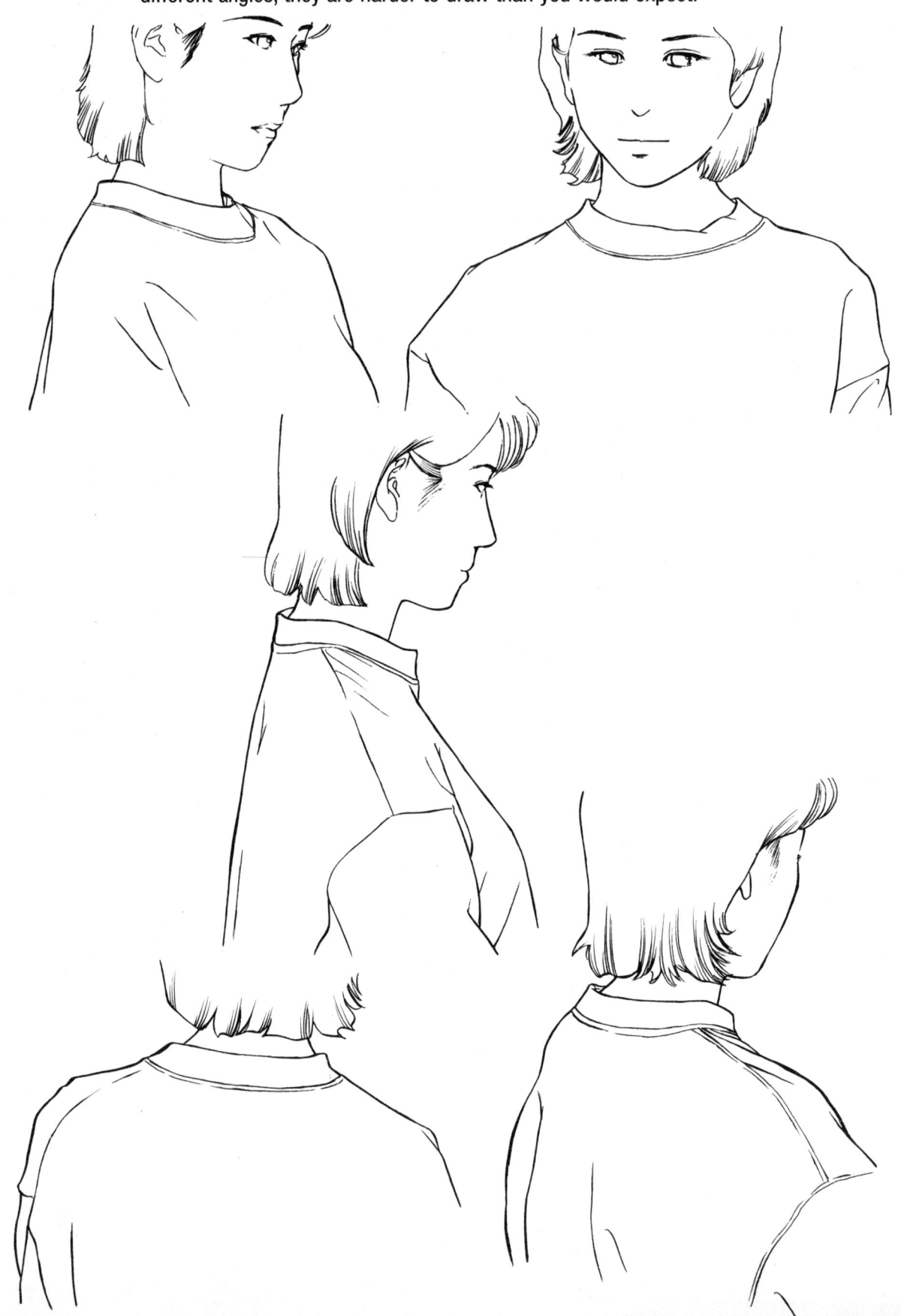

Crewnecks | High Angle

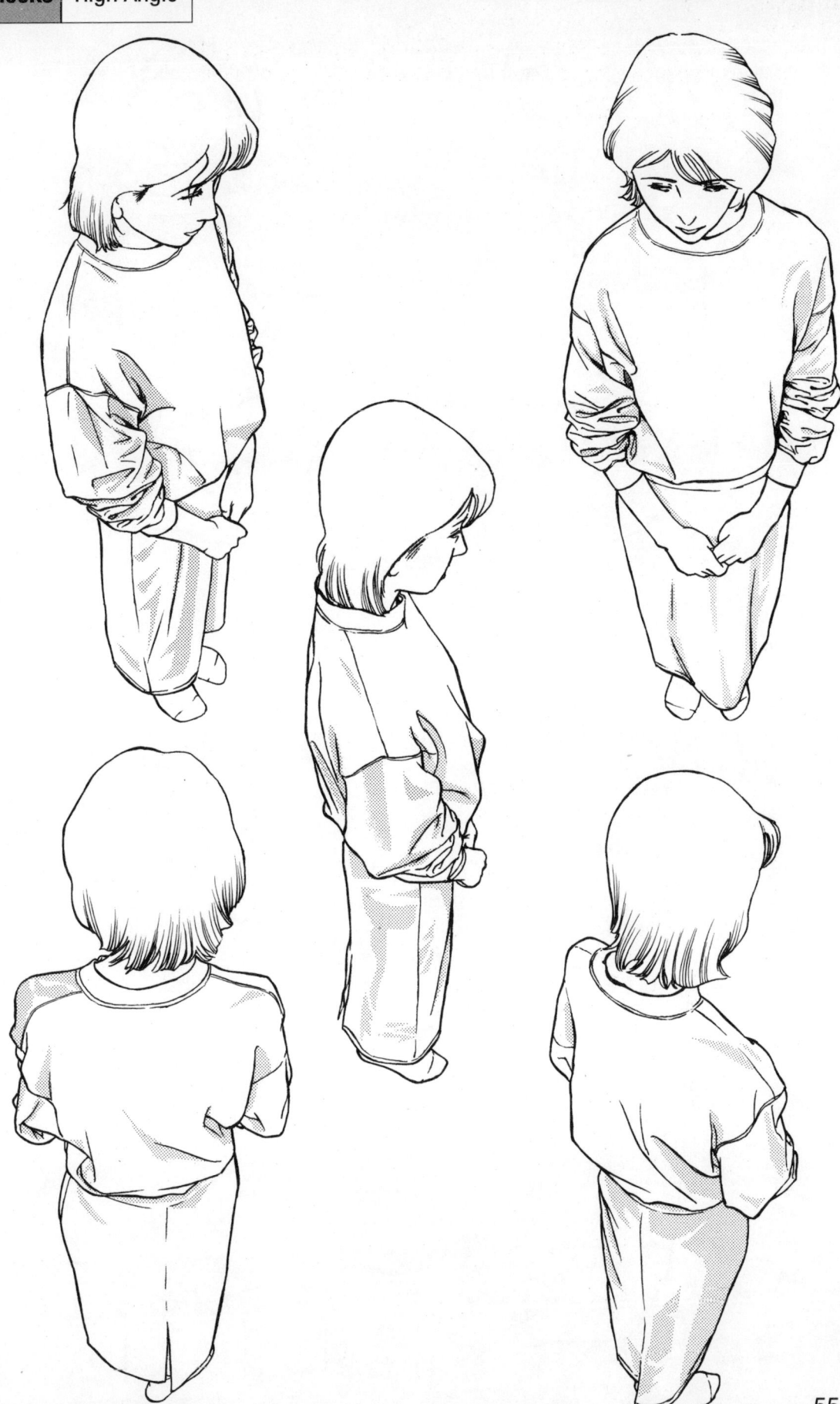

Folding the Arms

Let's take a look at how the wrinkles change with the pose.

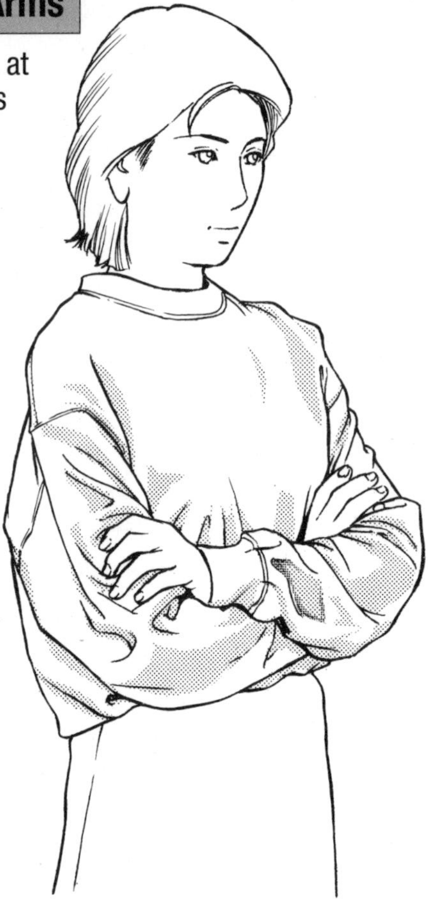

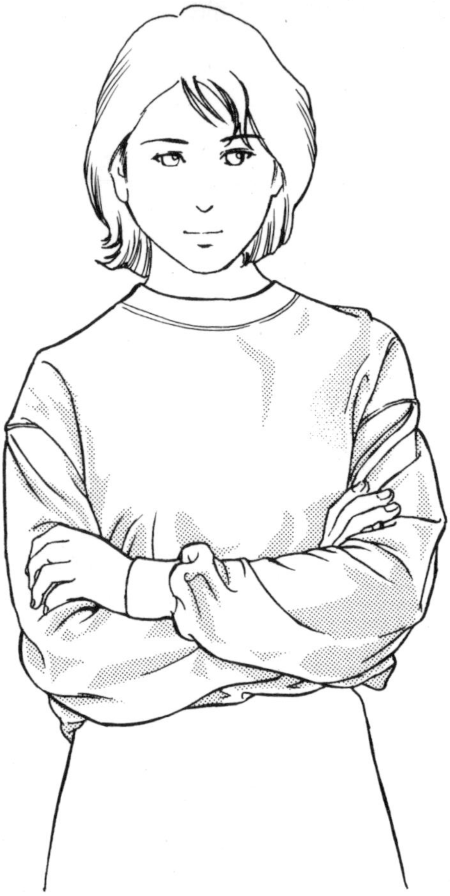

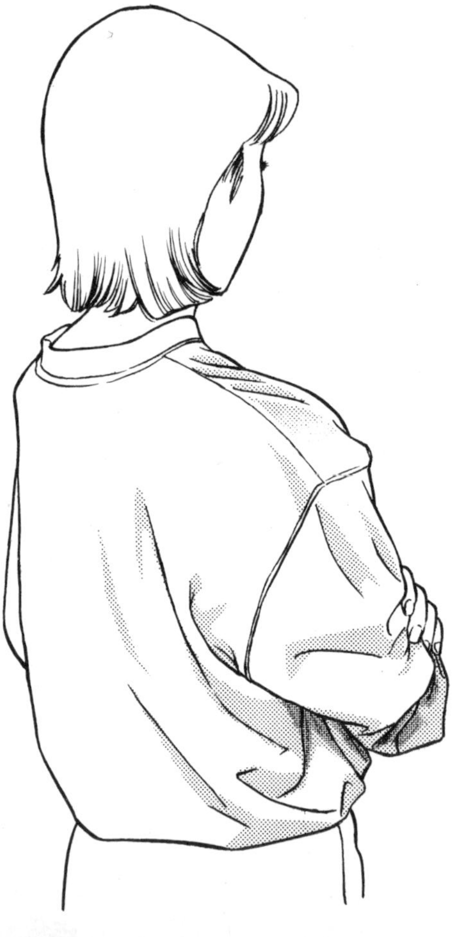

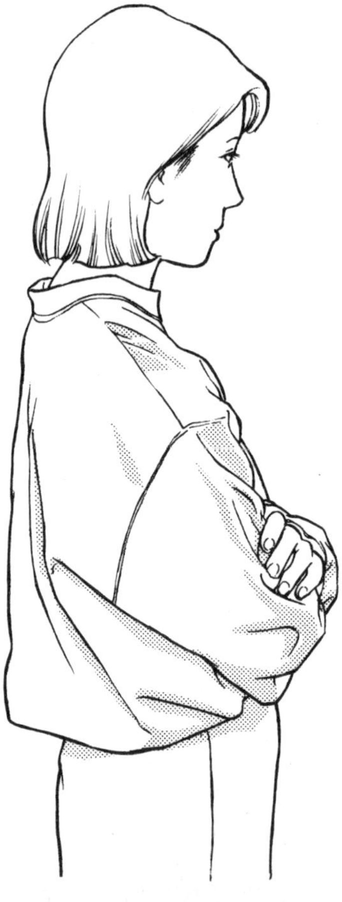

Folding the Arms — High Angle

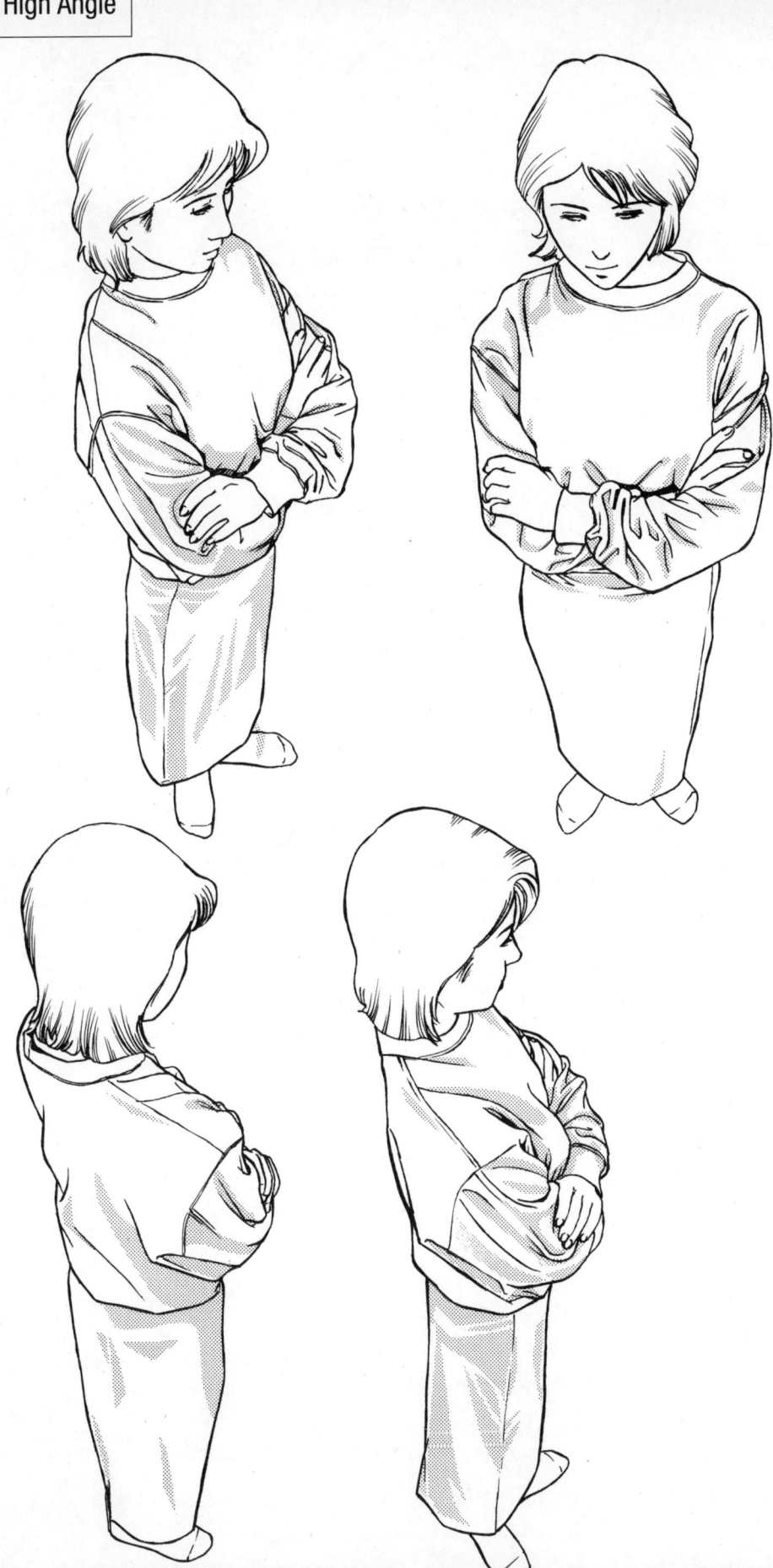

Bending to the Side

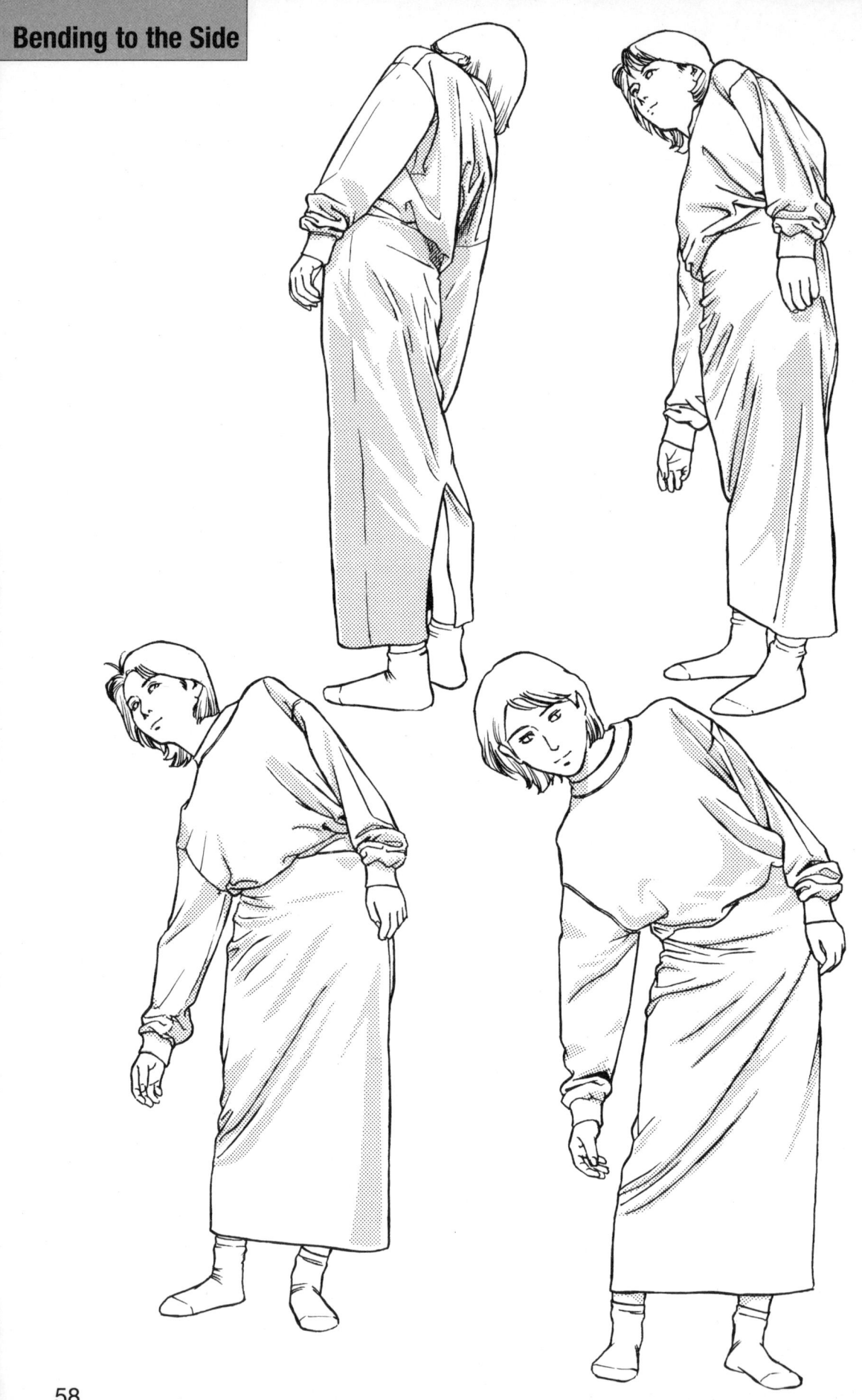

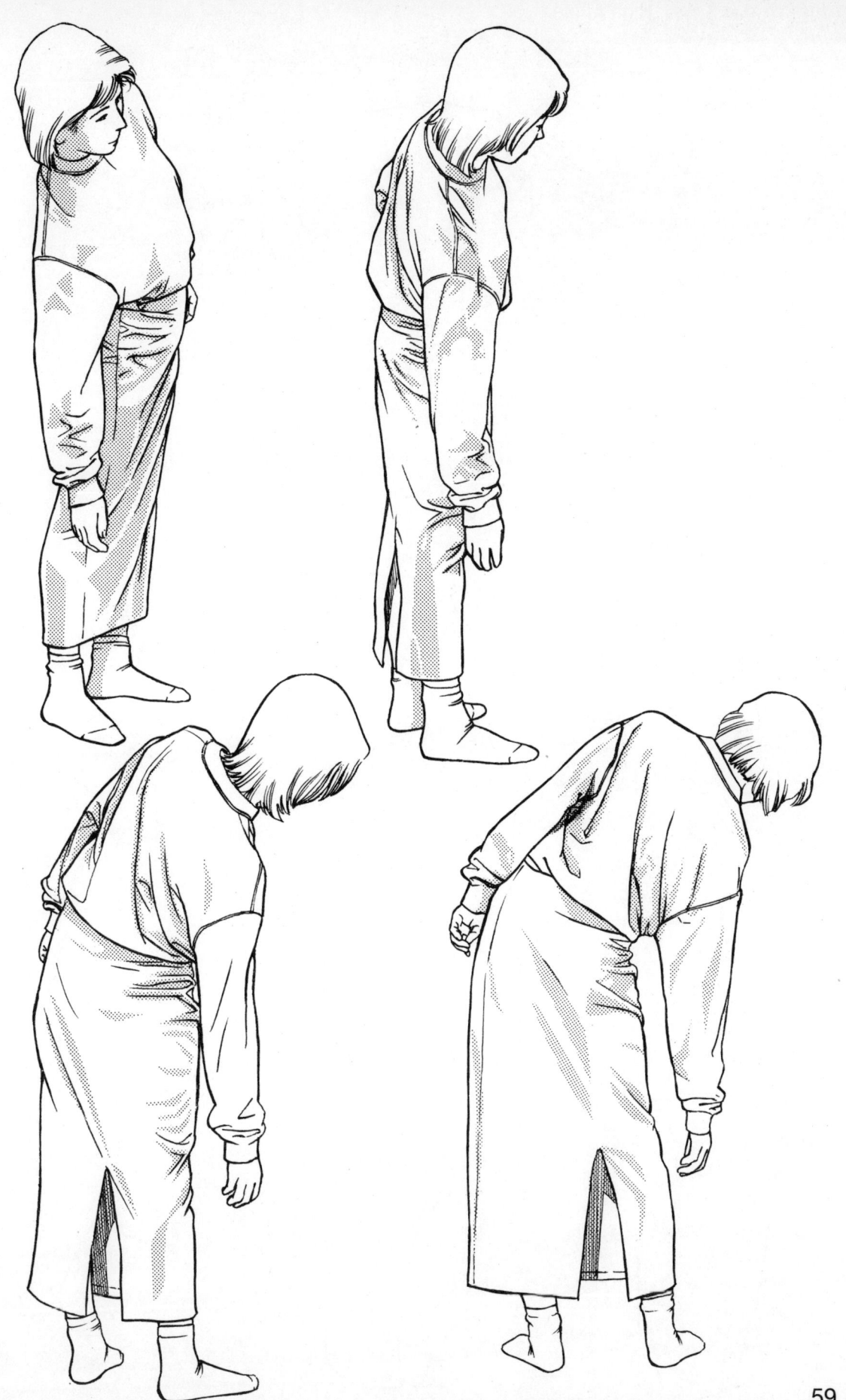

Bending to the Side | High Angle

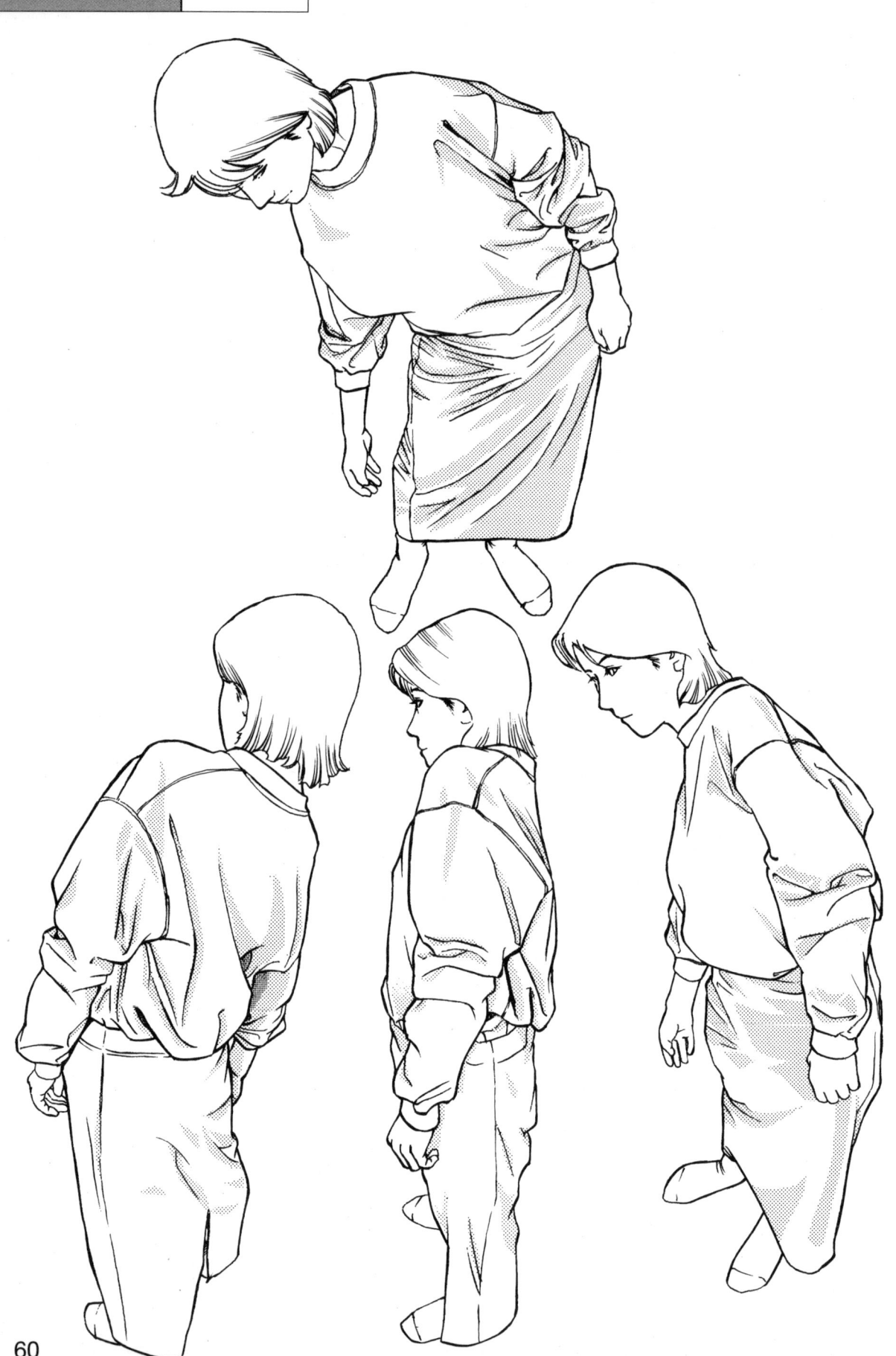

60

Bending to the Side | High Angle

Turning the Body

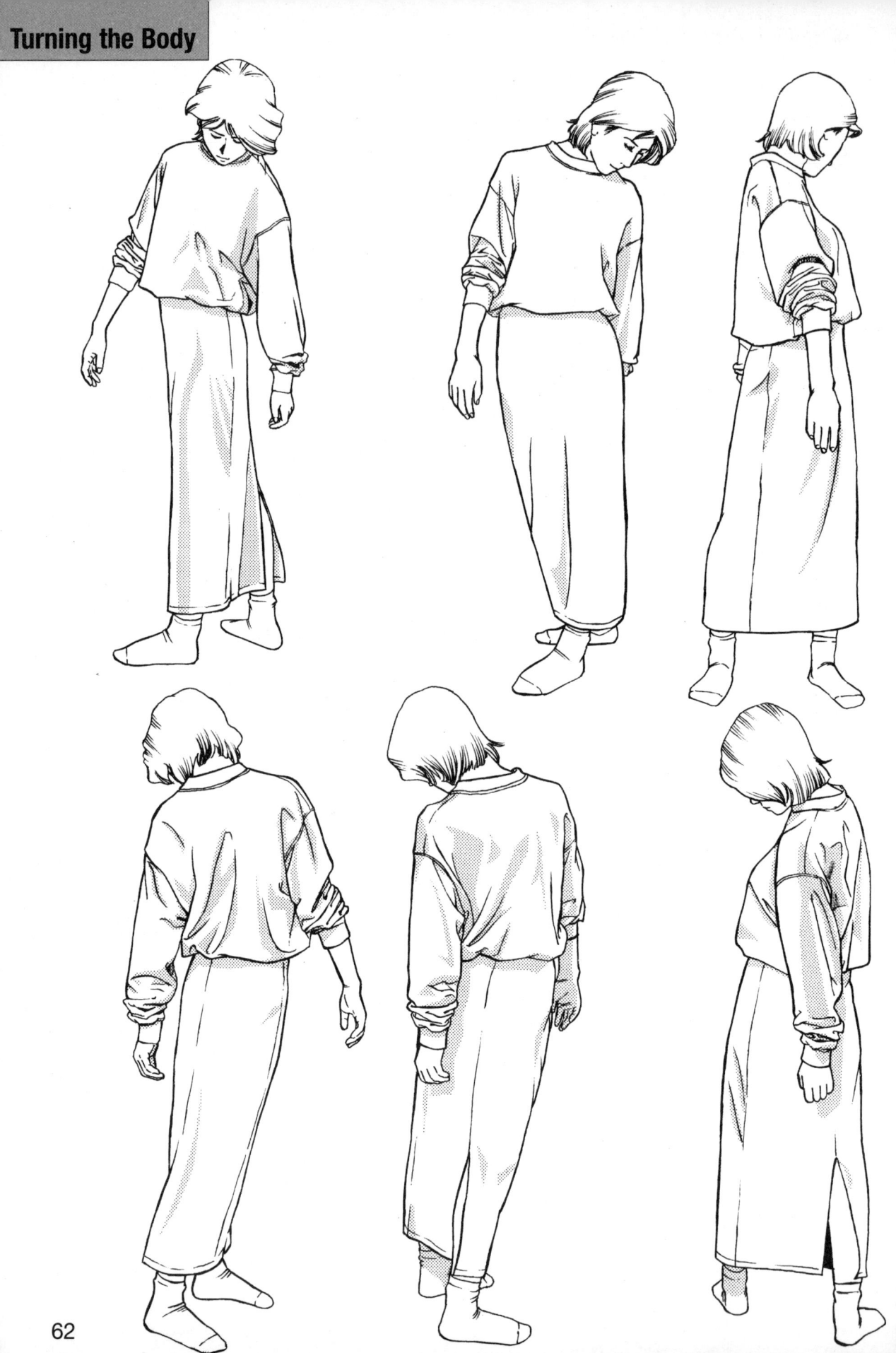

Turning the Body | High Angle

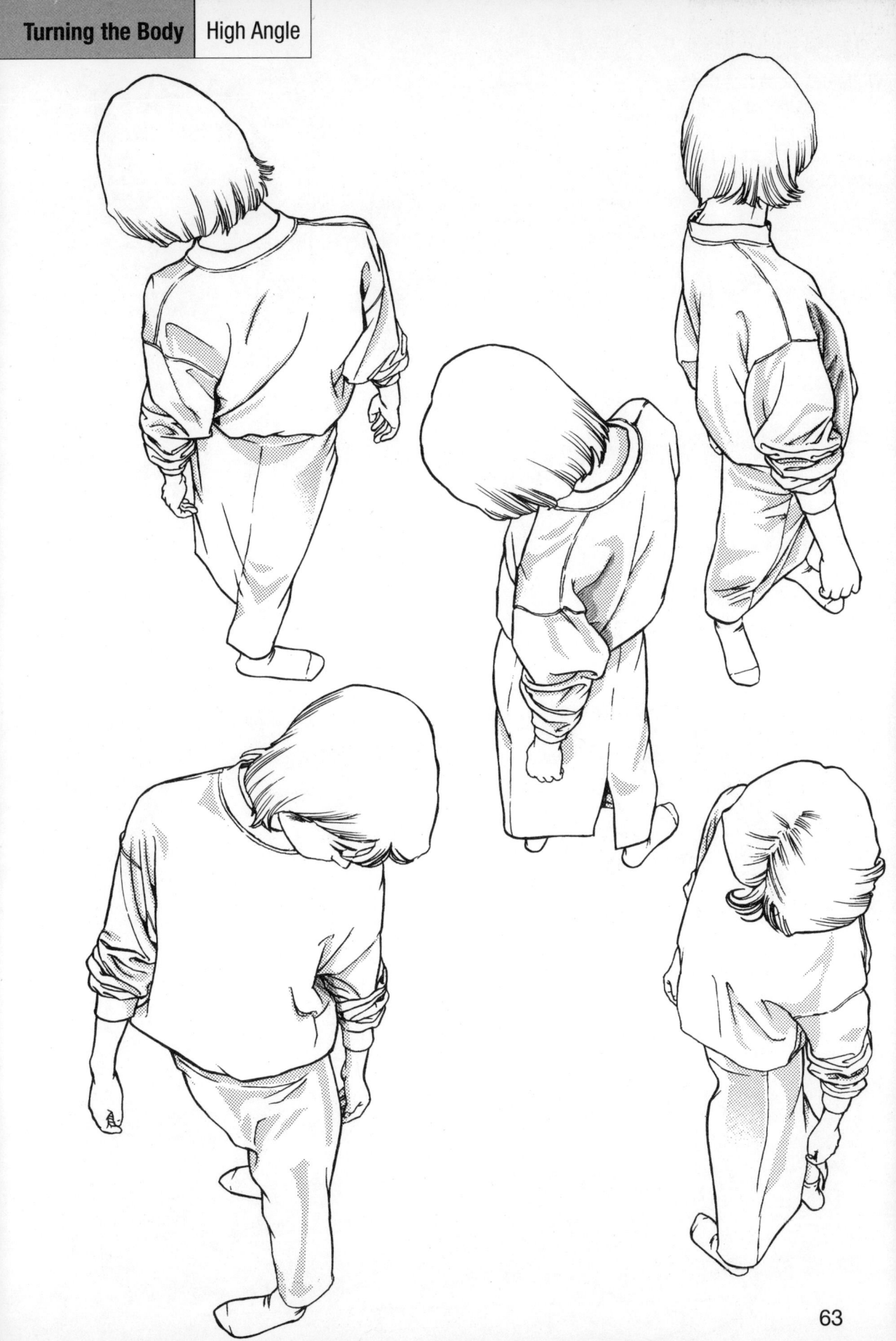

Picking Something Up – Part 1

While this pose has the model picking something up, please also make reference to the stooping forward pose.

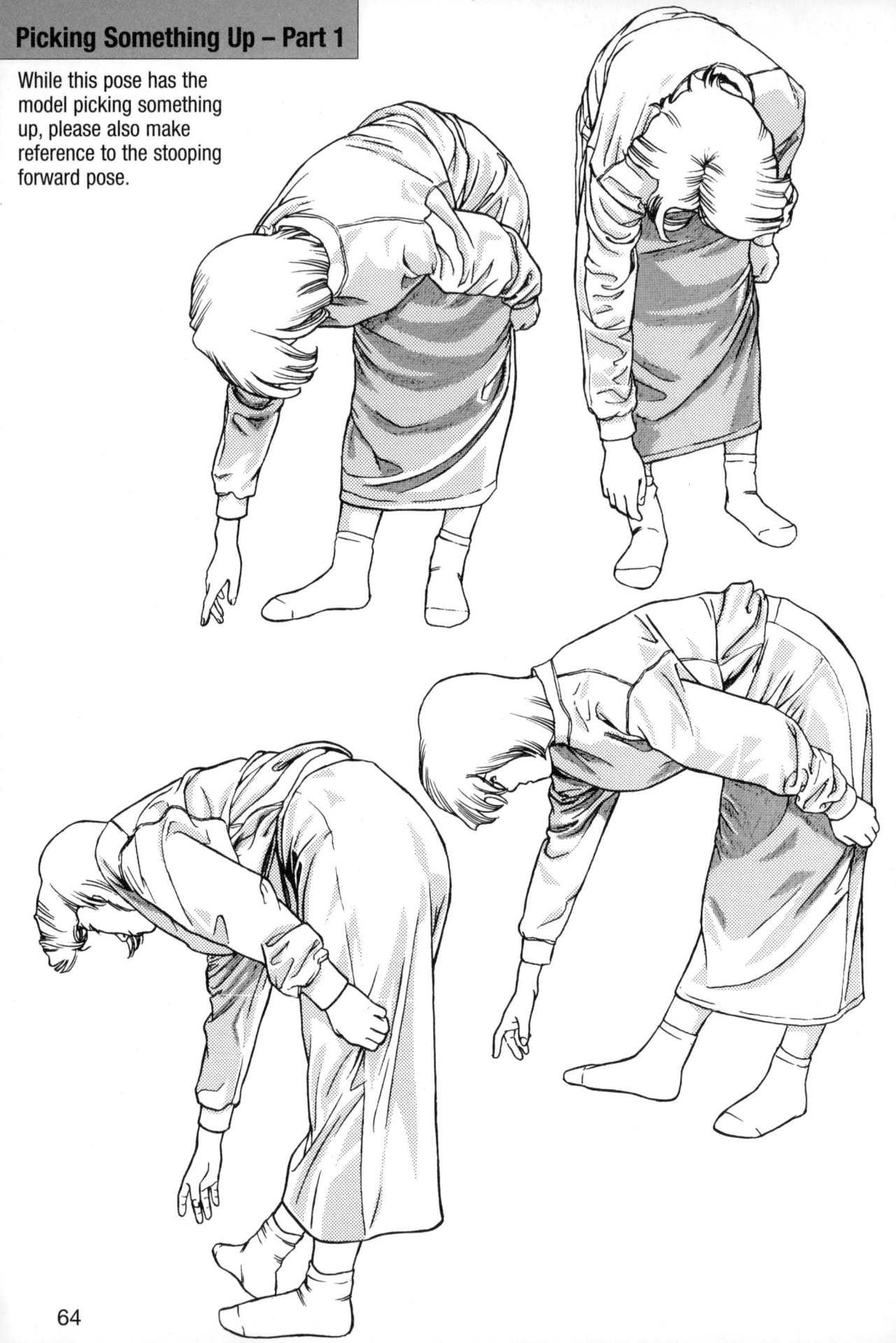

Picking Something Up – Part 2

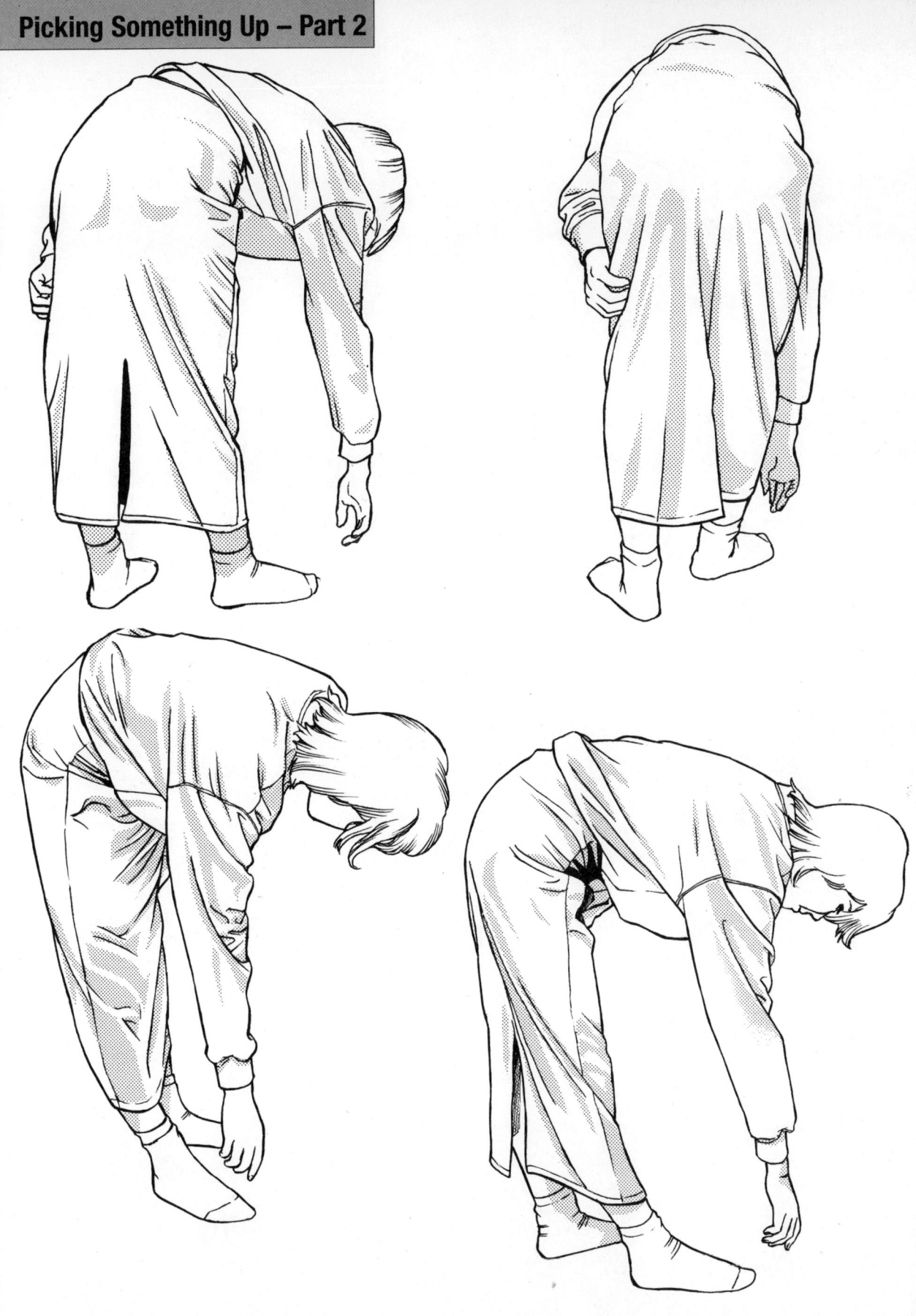

Picking Something Up – Part 3 | High Angle

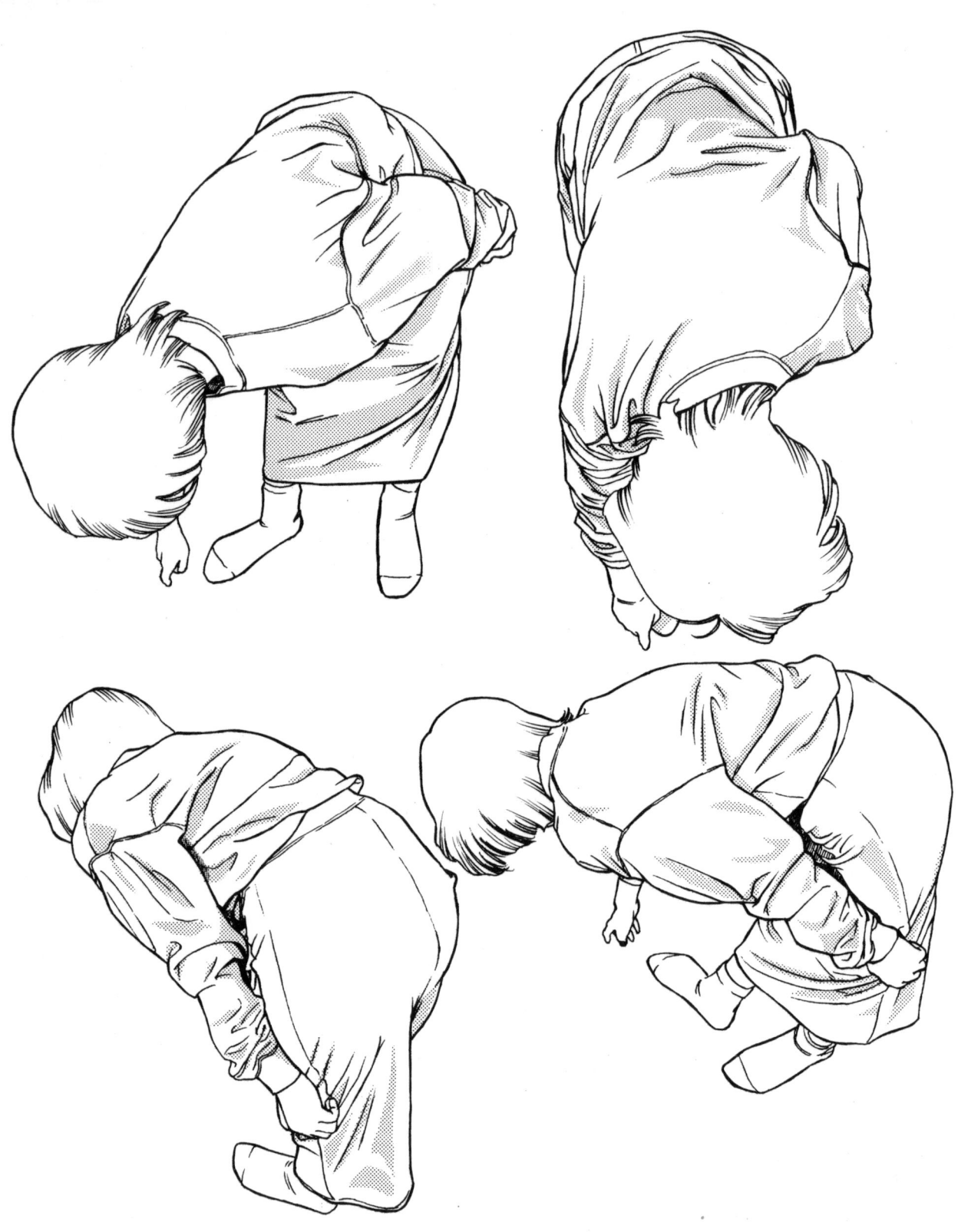

Picking Something Up – Part 4 | High Angle

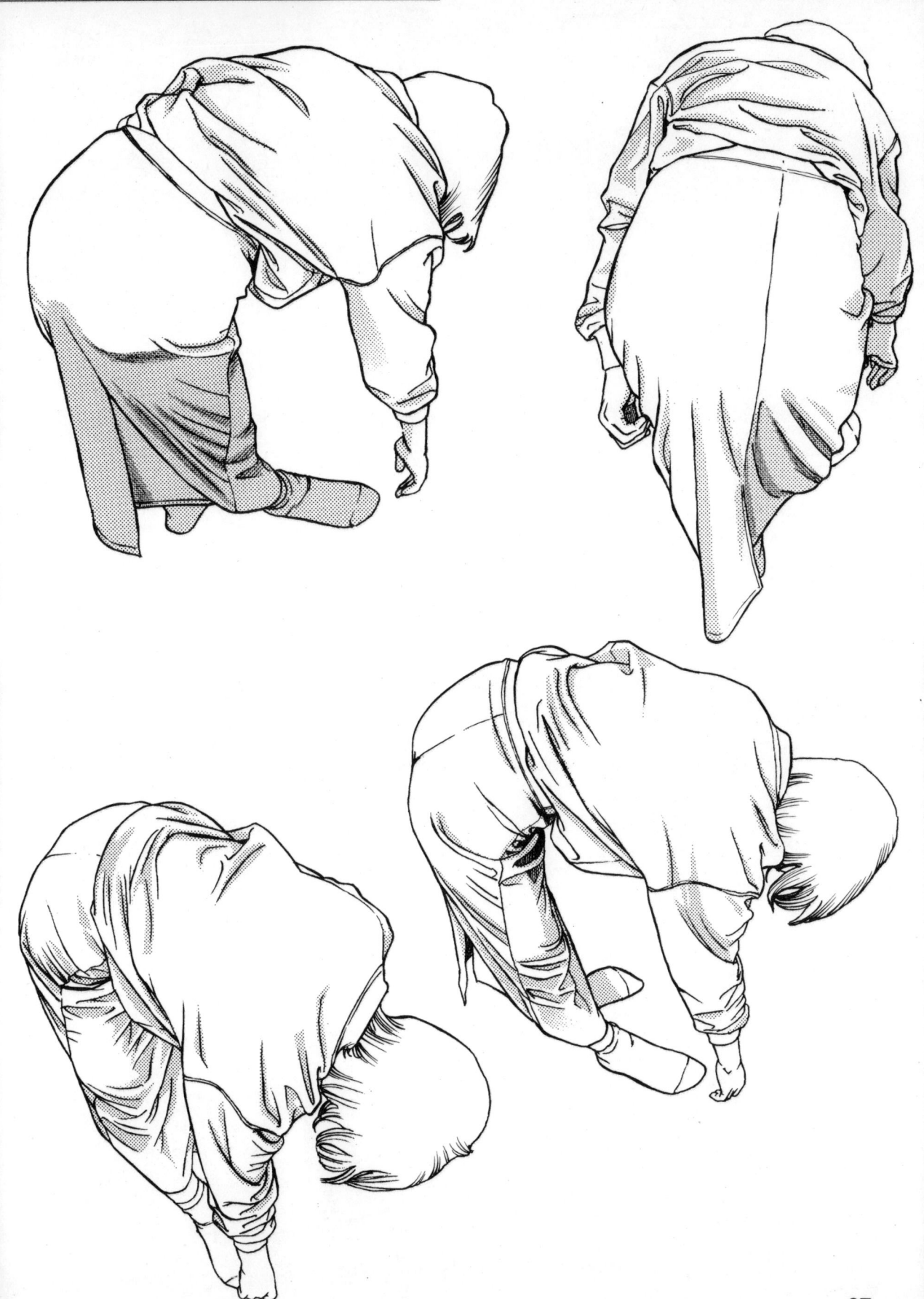

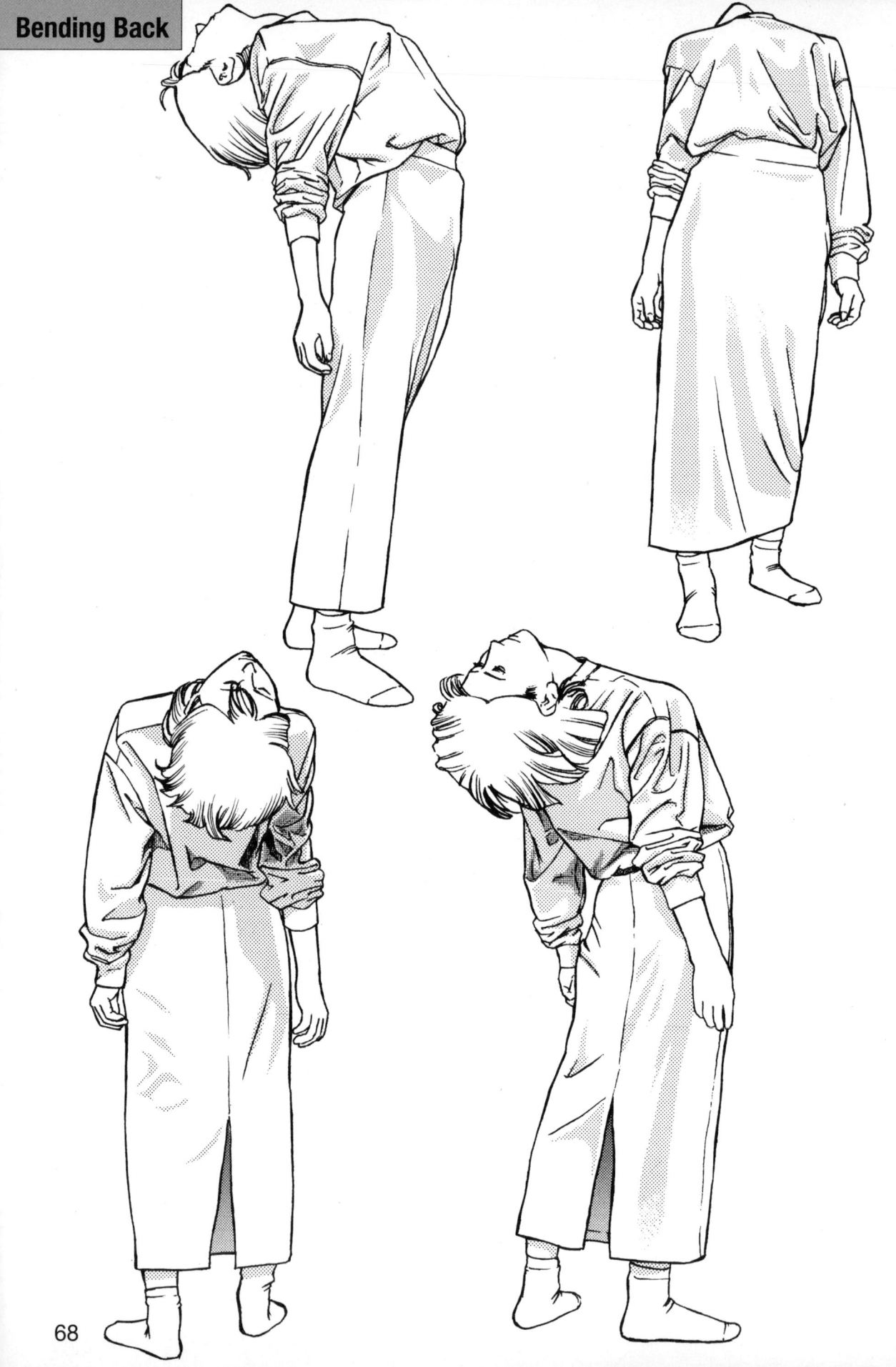

Bending Back | High Angle

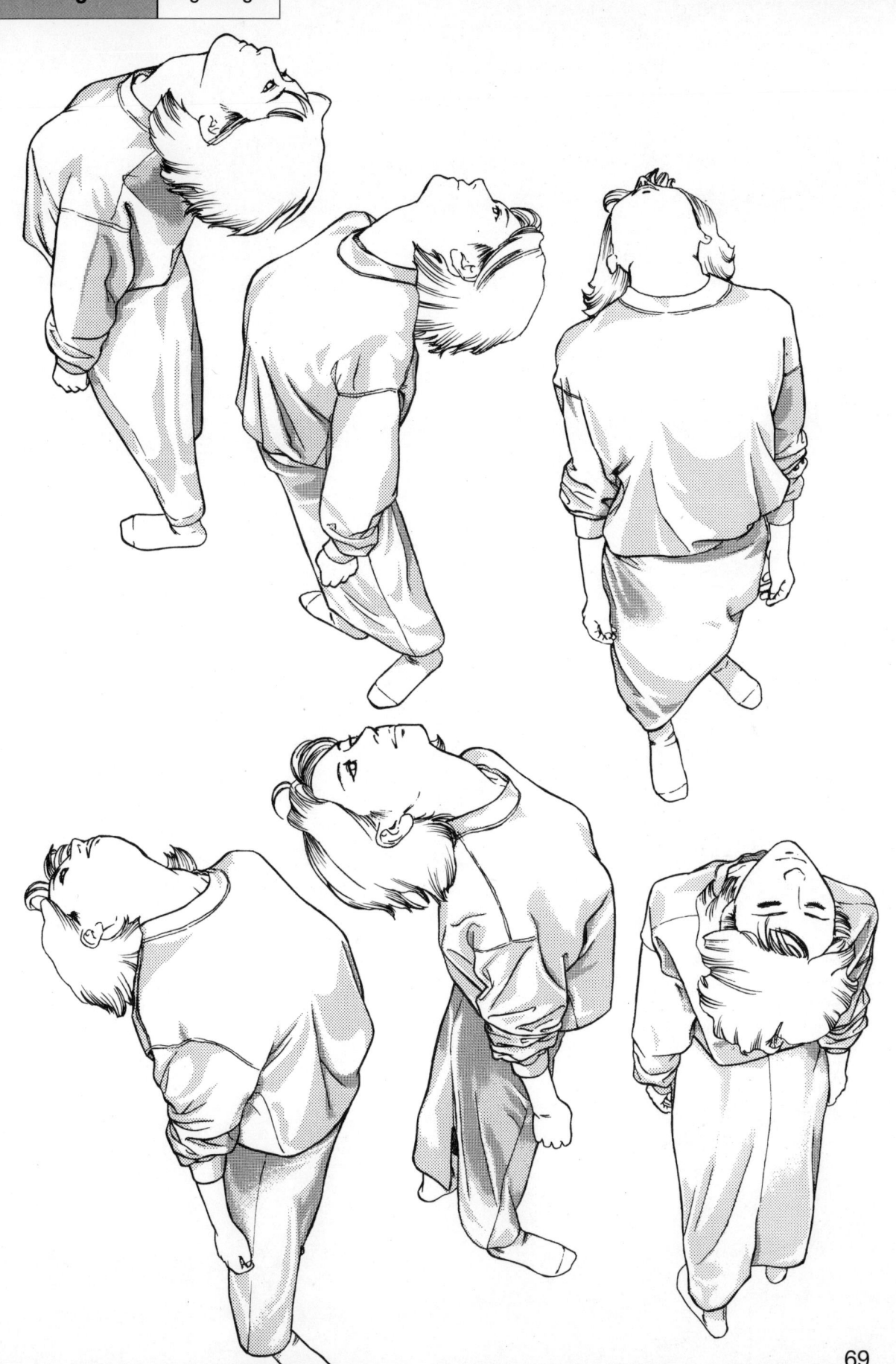

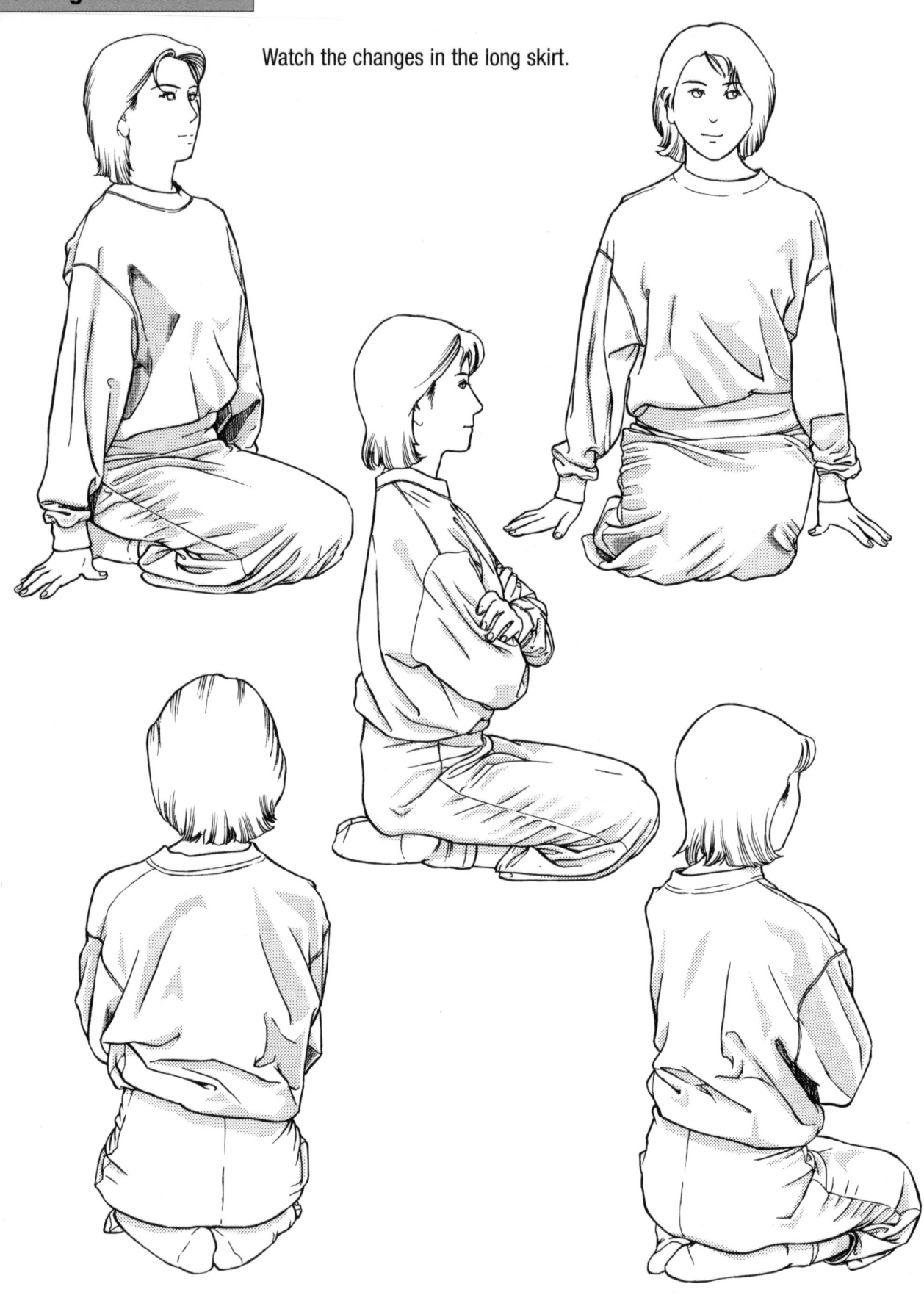

Sitting at Ease

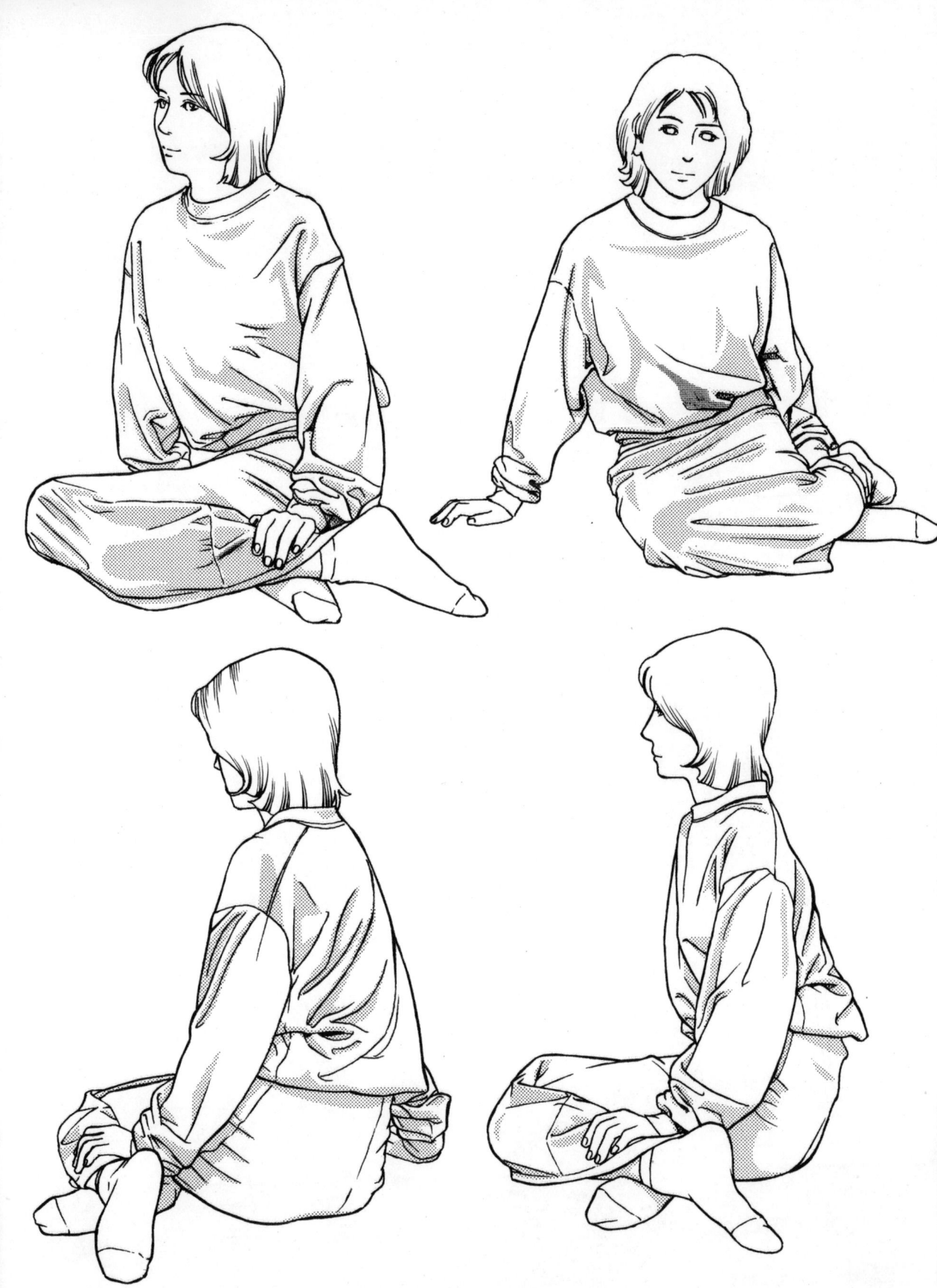

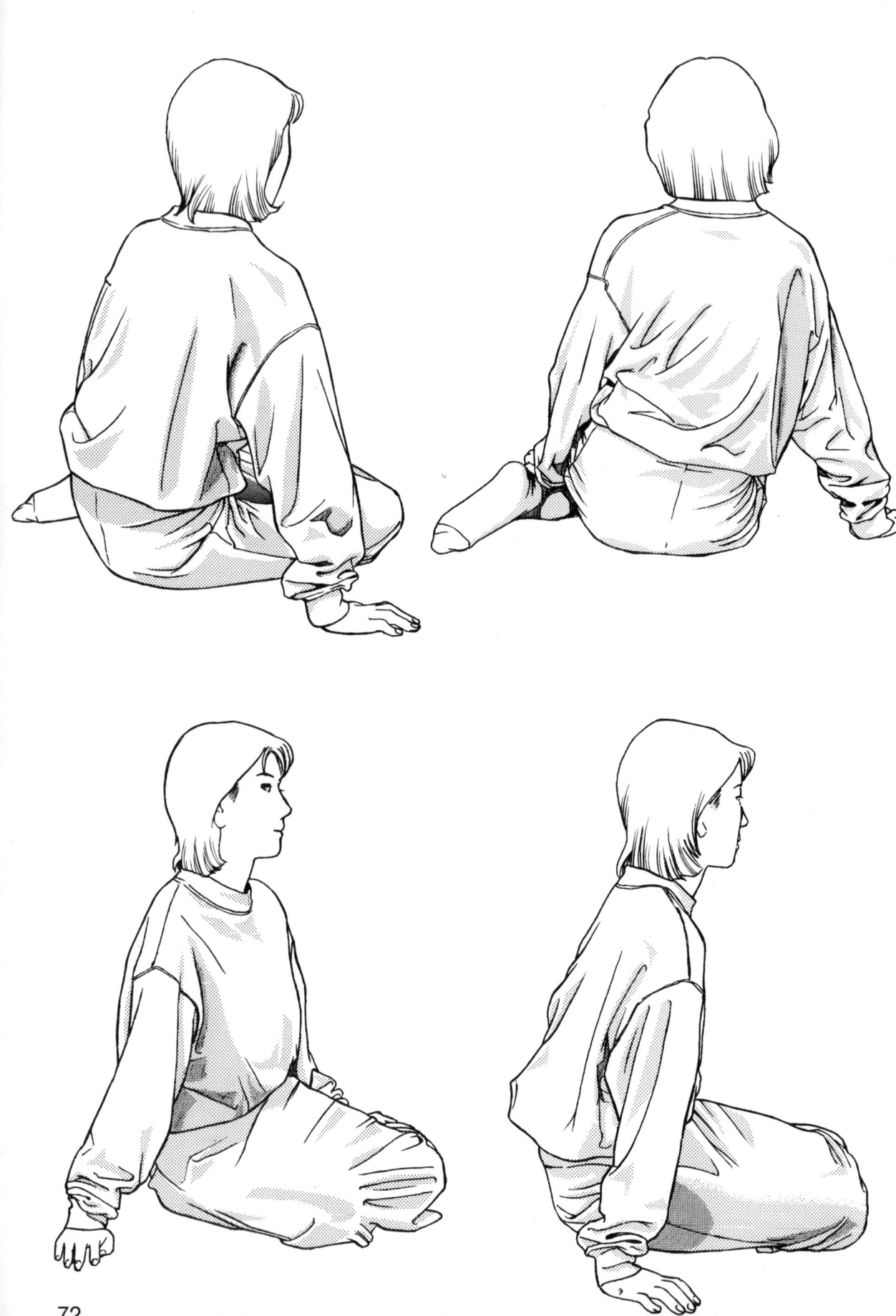

Sitting with the Legs Extended

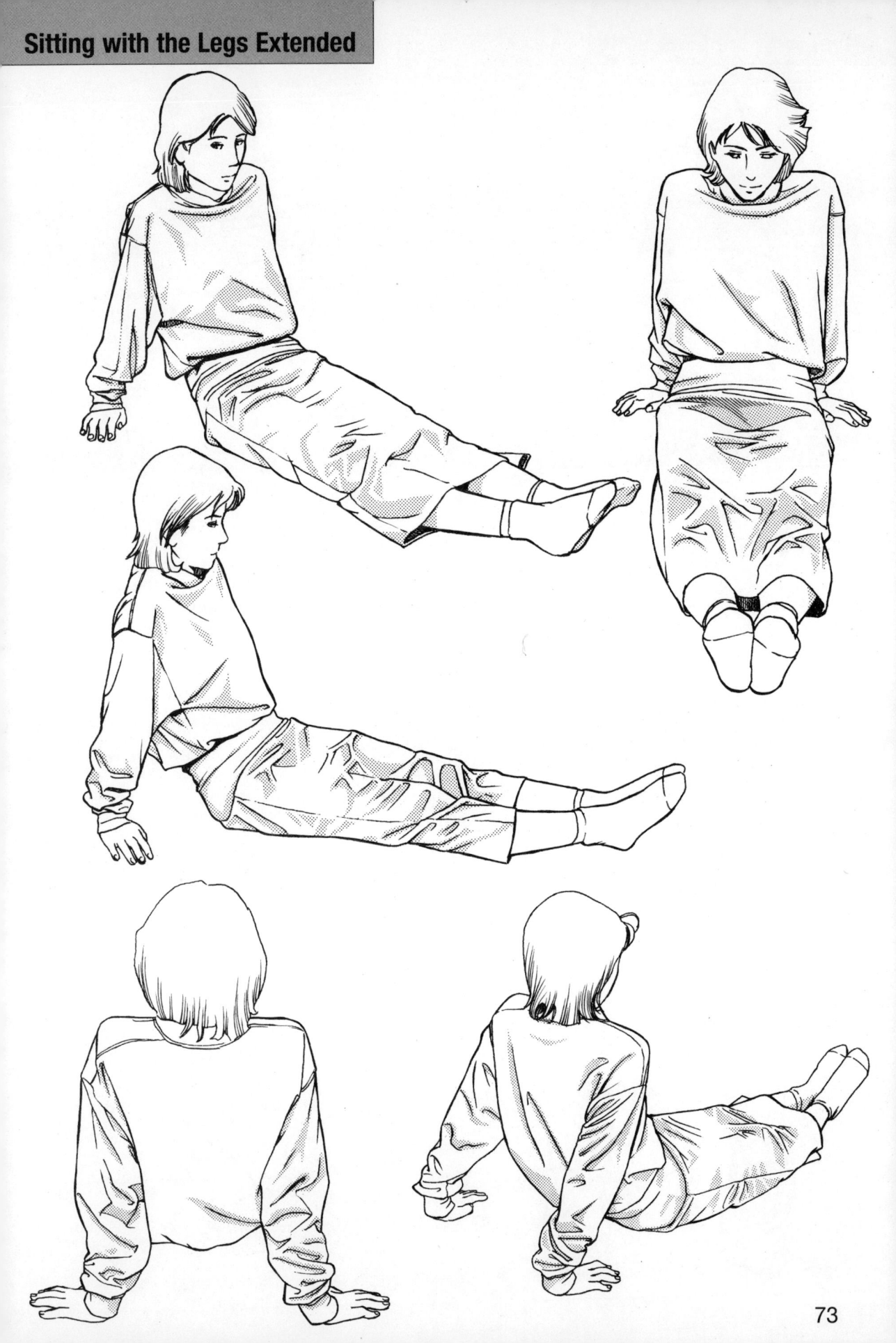

Sitting with the Legs Bent

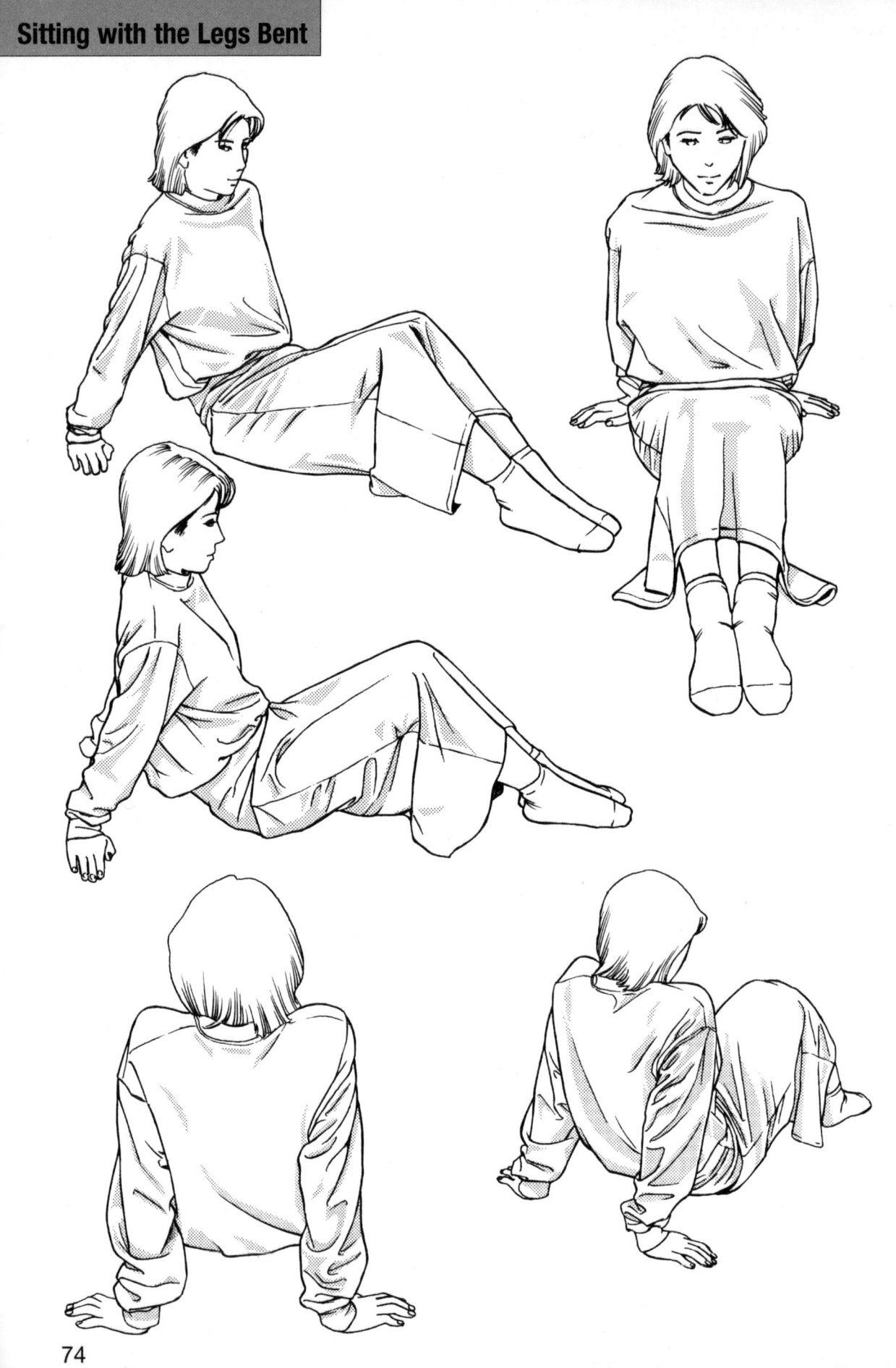

Standing on One Knee

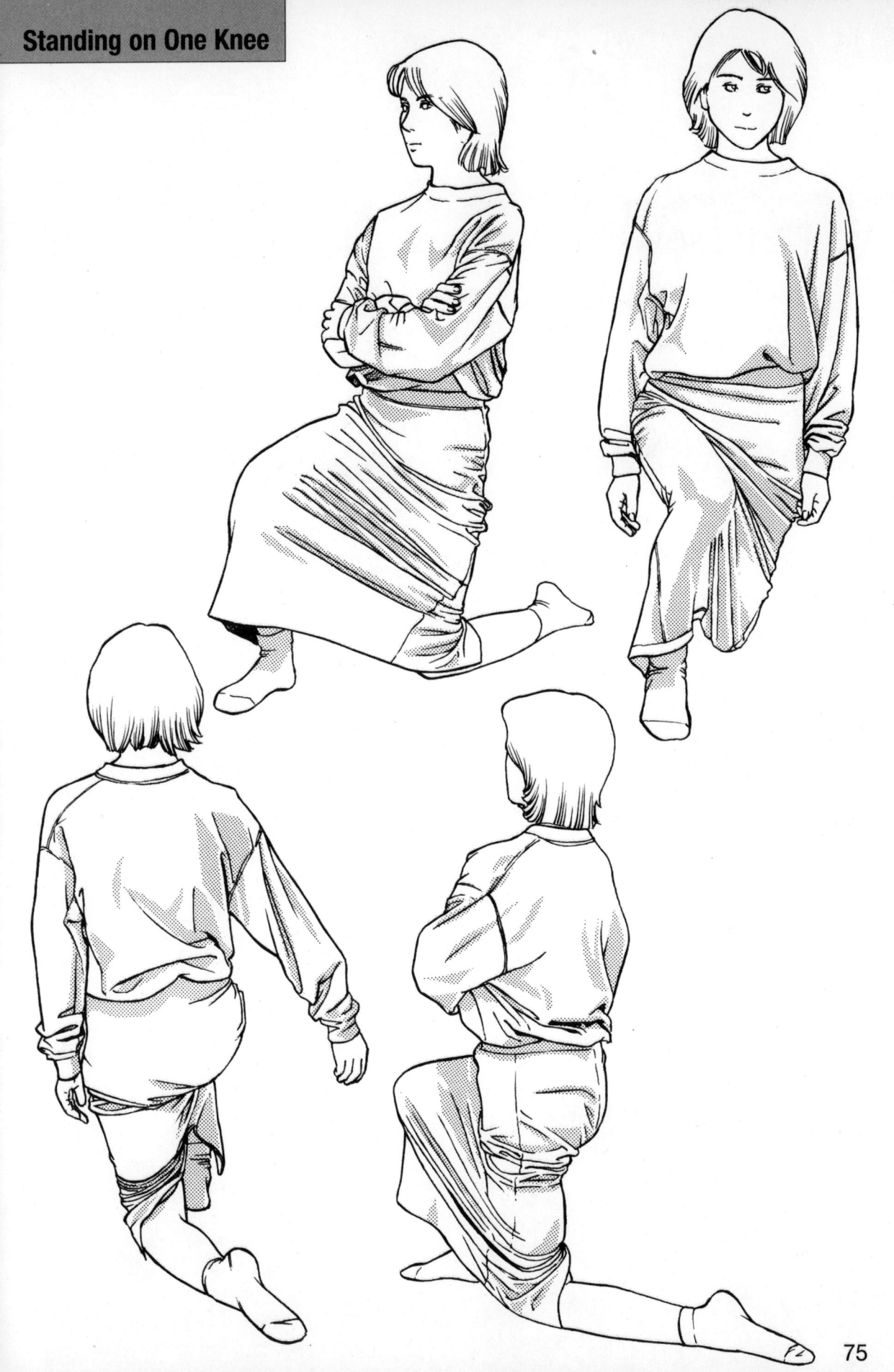

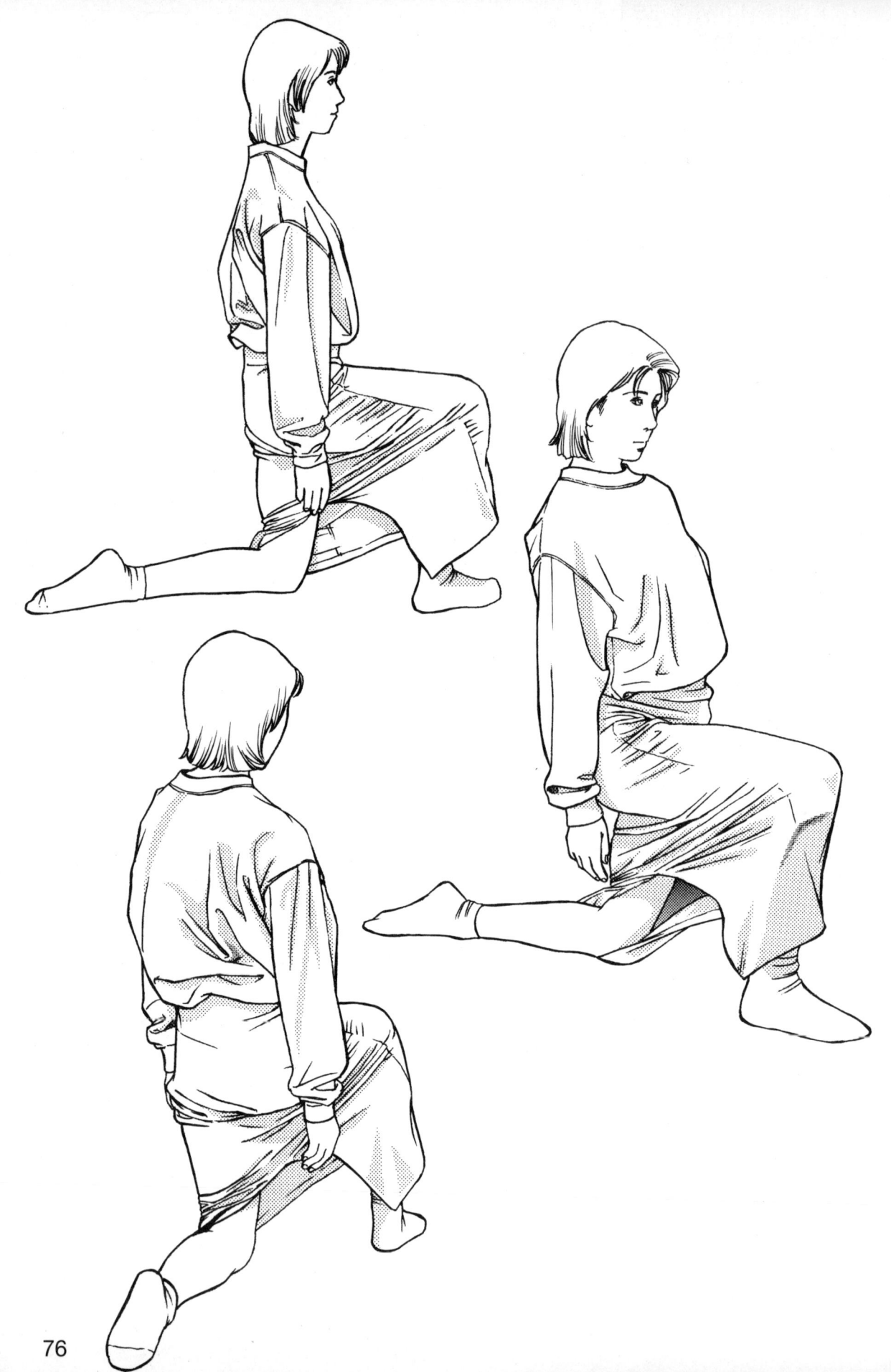

Putting On and Taking Off Sweatshirts — Front Angle

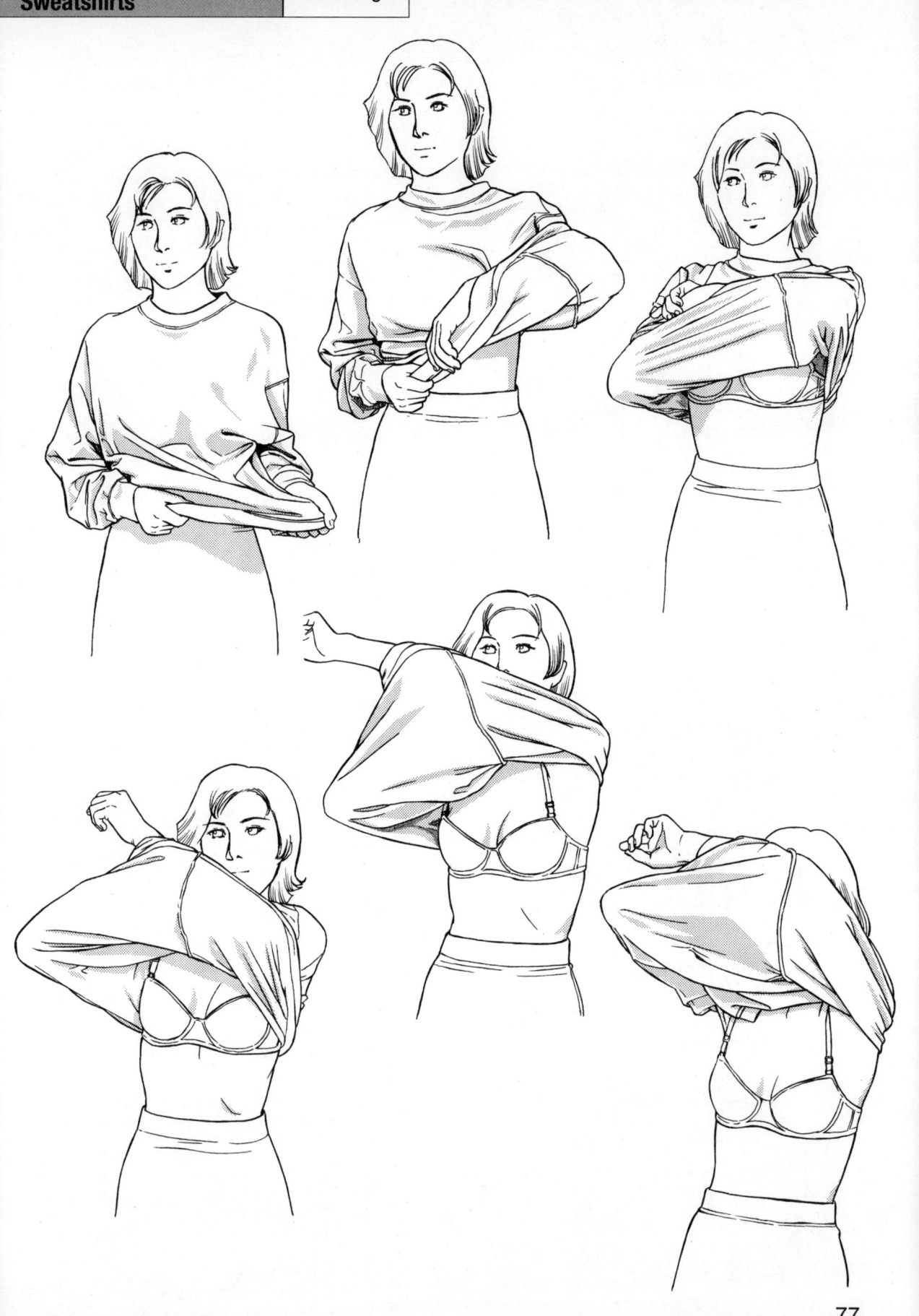

77

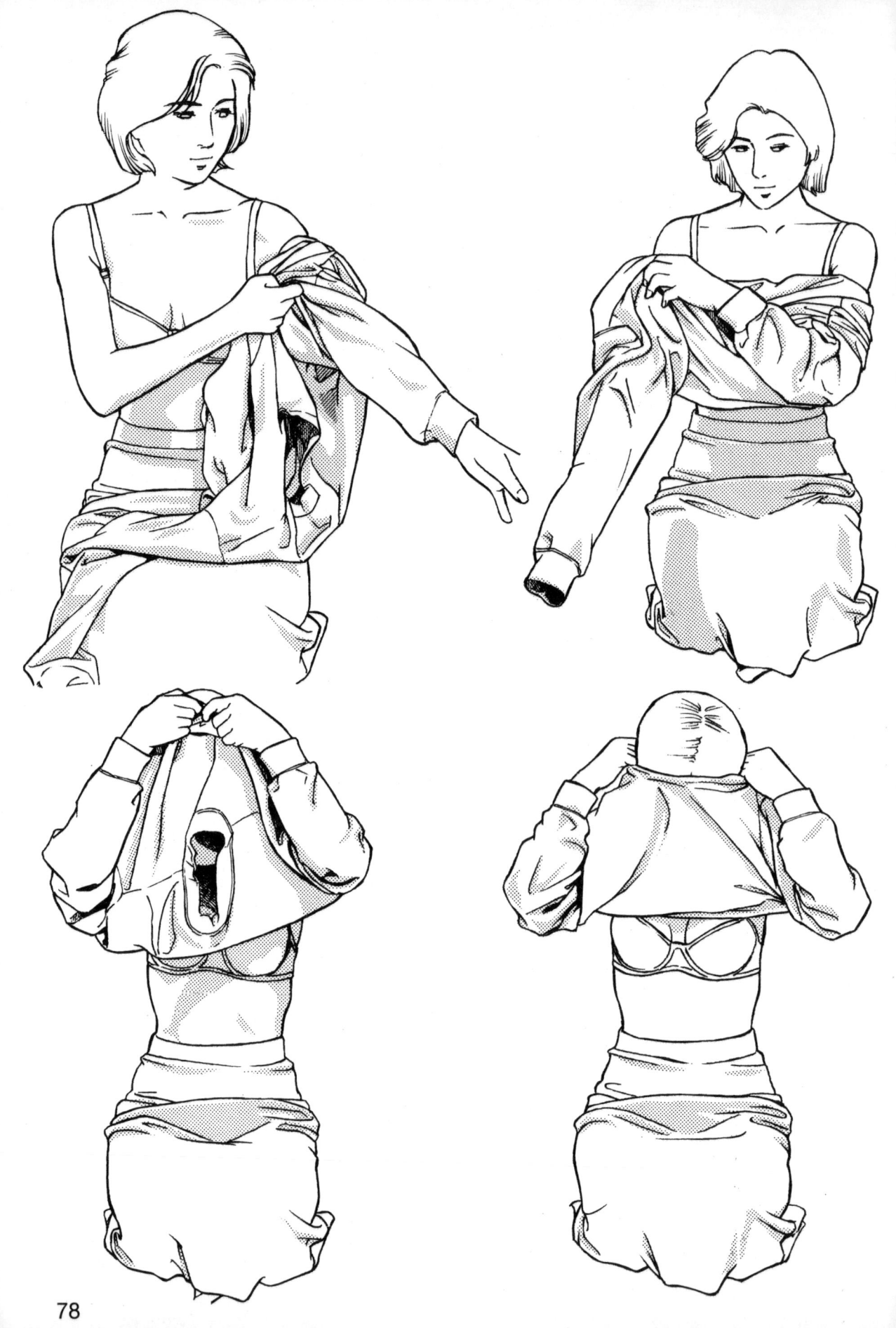

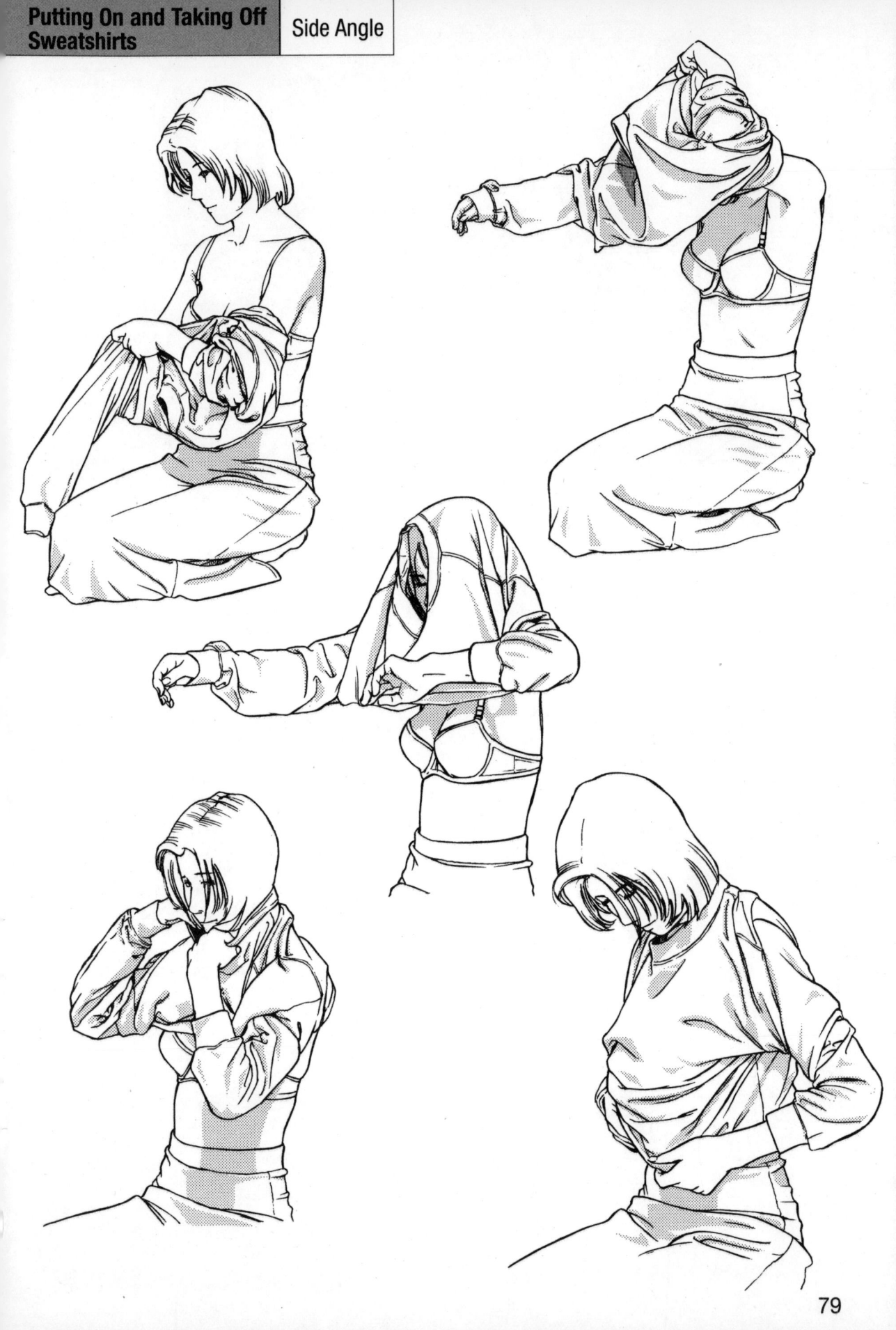

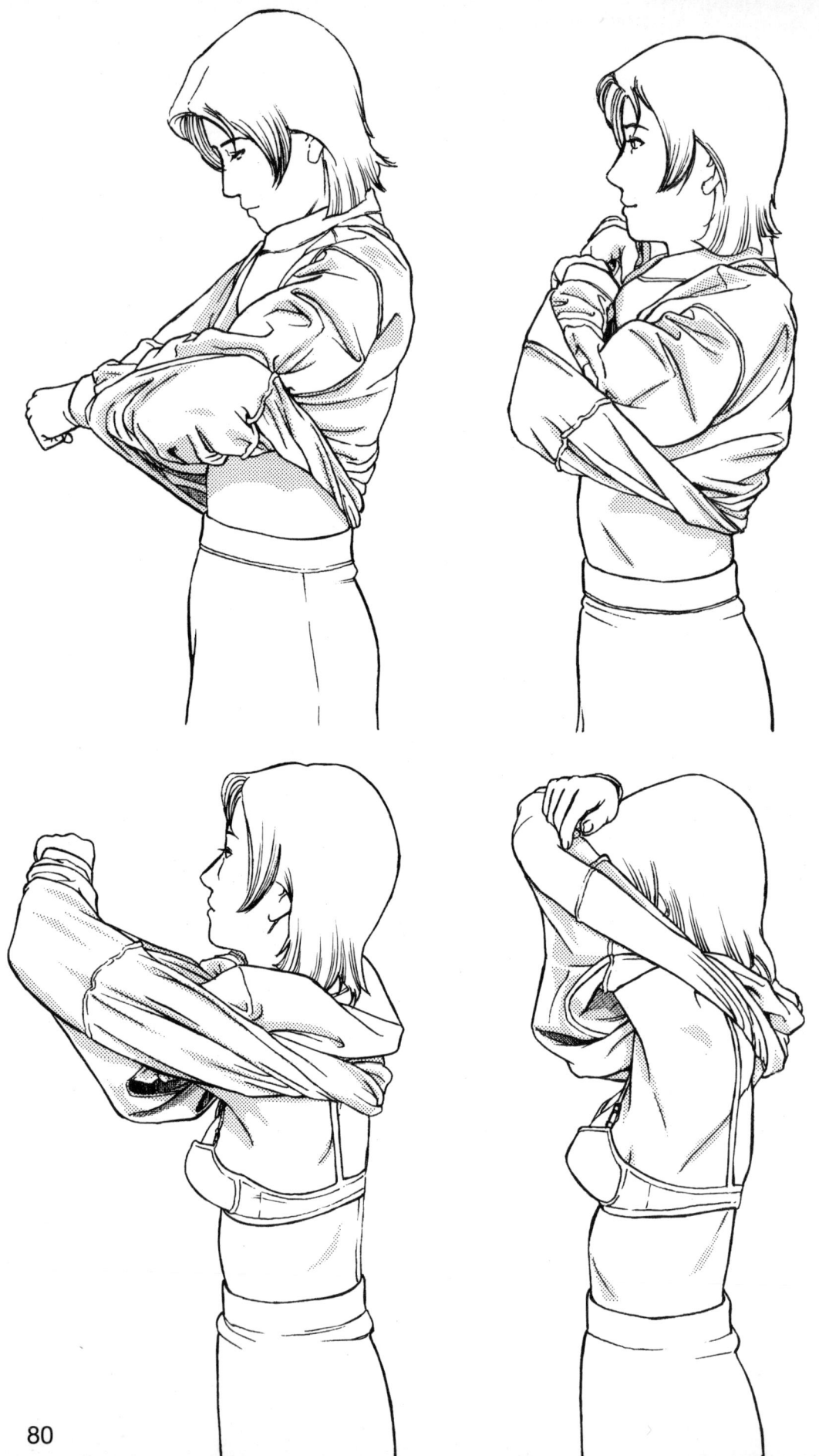

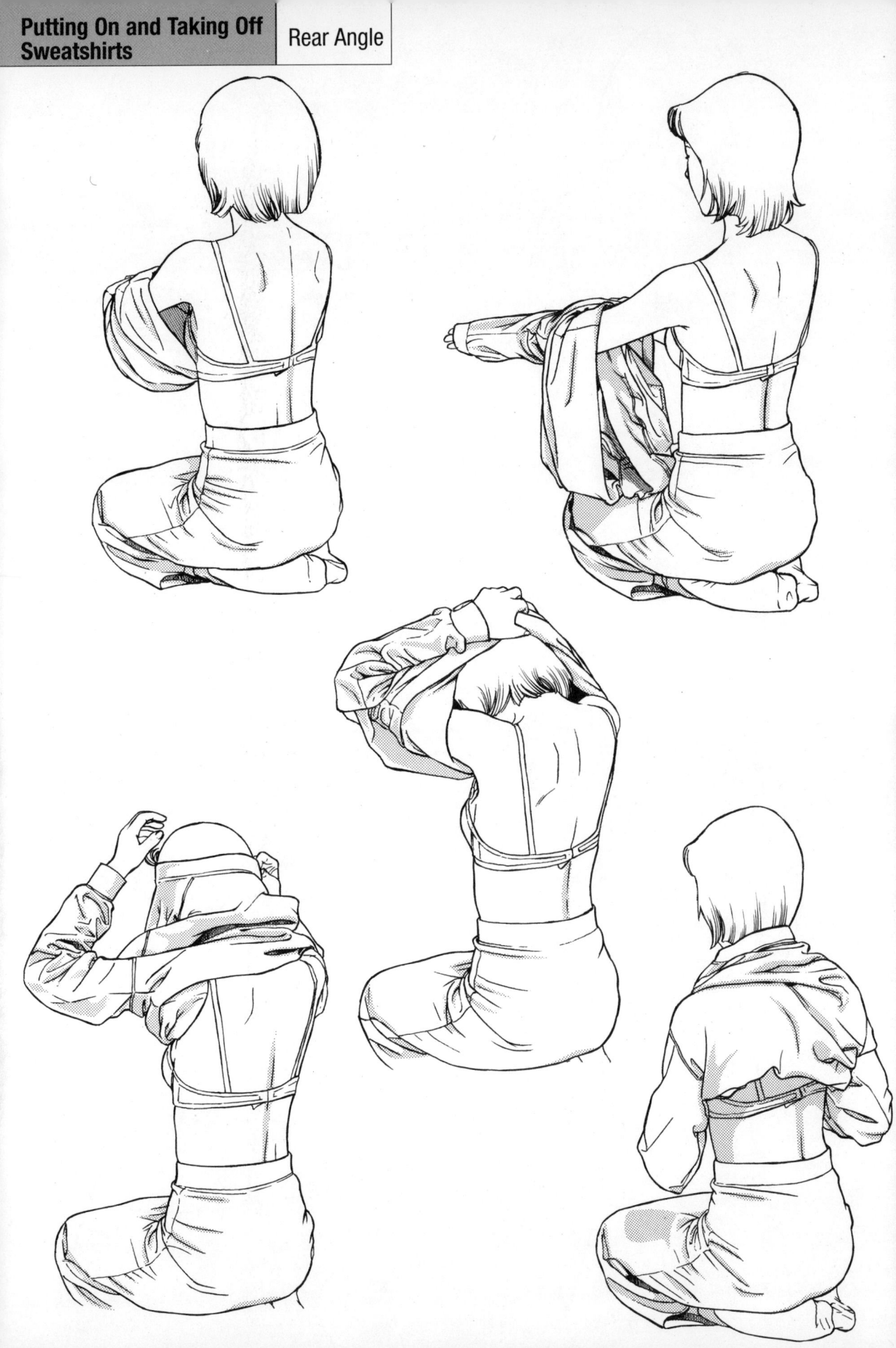

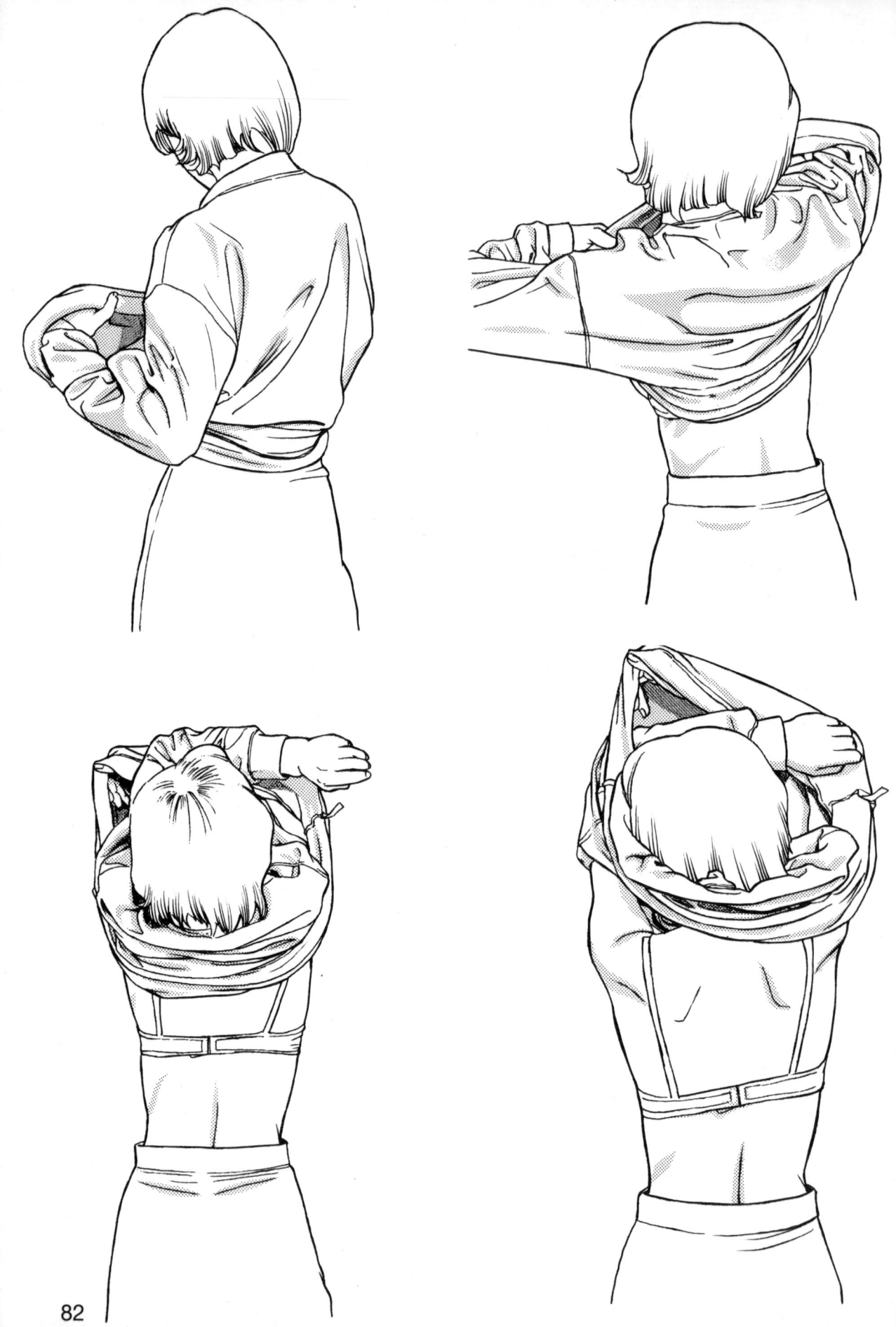

Sitting in a Chair

83

Crossing the Legs

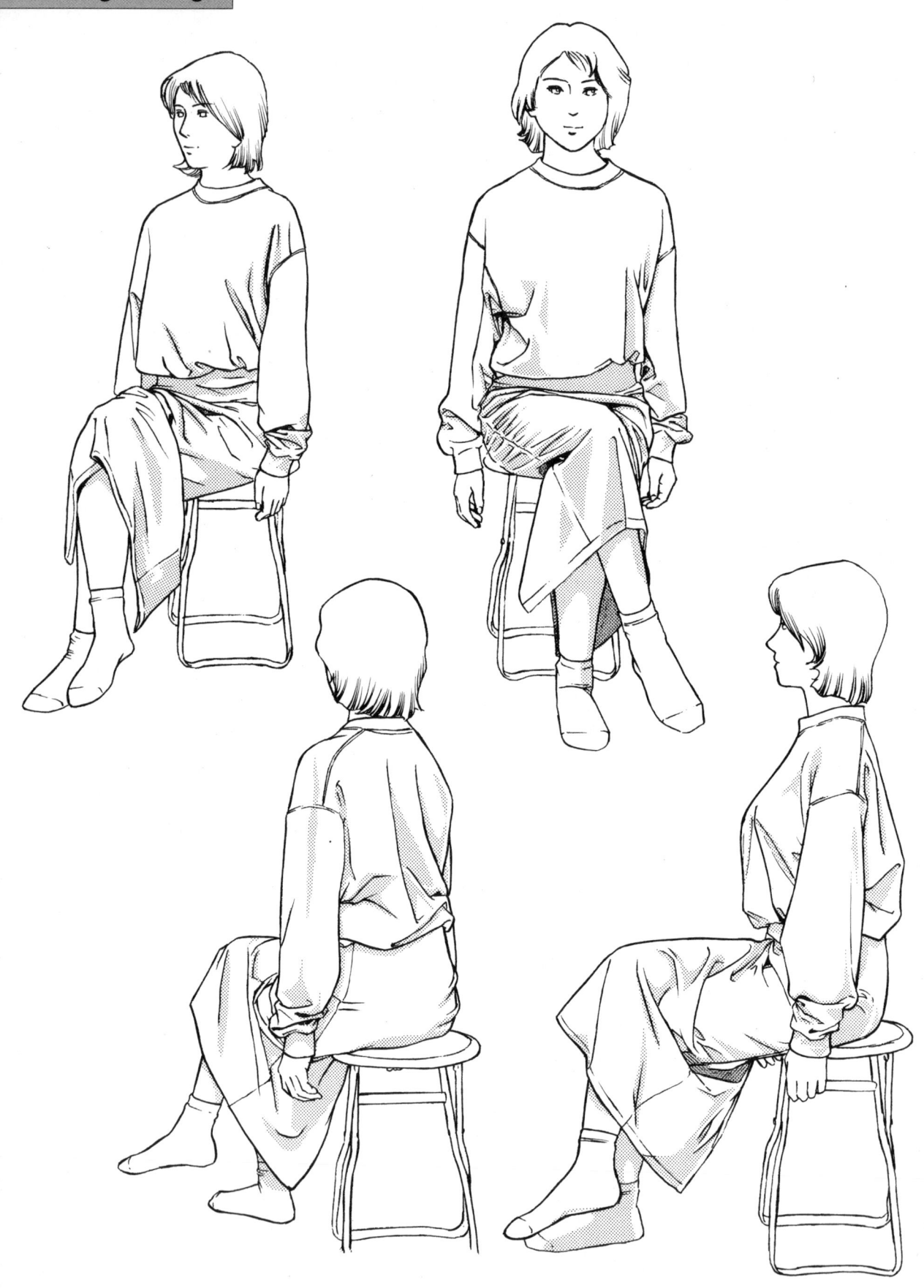

84

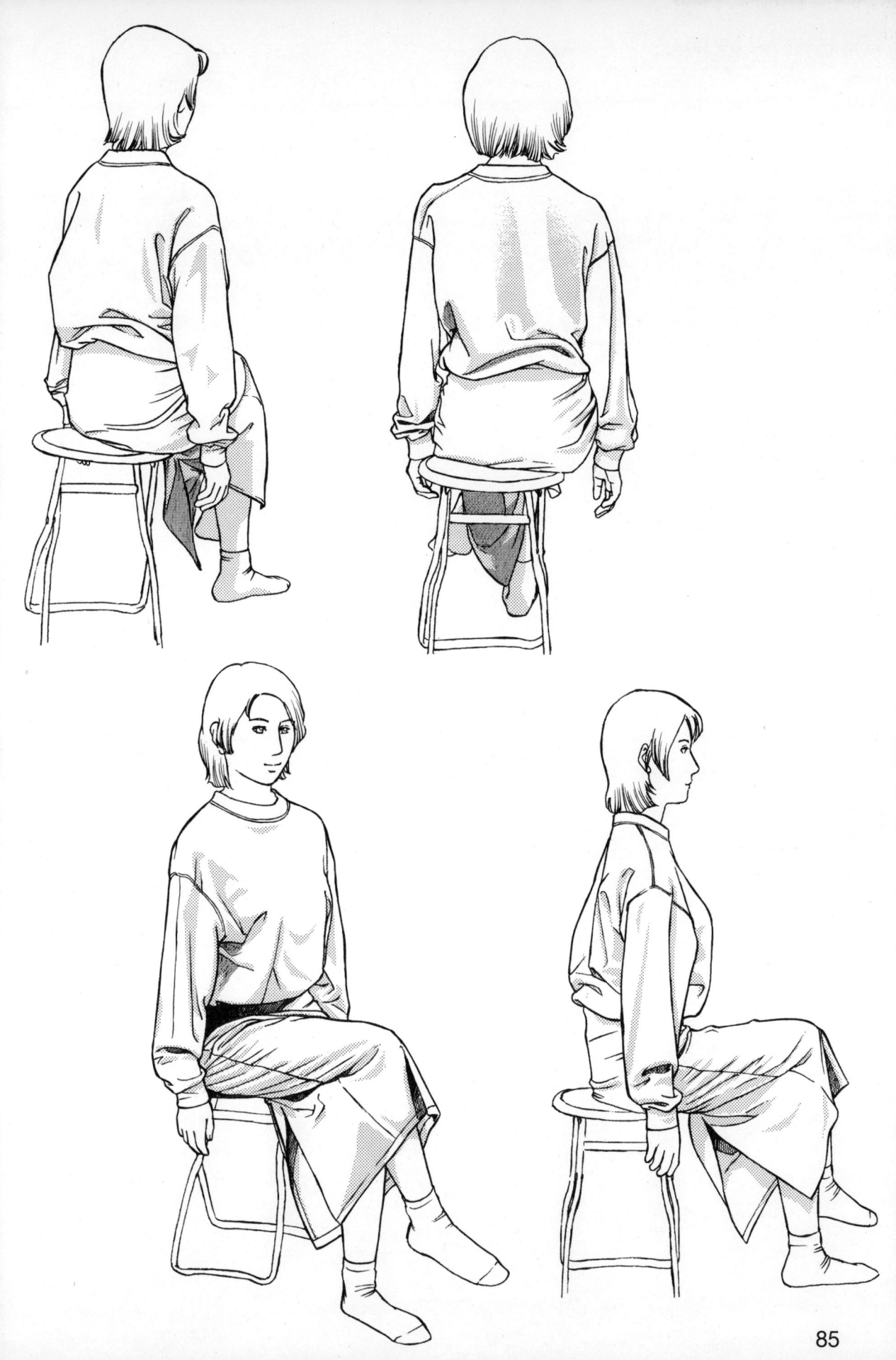

Standing on All Fours

Chapter 3
Jackets and Jeans

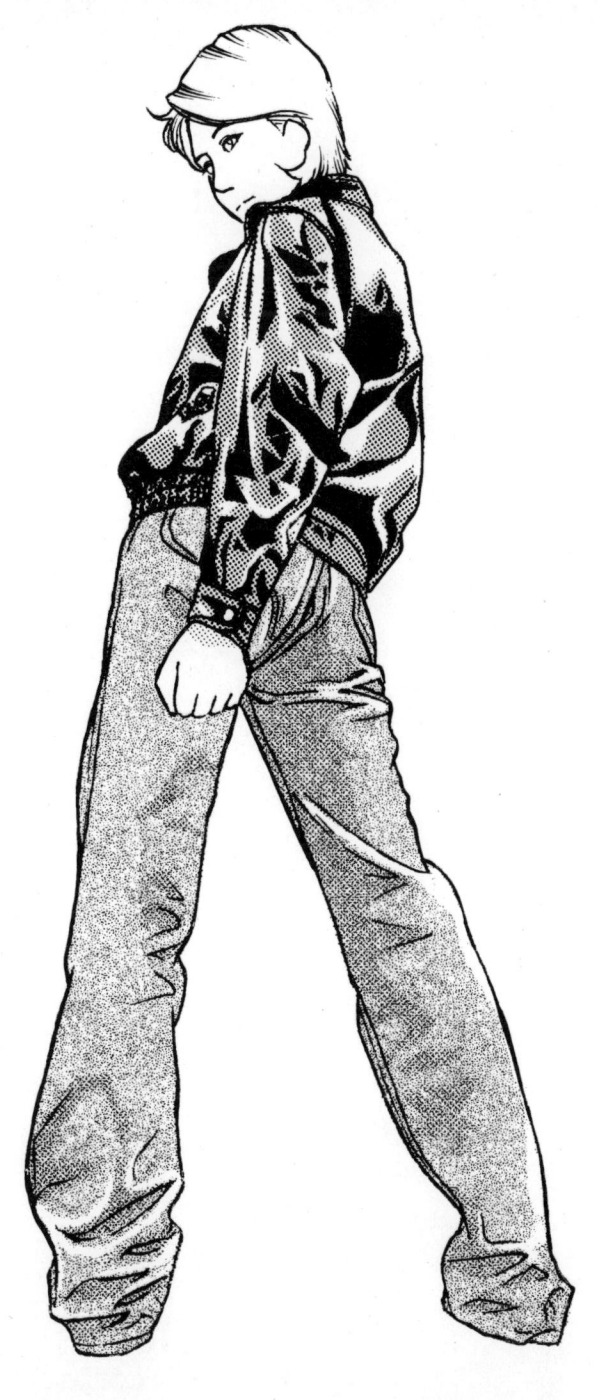

Jackets

Jackets come in a wide variety. Flight jackets and riders jackets are two commonly seen types.

In 1925, the U.S. military invented flight jackets to protect pilots from cold temperatures at high altitudes. It seems the style grew in popularity and was utilized in civilian fashion for riders jackets and stadium jackets.

Motorcycle enthusiasts make use of the anti-cold functionality and the collar and cuffs are usually fitted with elastics or belts to further protect the body from the wind. Other parts of the jacket are made of materials that permit the body to move easily.

Flight Jackets

The military probably thought these up with their easy-to-wear nature in mind. The collar and cuffs seem to be mostly made of rubber.

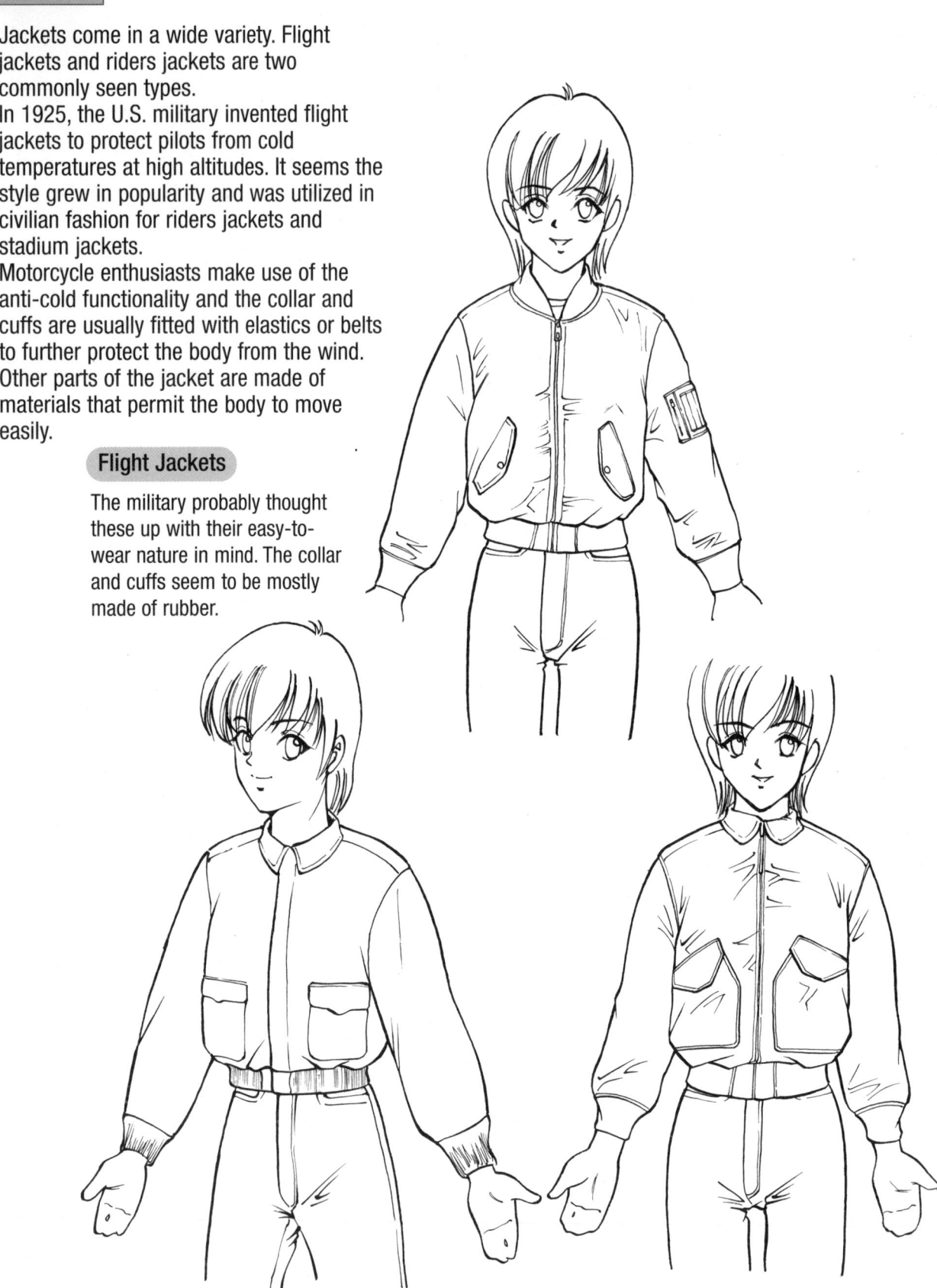

Jacket is a general term for clothing worn for outdoor use. The length extends a bit beyond the waist. Anything longer is generally not called a jacket.

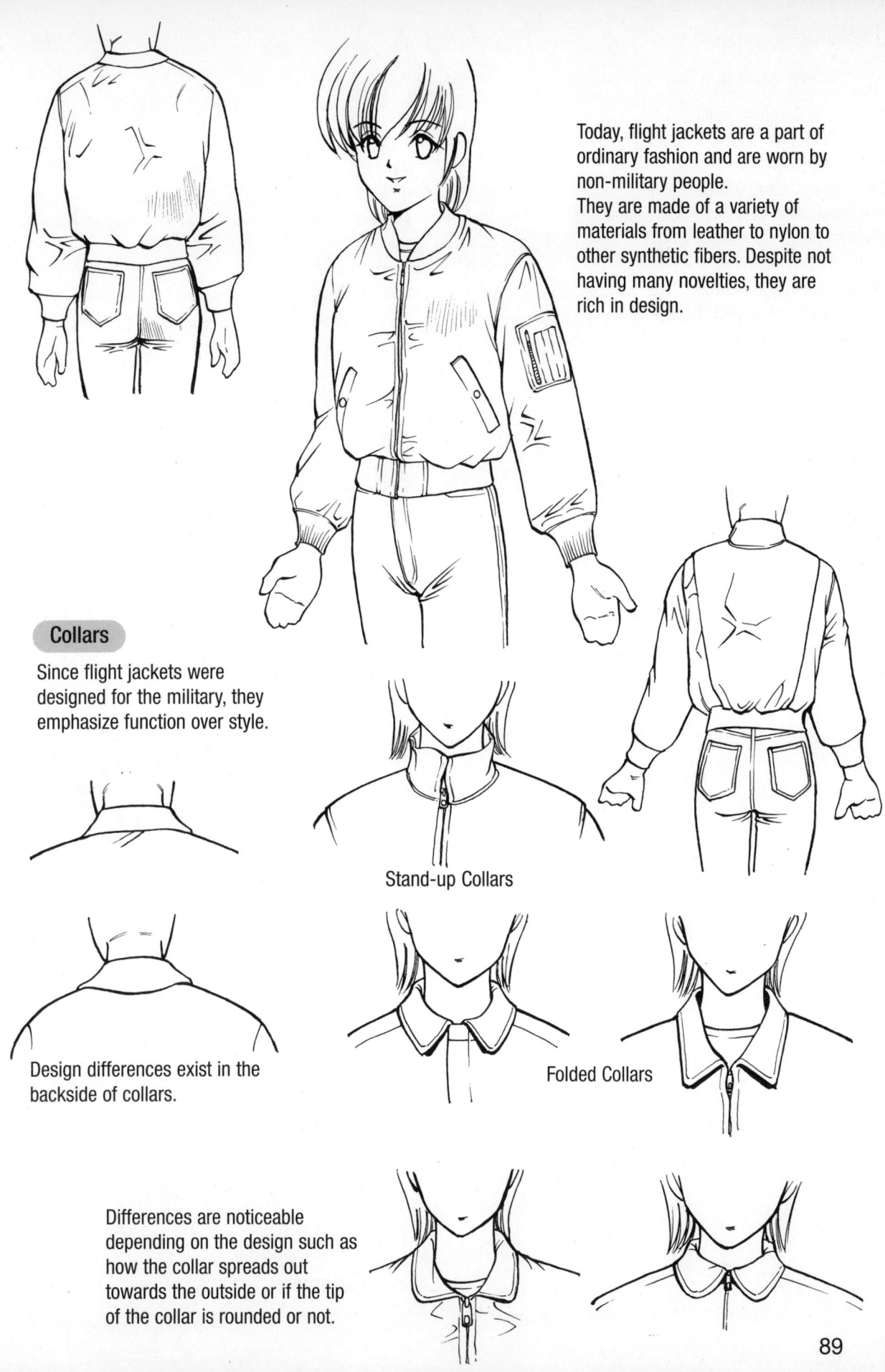

Today, flight jackets are a part of ordinary fashion and are worn by non-military people.
They are made of a variety of materials from leather to nylon to other synthetic fibers. Despite not having many novelties, they are rich in design.

Collars

Since flight jackets were designed for the military, they emphasize function over style.

Design differences exist in the backside of collars.

Stand-up Collars

Folded Collars

Differences are noticeable depending on the design such as how the collar spreads out towards the outside or if the tip of the collar is rounded or not.

Riders Jackets

As the name suggests, these jackets were thought up for motorcycle riders. Simple, as well as, lavish designs are commonplace.
The design of the collar and cuffs has been tightened with heat insulation in mind. While flight jackets place a preference on easy wear using mainly elastic and/or strings to tighten the clothing, riders jackets make use of belts and straps. This difference is probably decorative and interesting designs exist.

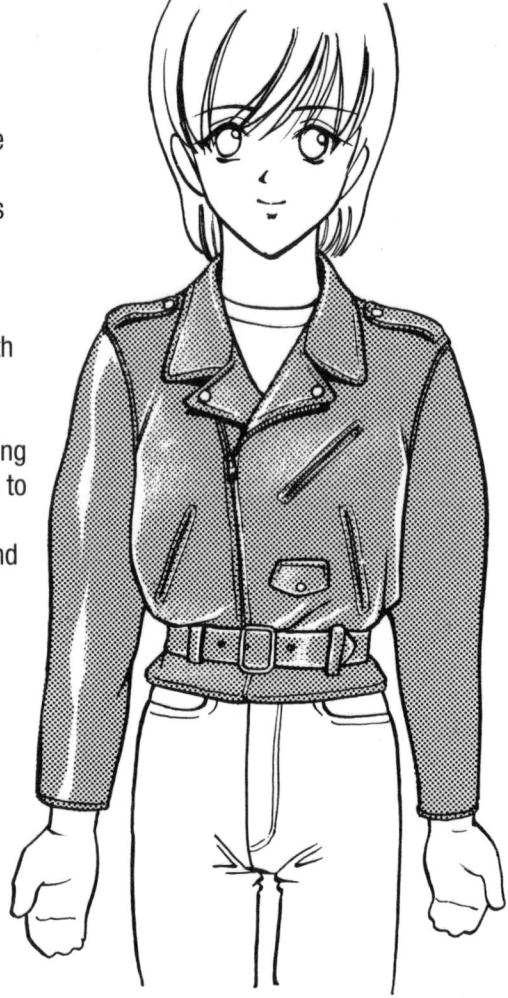

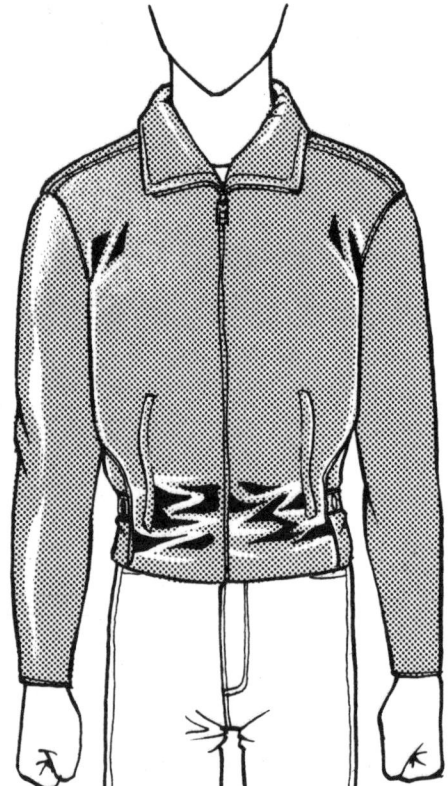

This jacket is fitted with two belts. The sleeves are a bit on the long side with tightened cuffs.

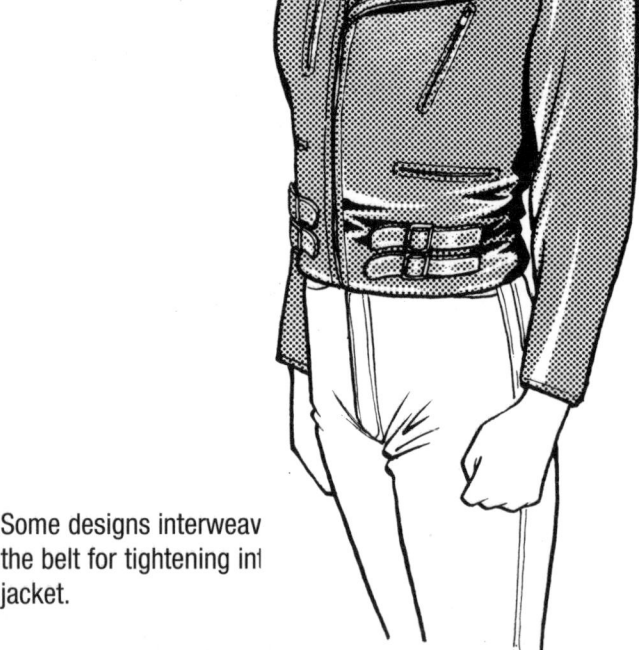

Some designs interweav the belt for tightening int jacket.

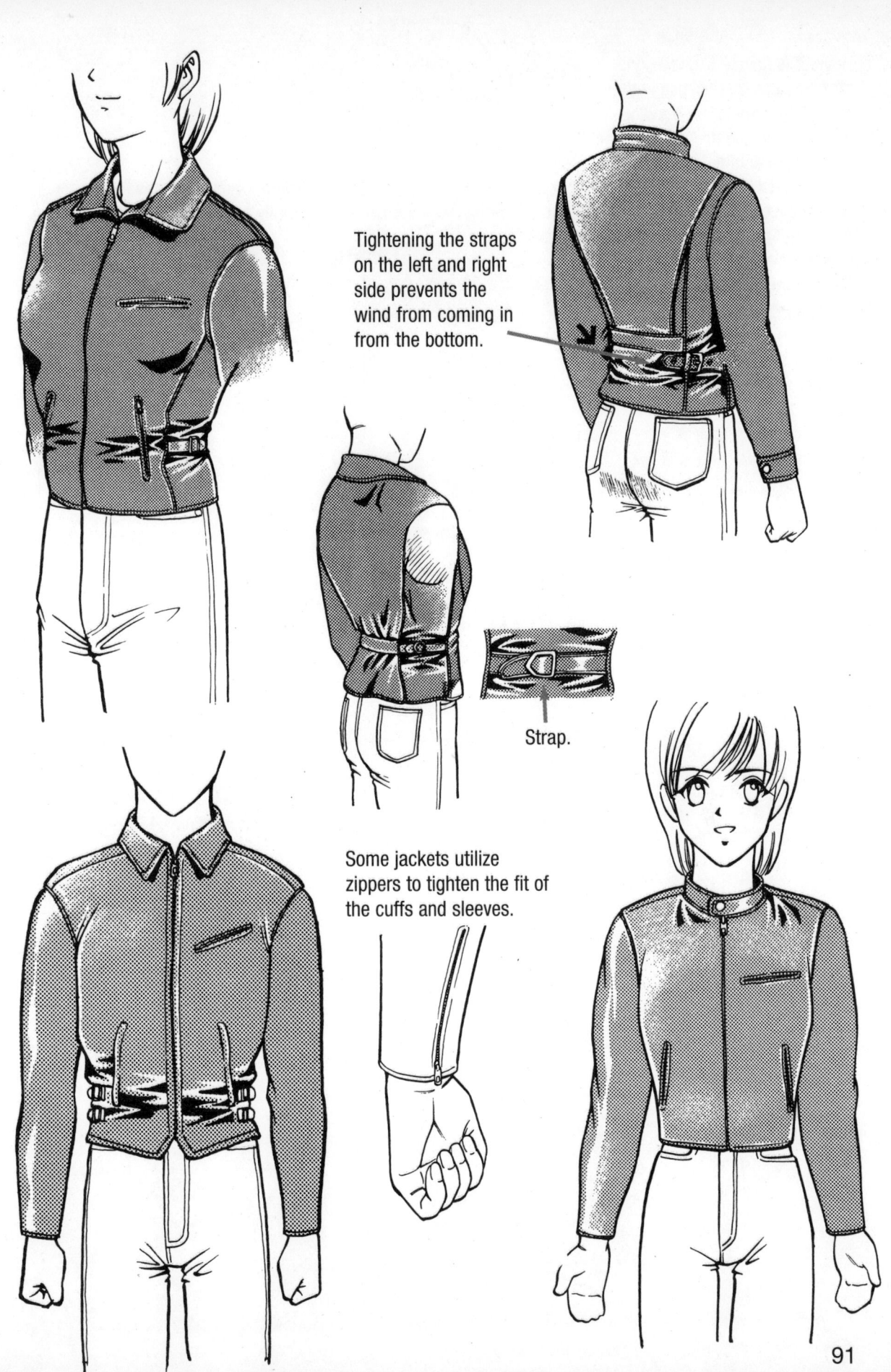

While it is fine to draw designs that actually exist for use in the worlds you create, try drawing your own unique designs. Use the basic parts of other designs for reference when creating the different parts of your design. While the example here is a riders jacket, the same principles can be applied to freely create other costume designs.

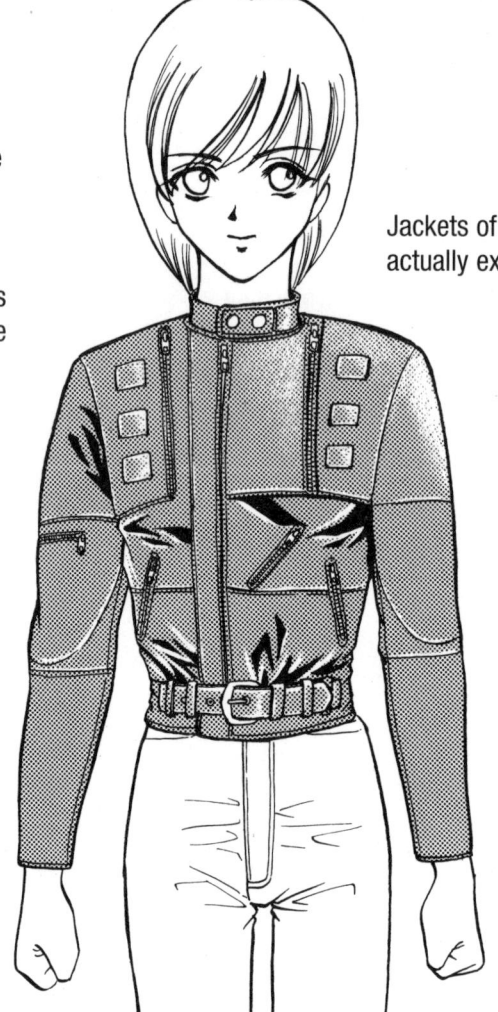

Jackets of this design seem to actually exist.

Here are a variety of collars in addition to the ones mentioned earlier.

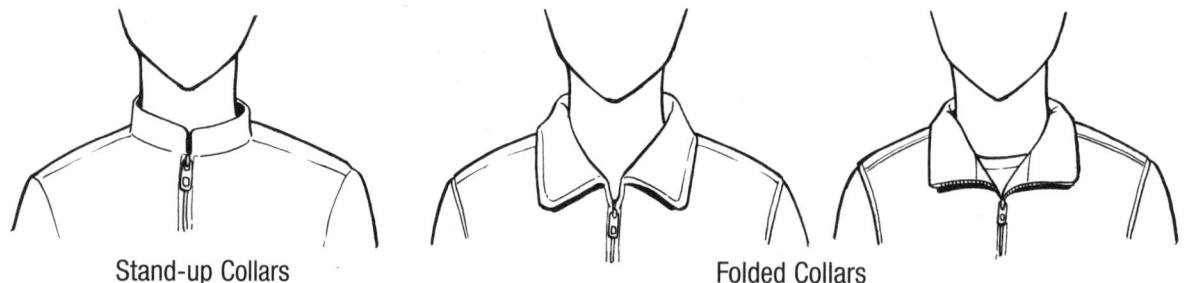

Stand-up Collars

Folded Collars

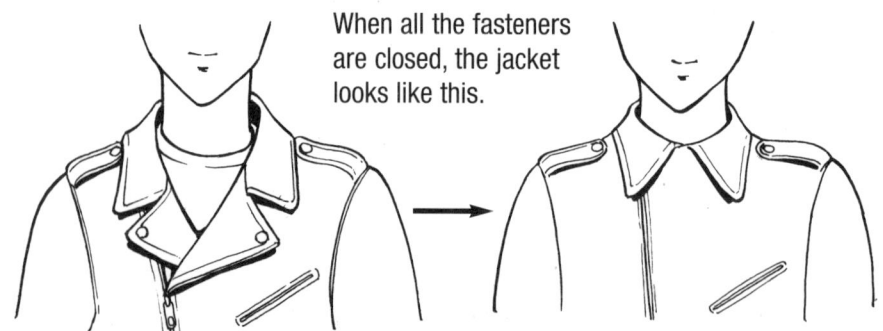

When all the fasteners are closed, the jacket looks like this.

Button-up Collars

Stadium Jackets

Stadium jackets originally came into existence as American sportswear and have a variety of uses like letterman jackets. In Japan, these jackets are often worn as casual wear.

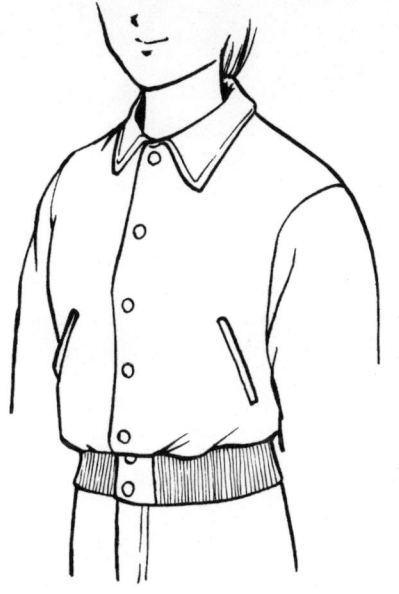

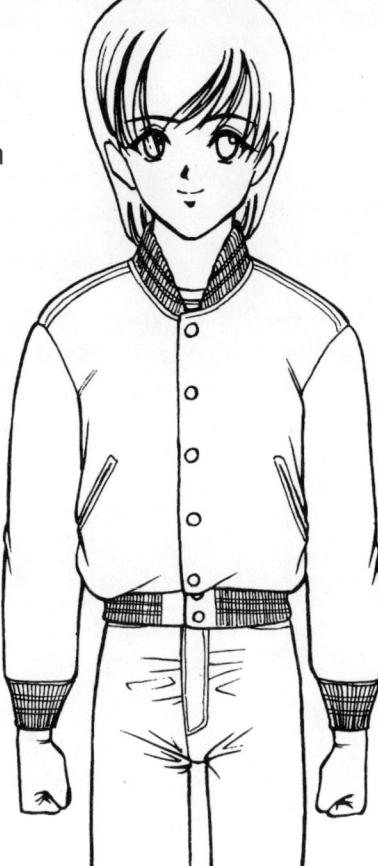

Swiss Collars
The collar is folded in two.

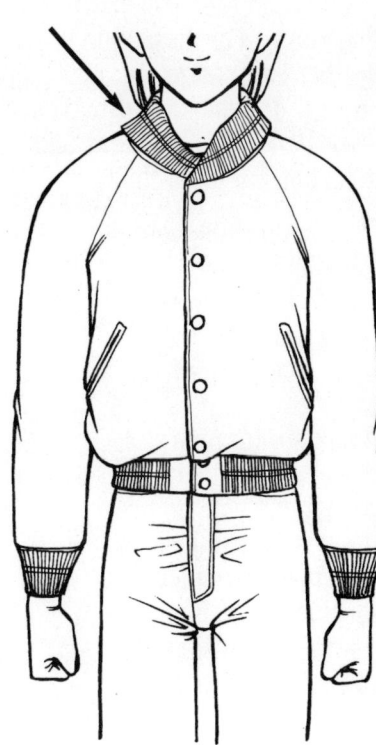

The buttons on women's jacket are on the opposite side from men's jackets. Please note that most of the examples found in this book are for men's jackets. Also be aware that some women prefer to wear men's jackets even when women's designs exist. The decision on where to place the buttons is yours.

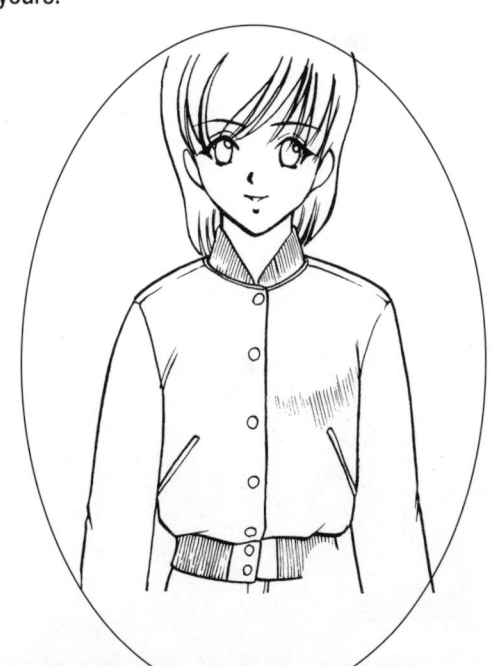

This jacket with a sailor collar is a rare design.

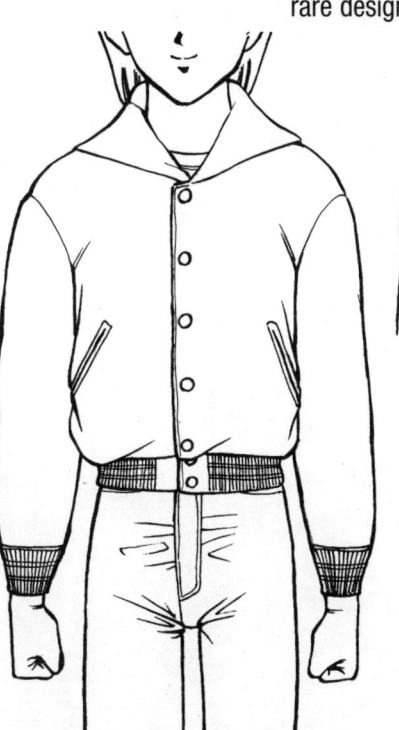

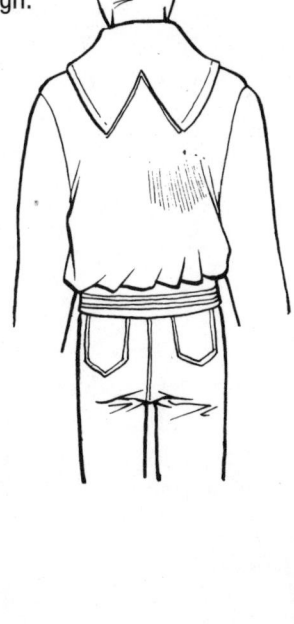

Quality and Feel

If a jacket you draw looks like a jacket, most readers will be able to imagine it as such and ascertain the quality and feel of clothing based on the shape. For those who want to further emphasize the quality and feel in your drawings, start by first considering the hardness and thickness of the clothing.

The buttons on women's jacket are on the opposite side from men's jackets. Please note that most of the examples found in this book are for men's jackets. Also be aware that some women prefer to wear men's jackets even when women's designs exist. The decision on where to place the buttons is yours.

The lines of the wrinkles change depending on the thickness of the material. Thick materials produce fat lines; thin materials produce detailed lines. Leather is considered to be a thick material.

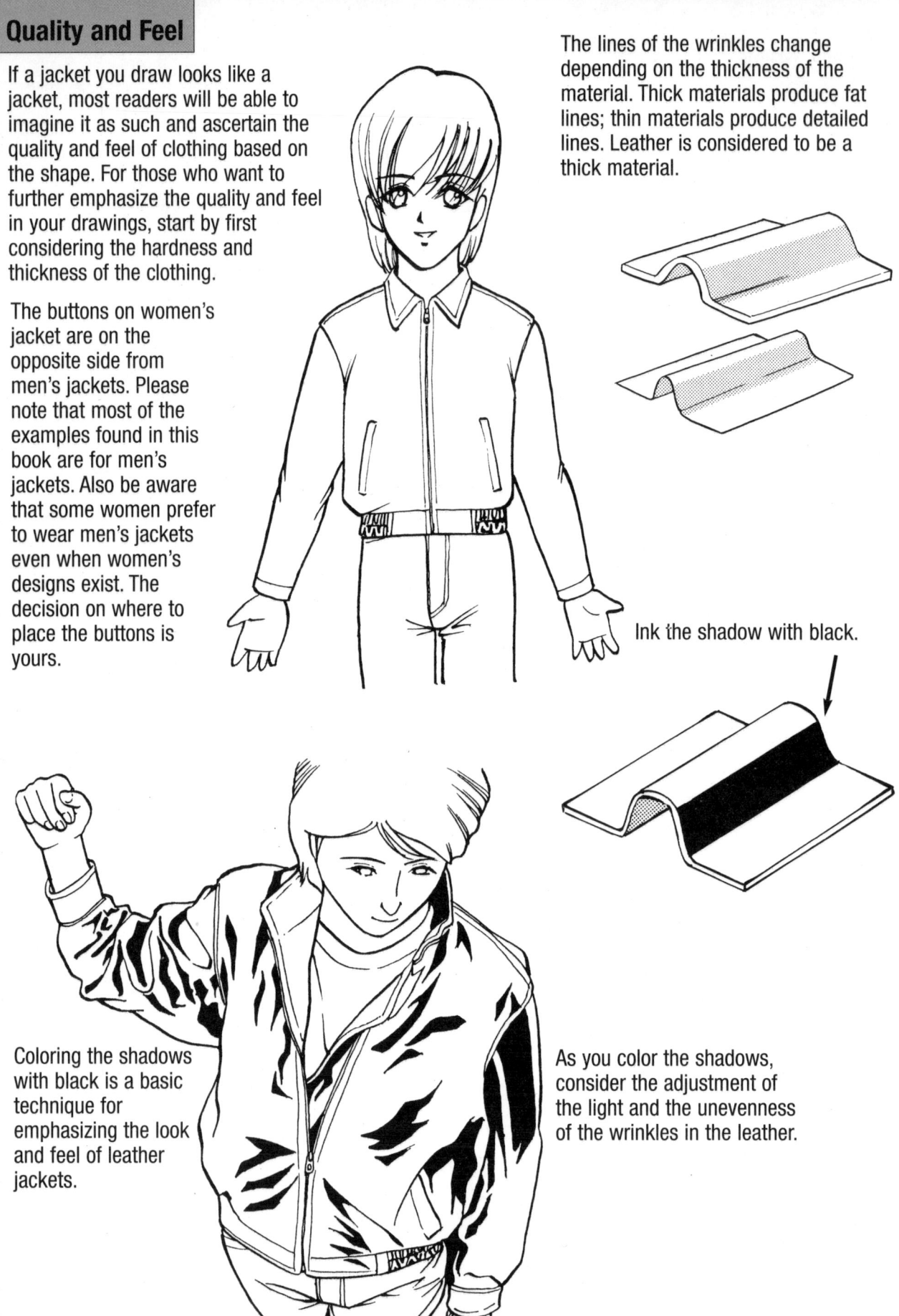

Ink the shadow with black.

Coloring the shadows with black is a basic technique for emphasizing the look and feel of leather jackets.

As you color the shadows, consider the adjustment of the light and the unevenness of the wrinkles in the leather.

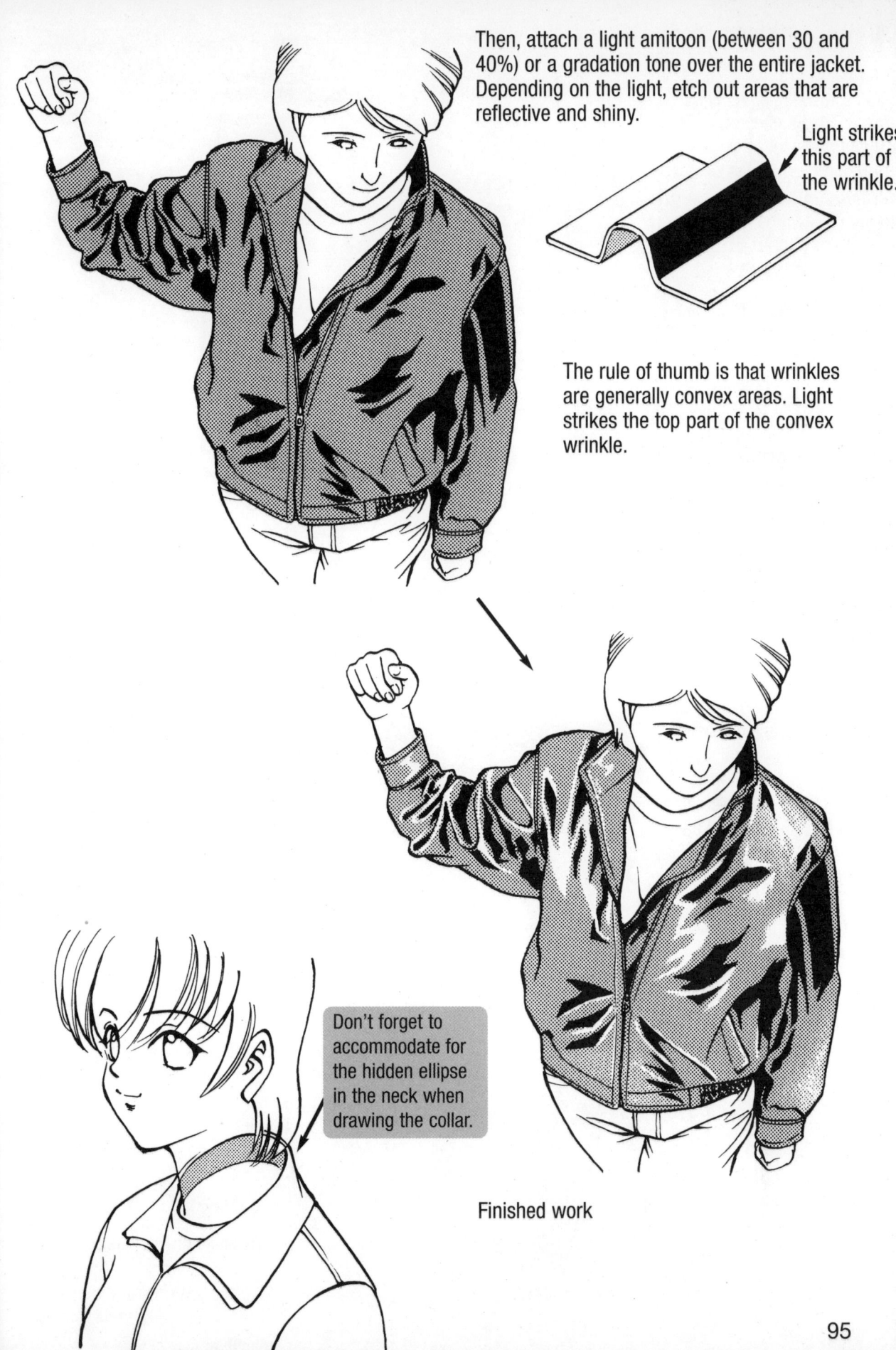

Then, attach a light amitoon (between 30 and 40%) or a gradation tone over the entire jacket. Depending on the light, etch out areas that are reflective and shiny.

Light strikes this part of the wrinkle.

The rule of thumb is that wrinkles are generally convex areas. Light strikes the top part of the convex wrinkle.

Don't forget to accommodate for the hidden ellipse in the neck when drawing the collar.

Finished work

Jeans

Jeans are one type of common clothing. Let's take a look at their basic design.

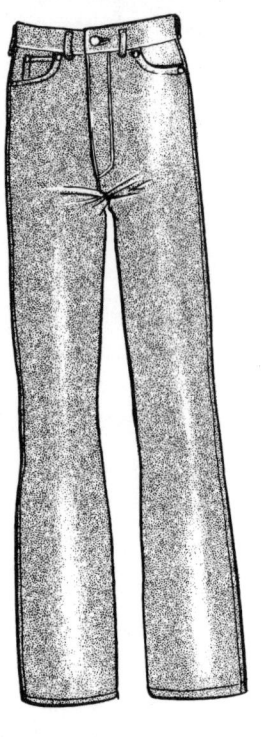

Boot Cut

These jeans were originally made for cowboys who wore boots. They were cut this way to ensure easy movement and maintain the masculine silhouette of the cowboy. The thigh area is a bit thin, and the knee area is tightened. The key characteristic of these jeans is the way they expand out from the knees down.

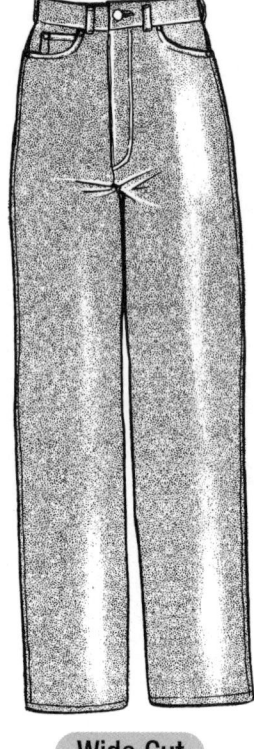

Wide Cut

These are the same shape as the straight cut but are a bit wider.

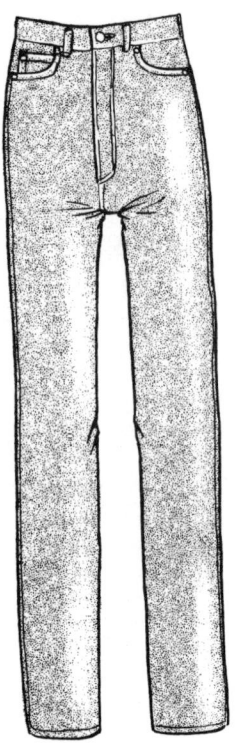

Straight Cut

This is the most basic shape.

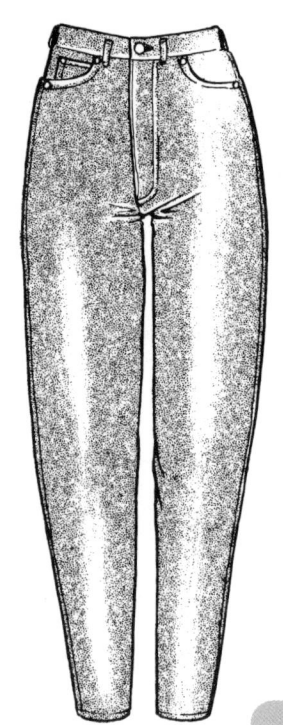

Slim cut jeans accent the leg lines.

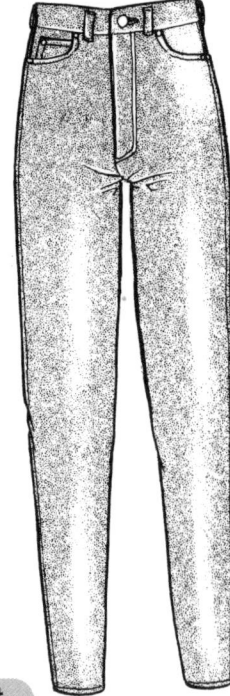

Slim Cut

These jeans get thinner towards the ankles. There are various designs for the upper area ranging from thin to thick diameters.

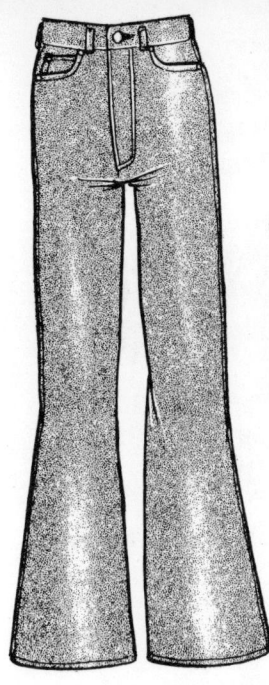

Bell Bottom Cut
This design, which was very popular in the 70s, widens out from the knees into the shape of a bell.

Baggy Cut
This design flows straight down from the waist with plenty of room all over.

A small pocket, known as a coin pocket, is often attached inside the right pocket.

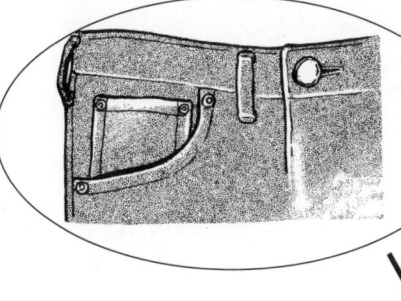

There are a variety of pocket lines on the front of the jeans.

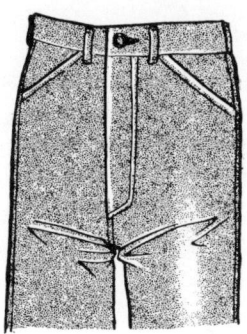
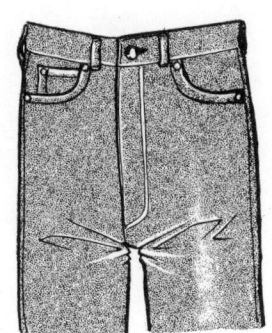
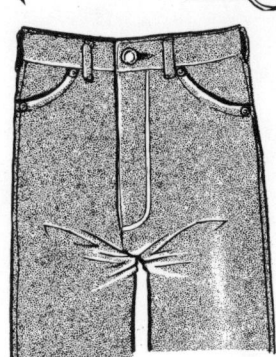

The stitching on the back pockets has a special design. These are different for each manufacturer and act as a trademark. Jeans with hidden stitches also exist.

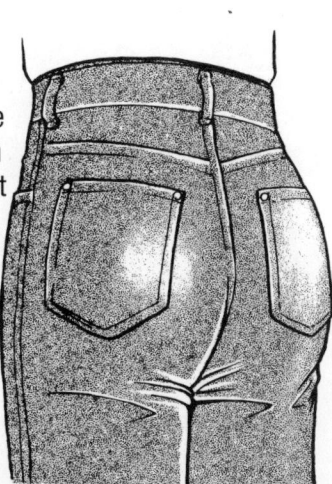
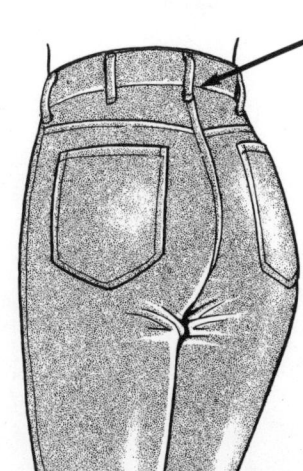

Belt Loops
A belt is threaded through these. There are usually five belt loops with two in the front, two on the side and one in the back. A design also exists with seven loops for extra strength.

Standing | Zipped

Let's take a look how the jeans and leather jacket change depending on the pose from a variety of angles.

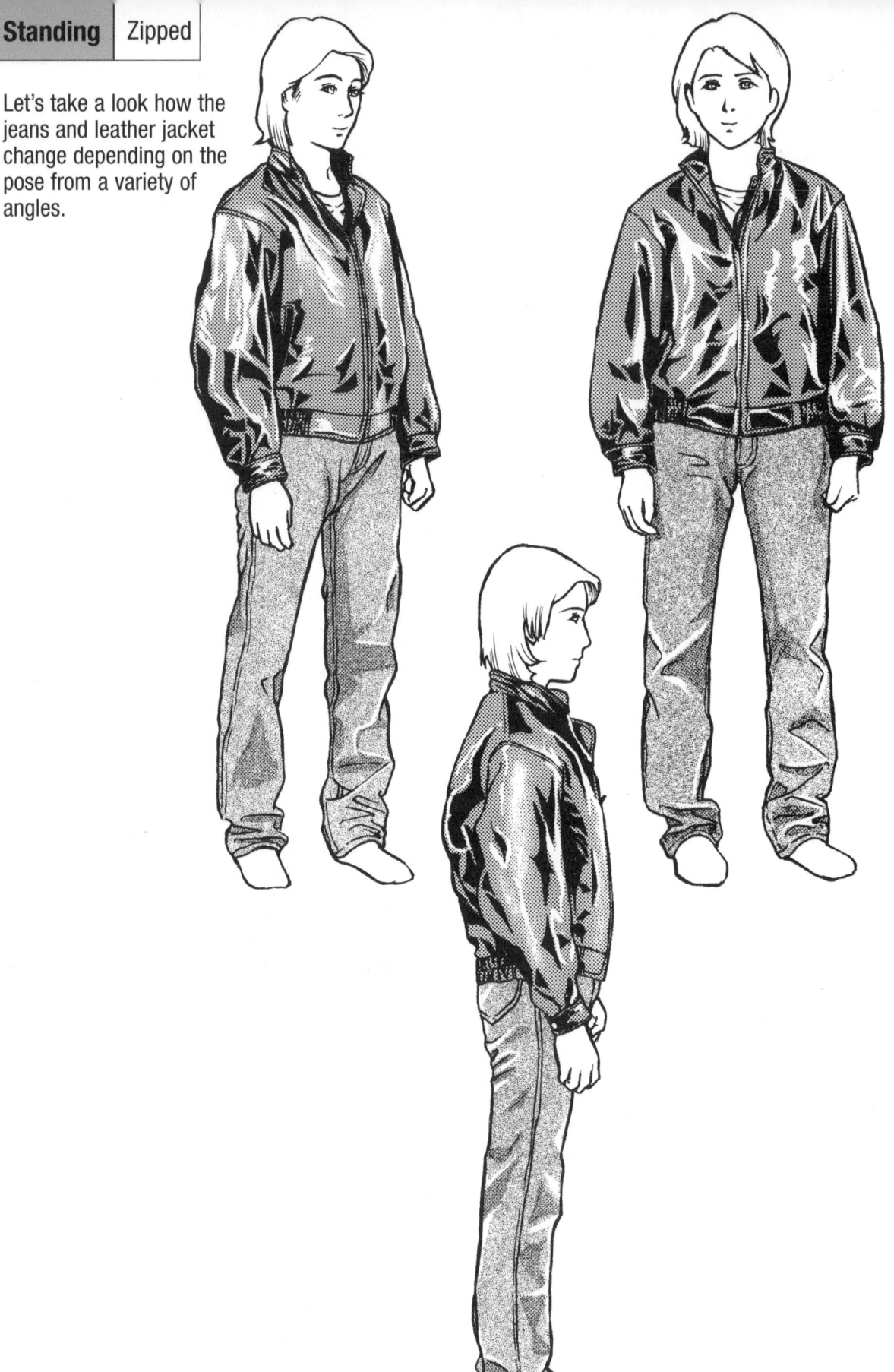

Standing | Unzipped

Standing | Zipped | Low Angle

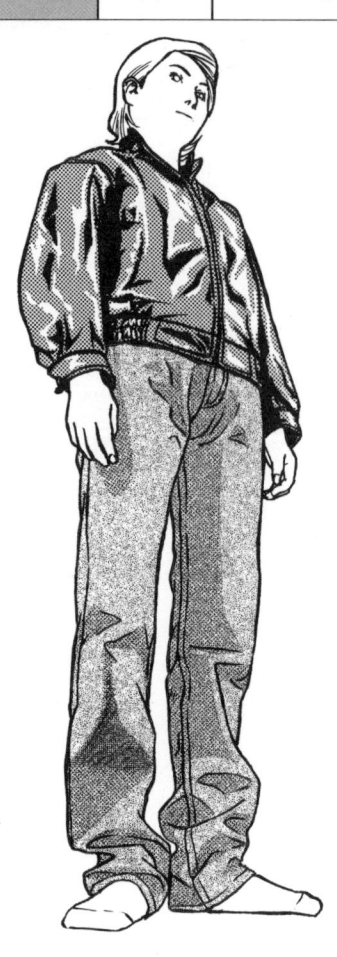
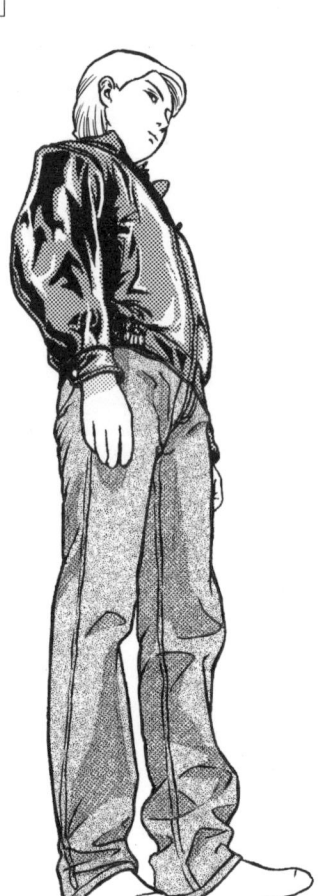
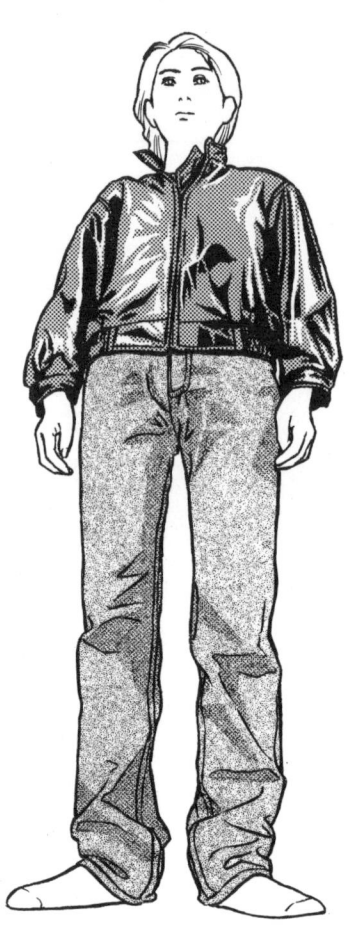
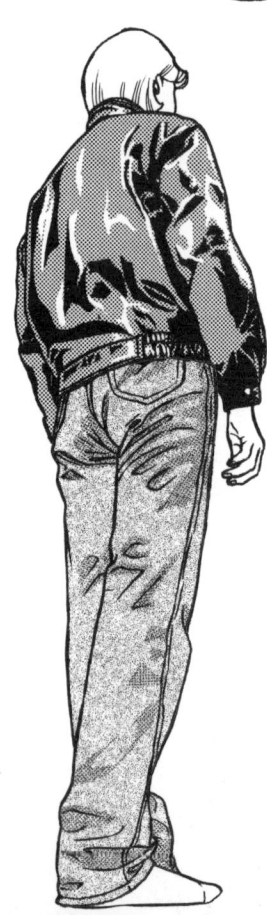
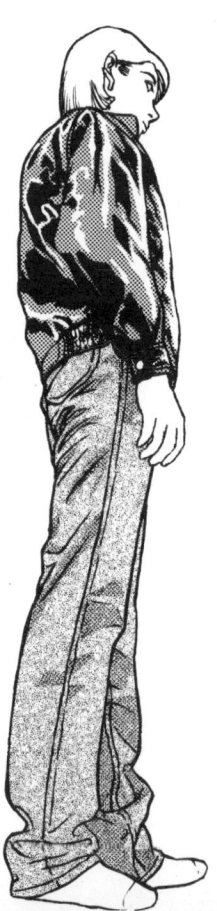

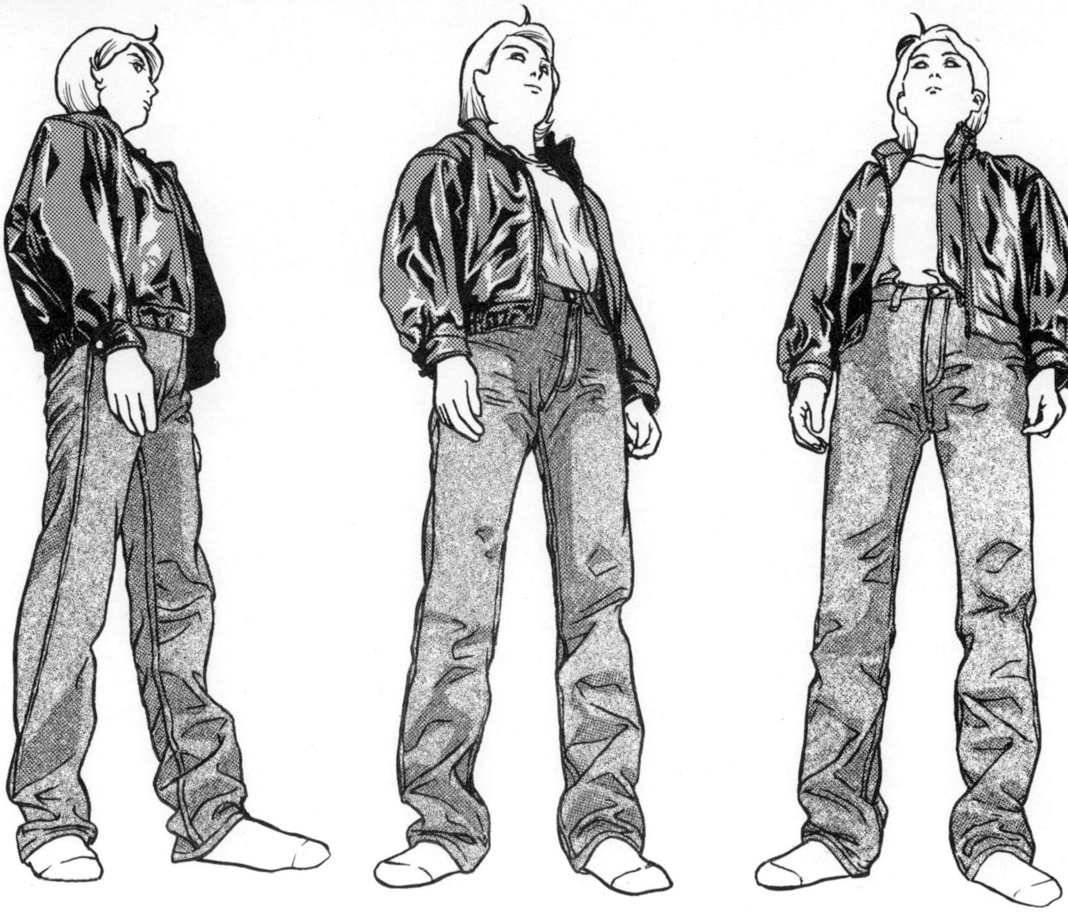

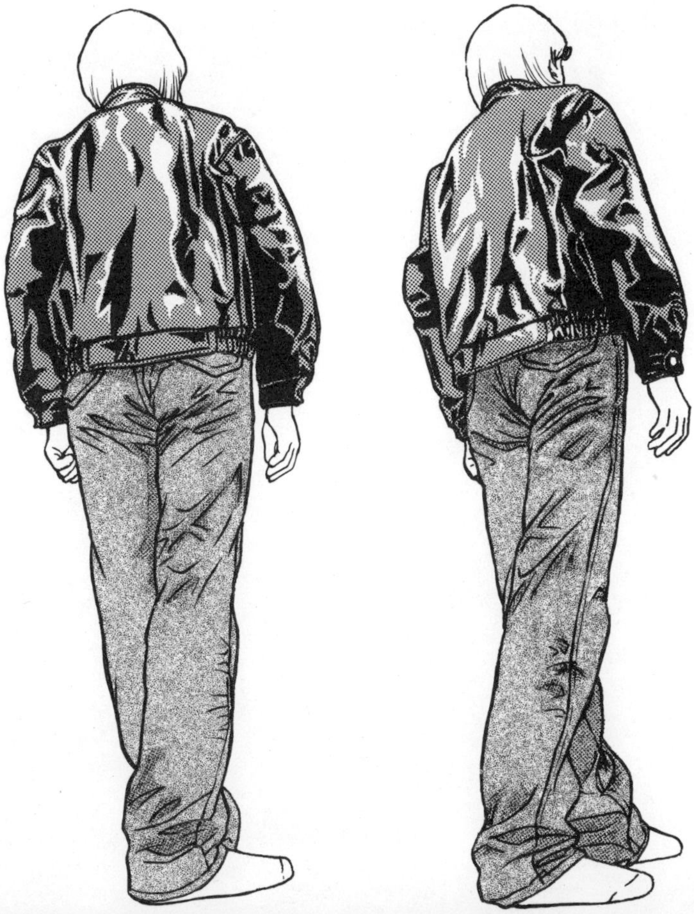

Standing | Unzipped | Low Angle

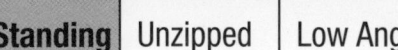

| One Arm Raised | Zipped | Slight Side Angle |

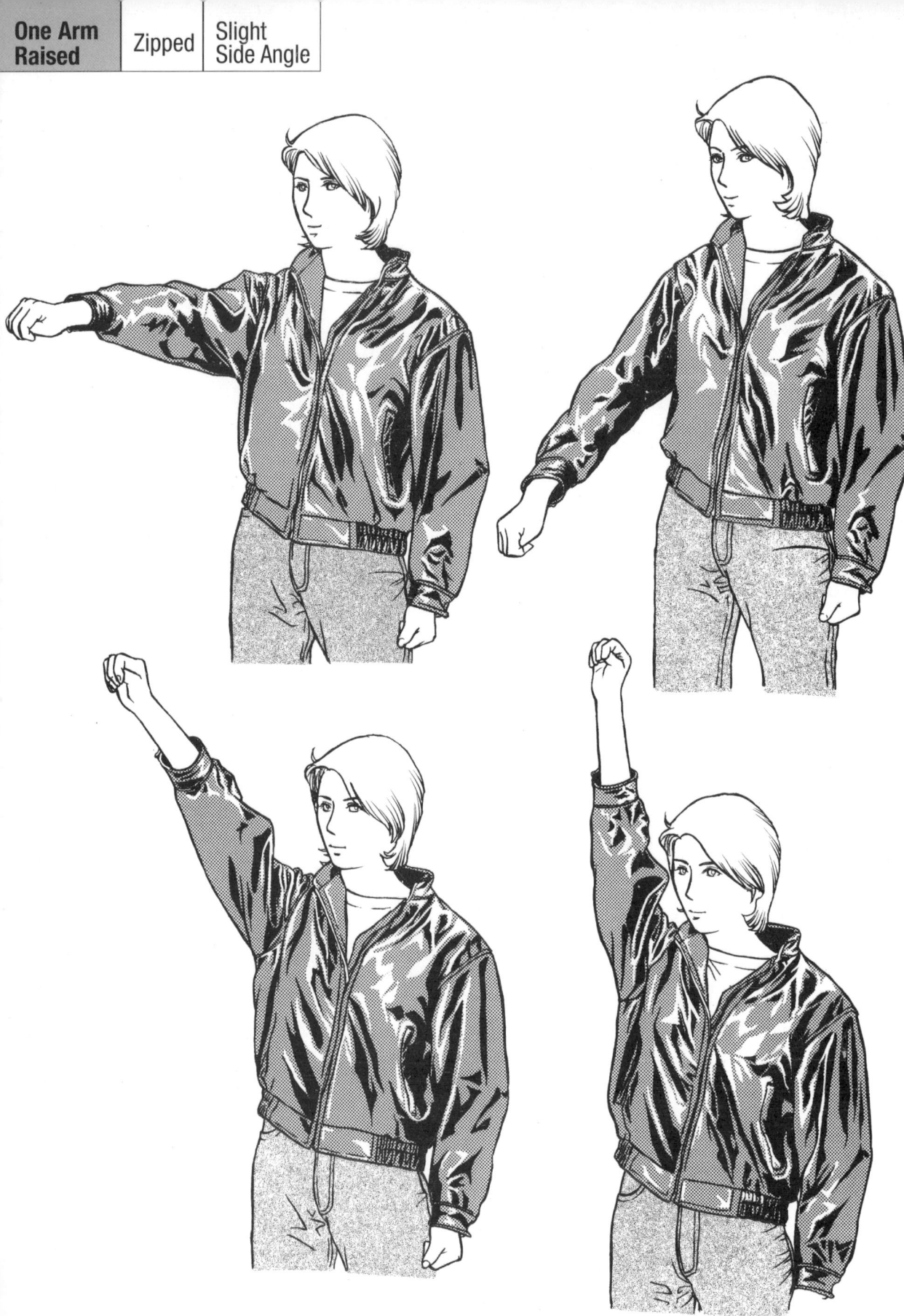

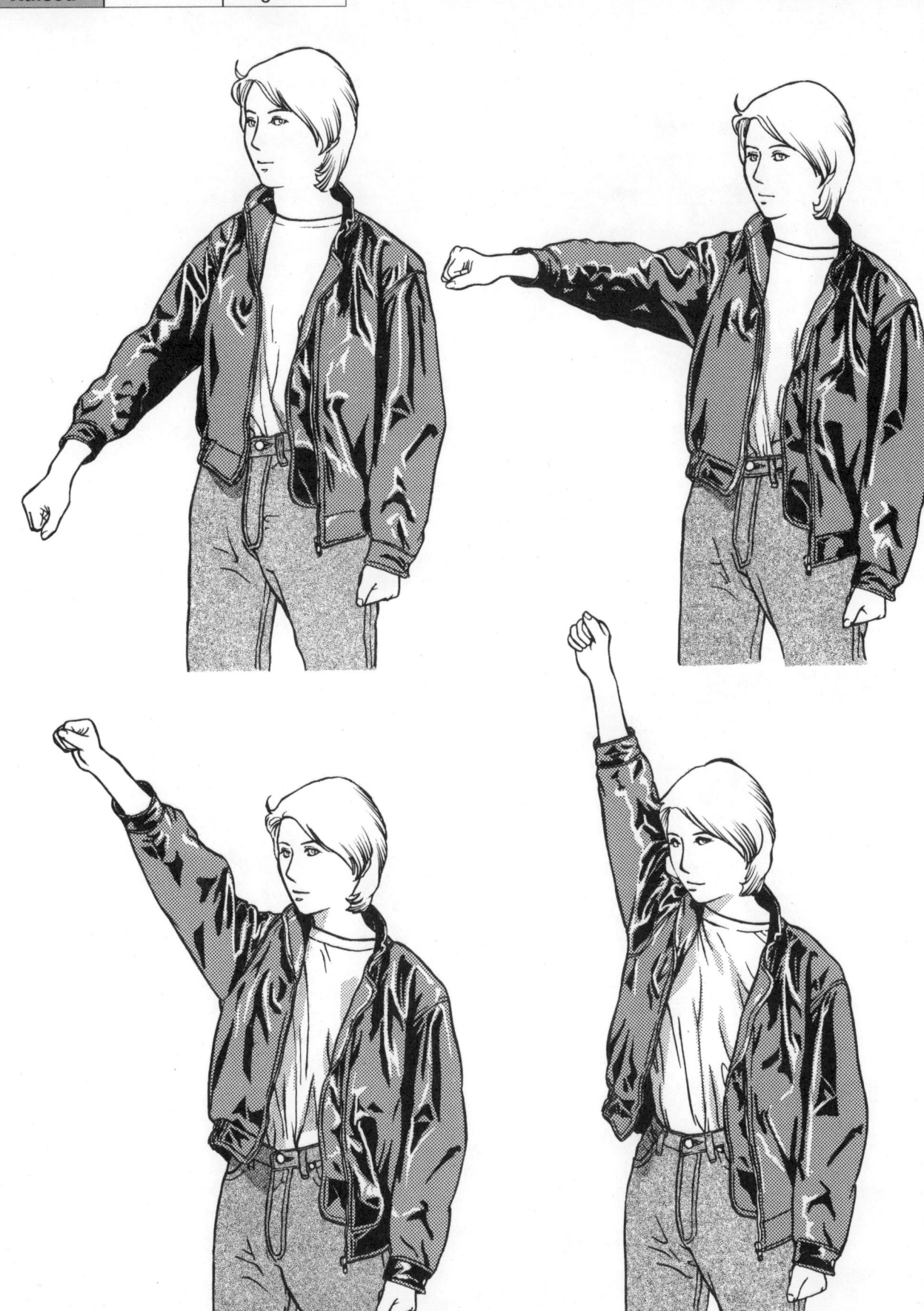

One Arm Raised to the Side | Zipped | Front Angle

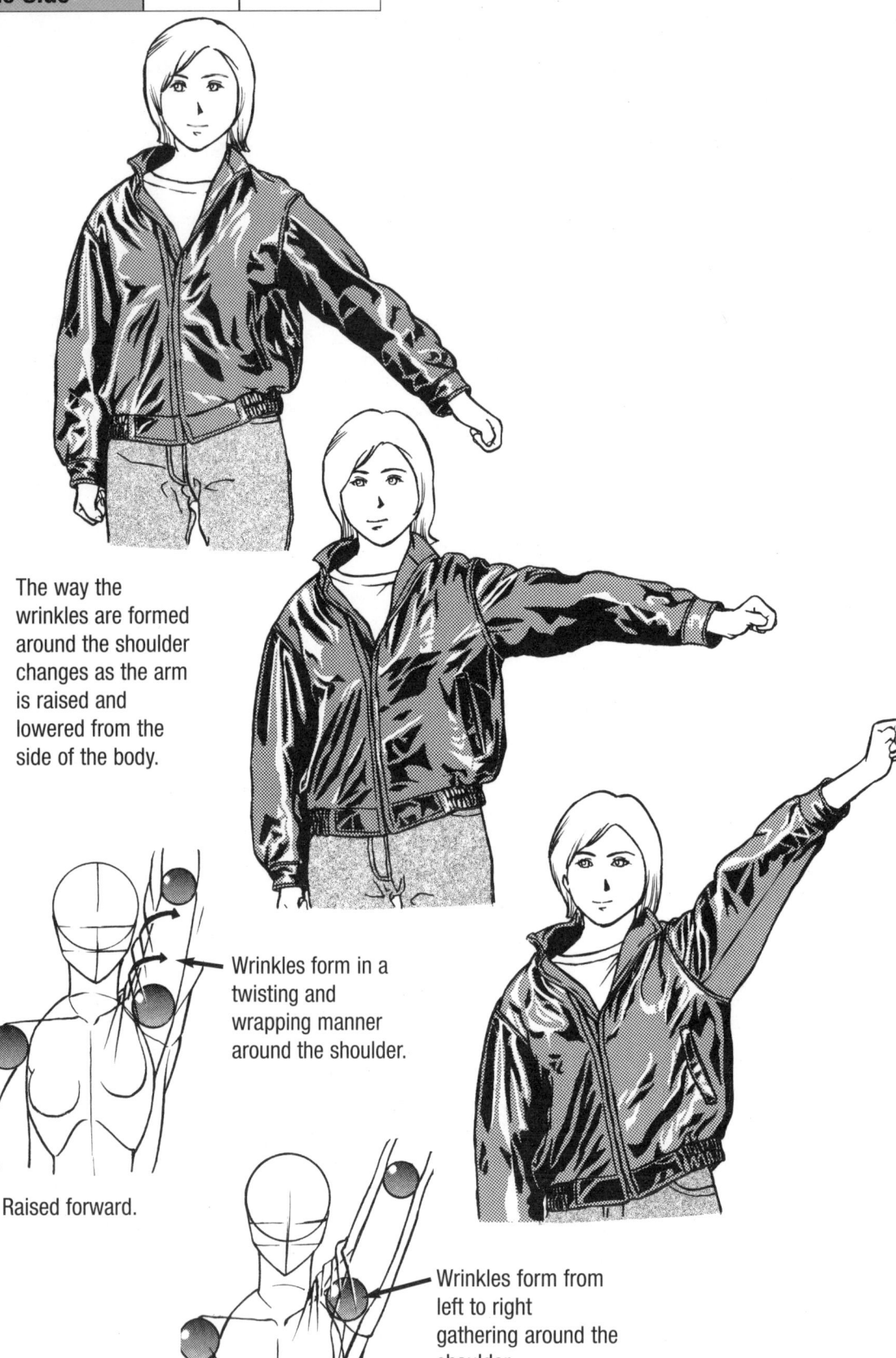

The way the wrinkles are formed around the shoulder changes as the arm is raised and lowered from the side of the body.

Wrinkles form in a twisting and wrapping manner around the shoulder.

Raised forward.

Wrinkles form from left to right gathering around the shoulder.

Raised to the side.

| One Arm Raised to the Side | Unzipped | Front Angle |

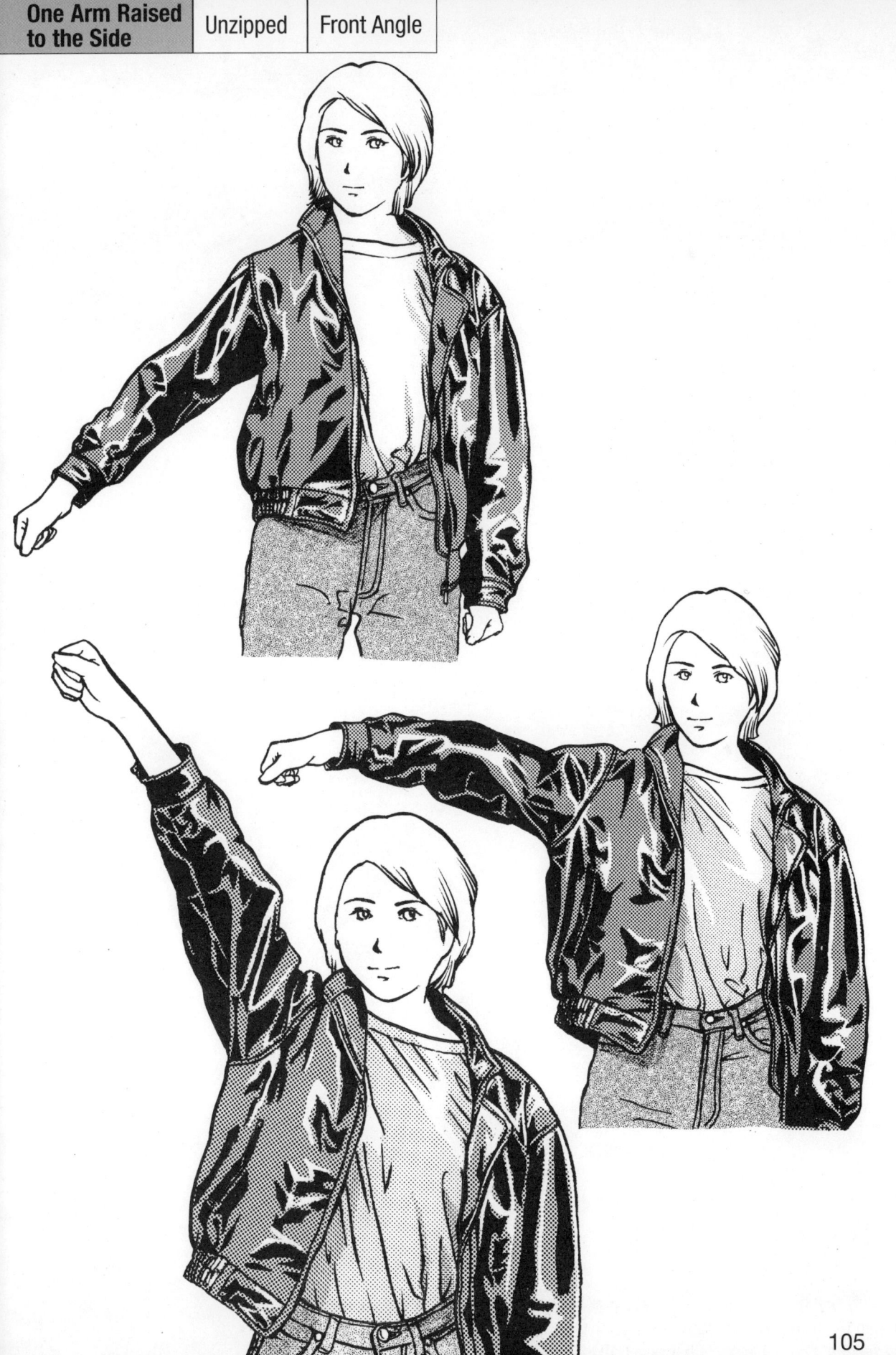

One Arm Raised to the Side | Unzipped | Rear Angle

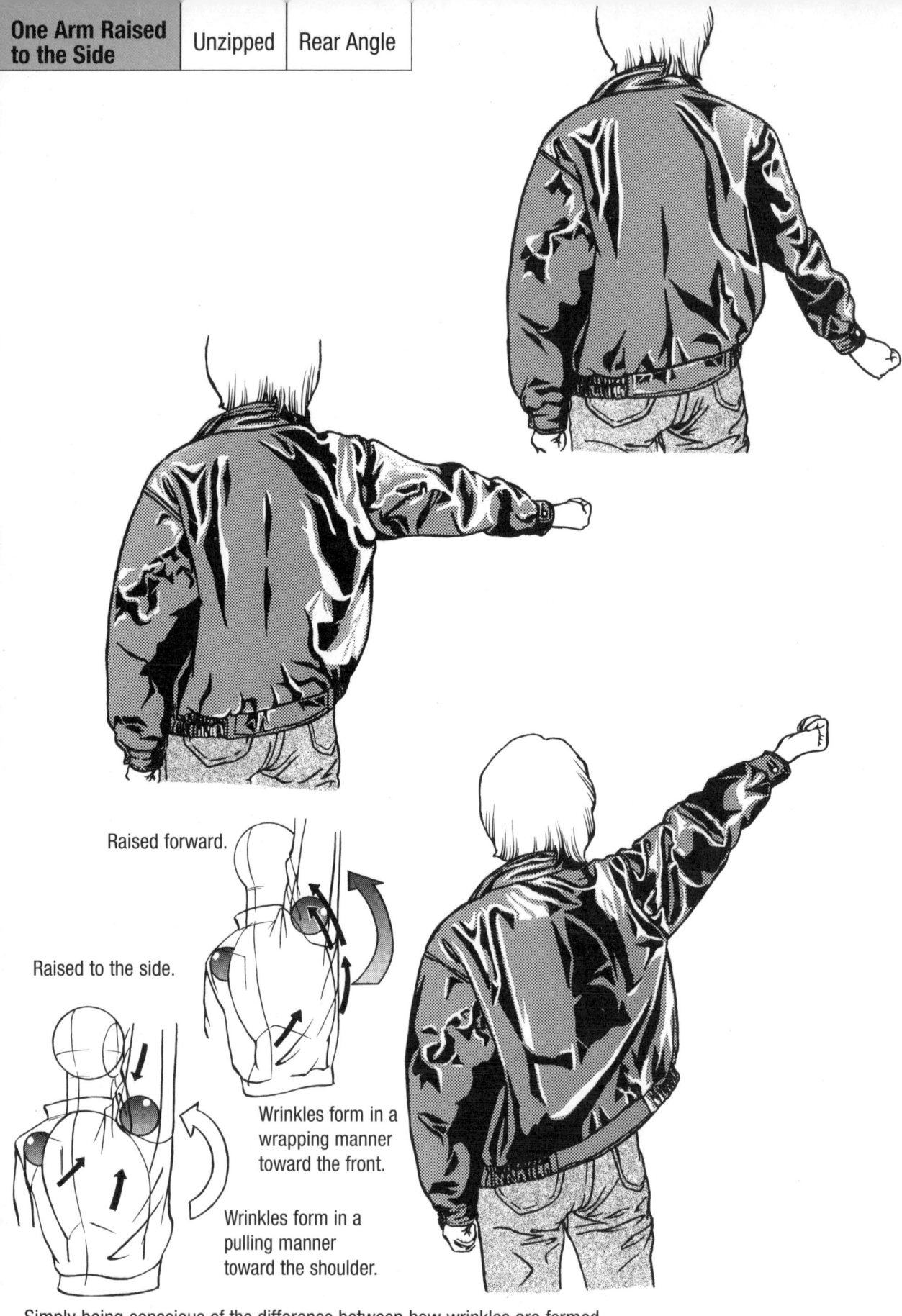

Raised forward.

Raised to the side.

Wrinkles form in a wrapping manner toward the front.

Wrinkles form in a pulling manner toward the shoulder.

Simply being conscious of the difference between how wrinkles are formed when the arm is raised from the front or the side will definitely improve your drawings. This will also help add a sense of motion to your work.

| One Arm Raised to the Side | Zipped | Rear Right Side Angle |

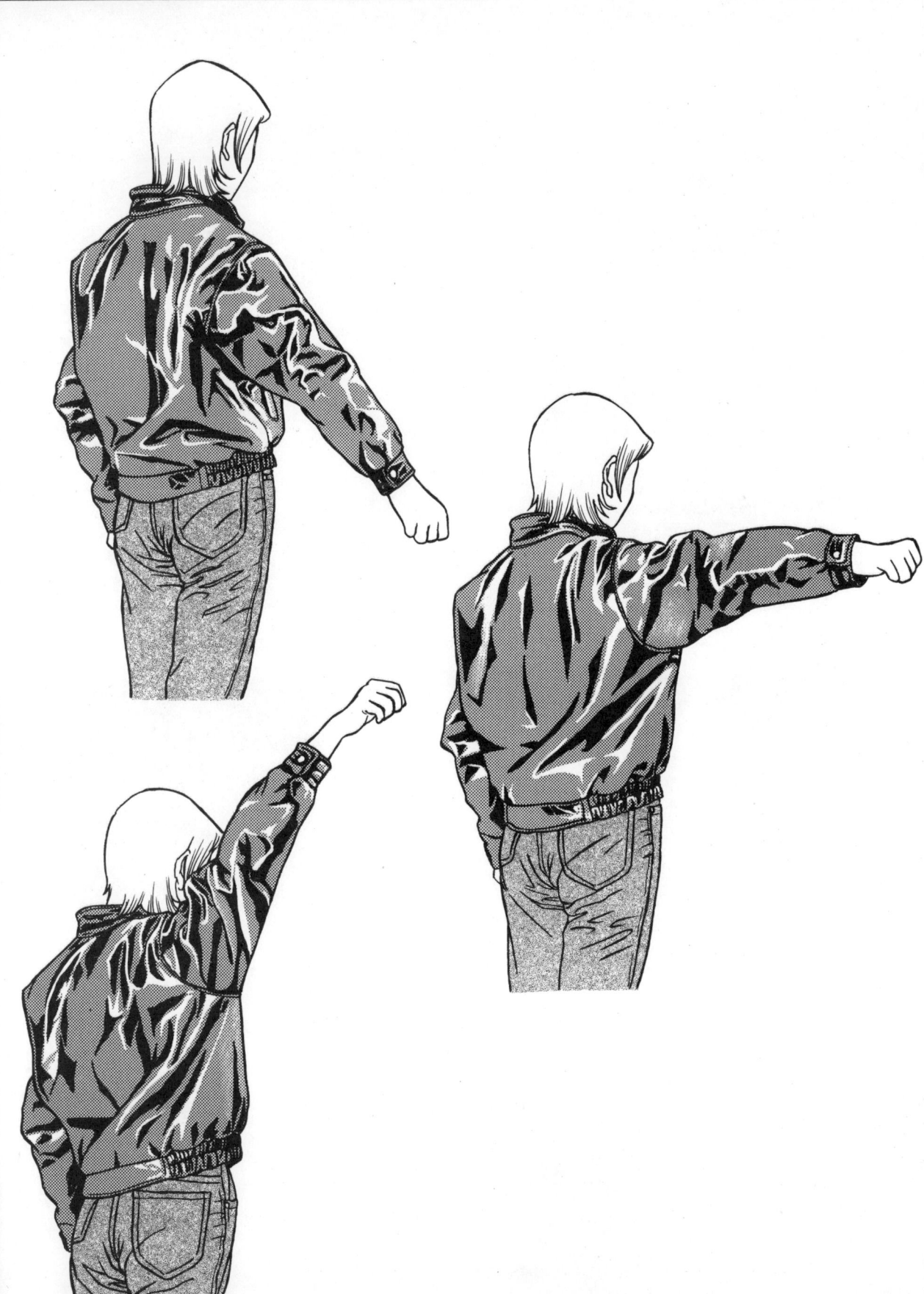

| One Arm Raised to the Side | Unzipped | Right Side Front Angle |

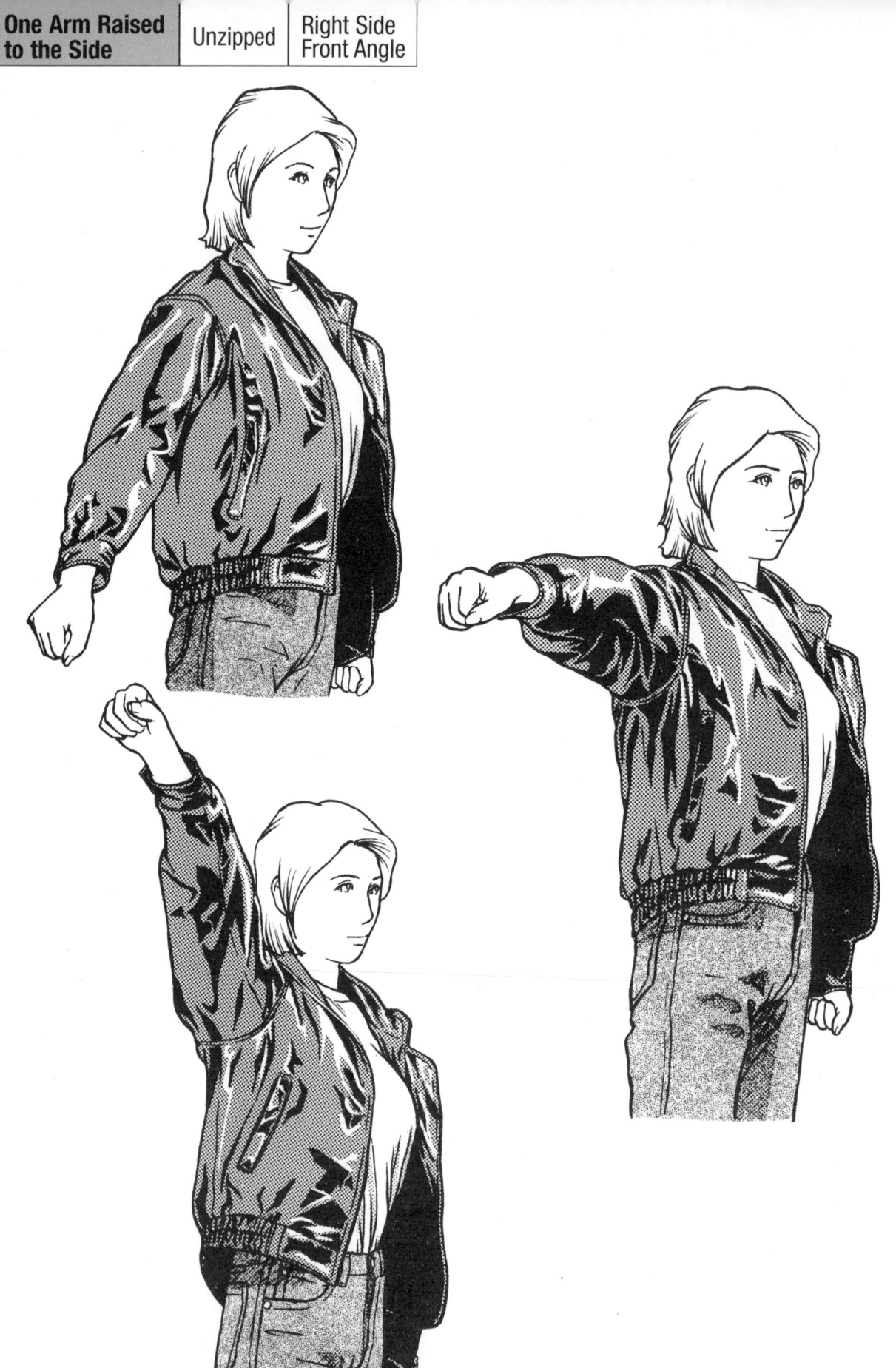

Both Arms Raised | Zipped

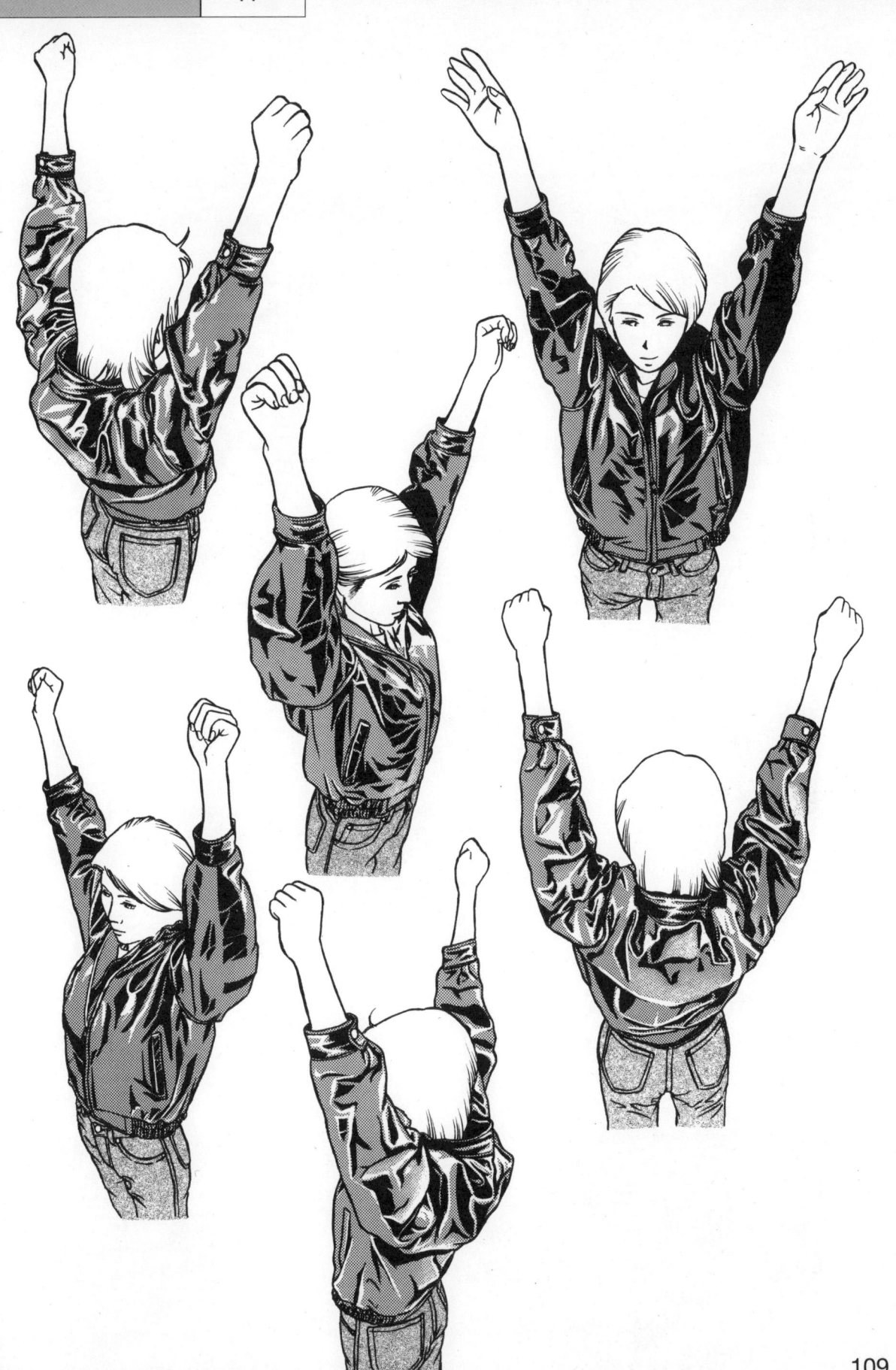

109

Both Arms Raised | Unzipped

Picking Something Up | Zipped

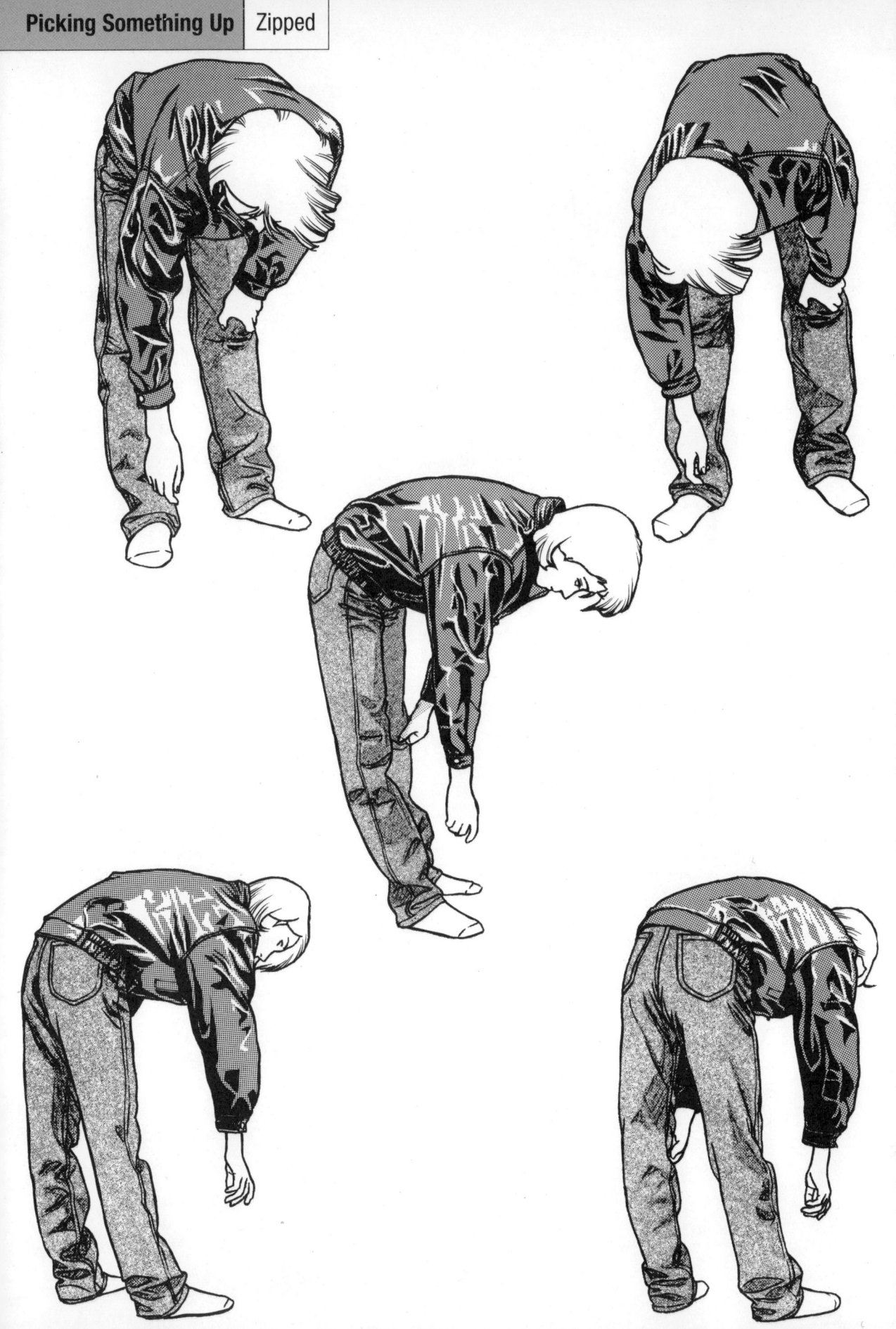

Turning the Body | Zipped

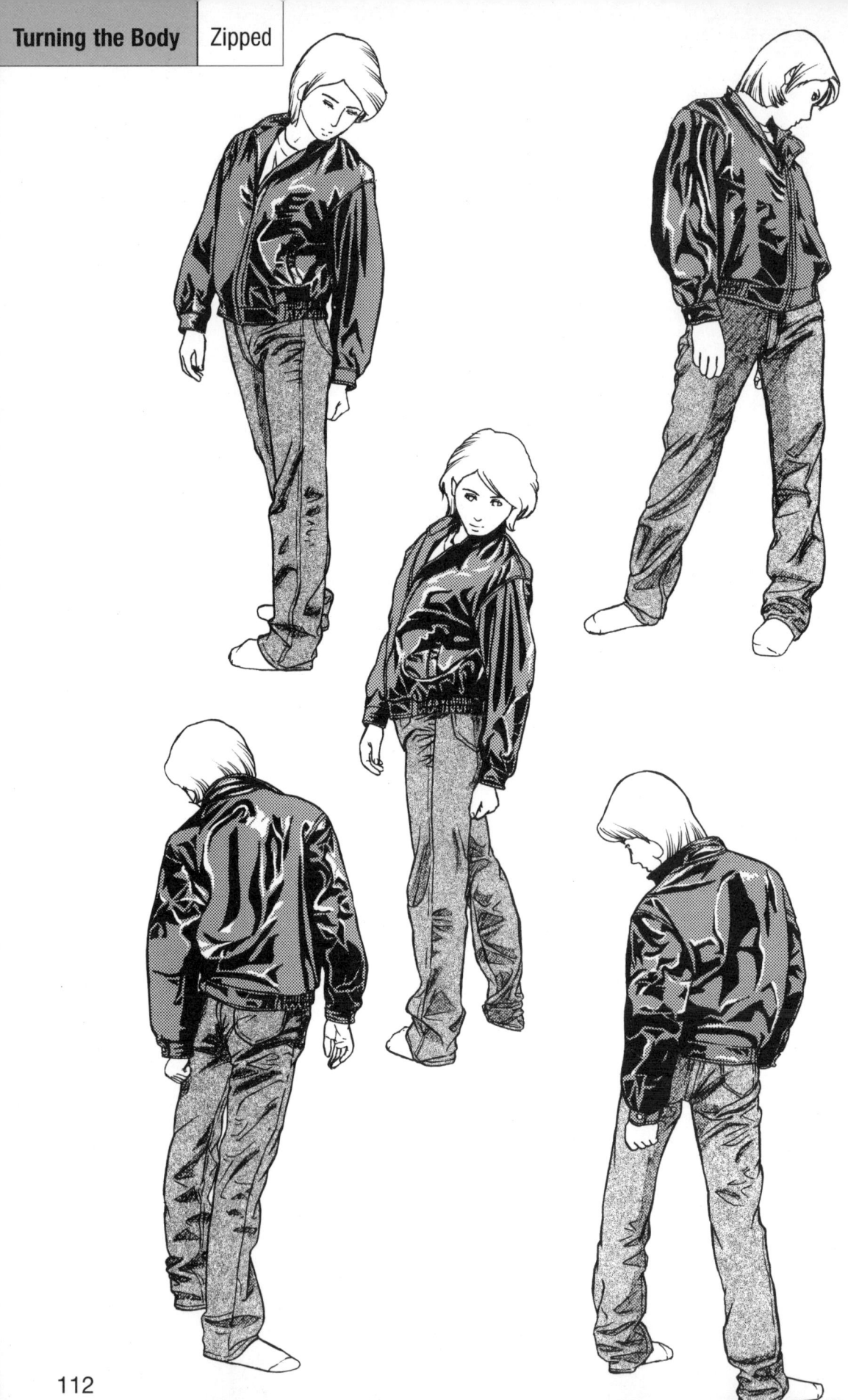

Turning the Body | Unzipped

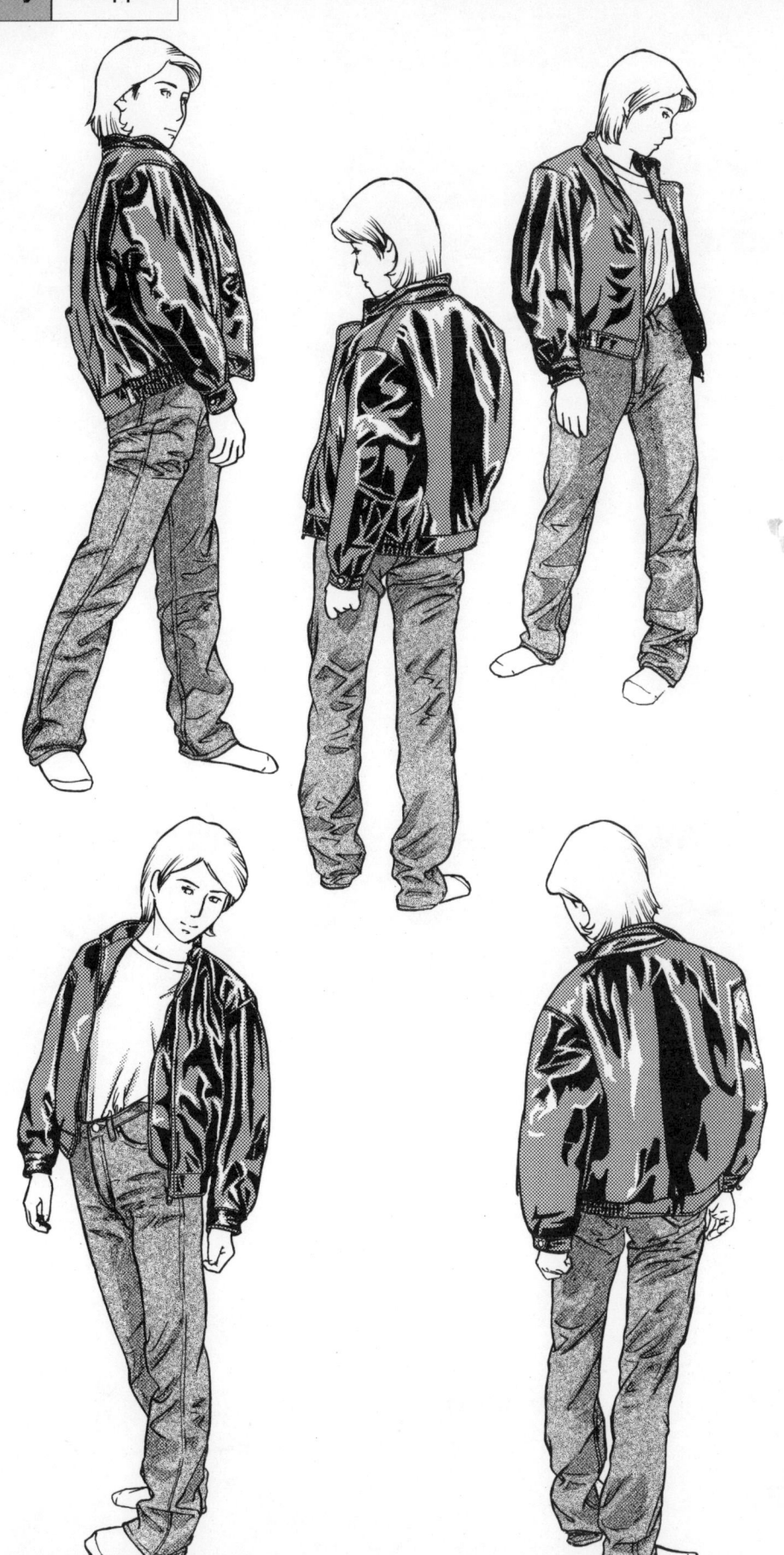

113

| Turning the Body | Zipped | Low Angle |

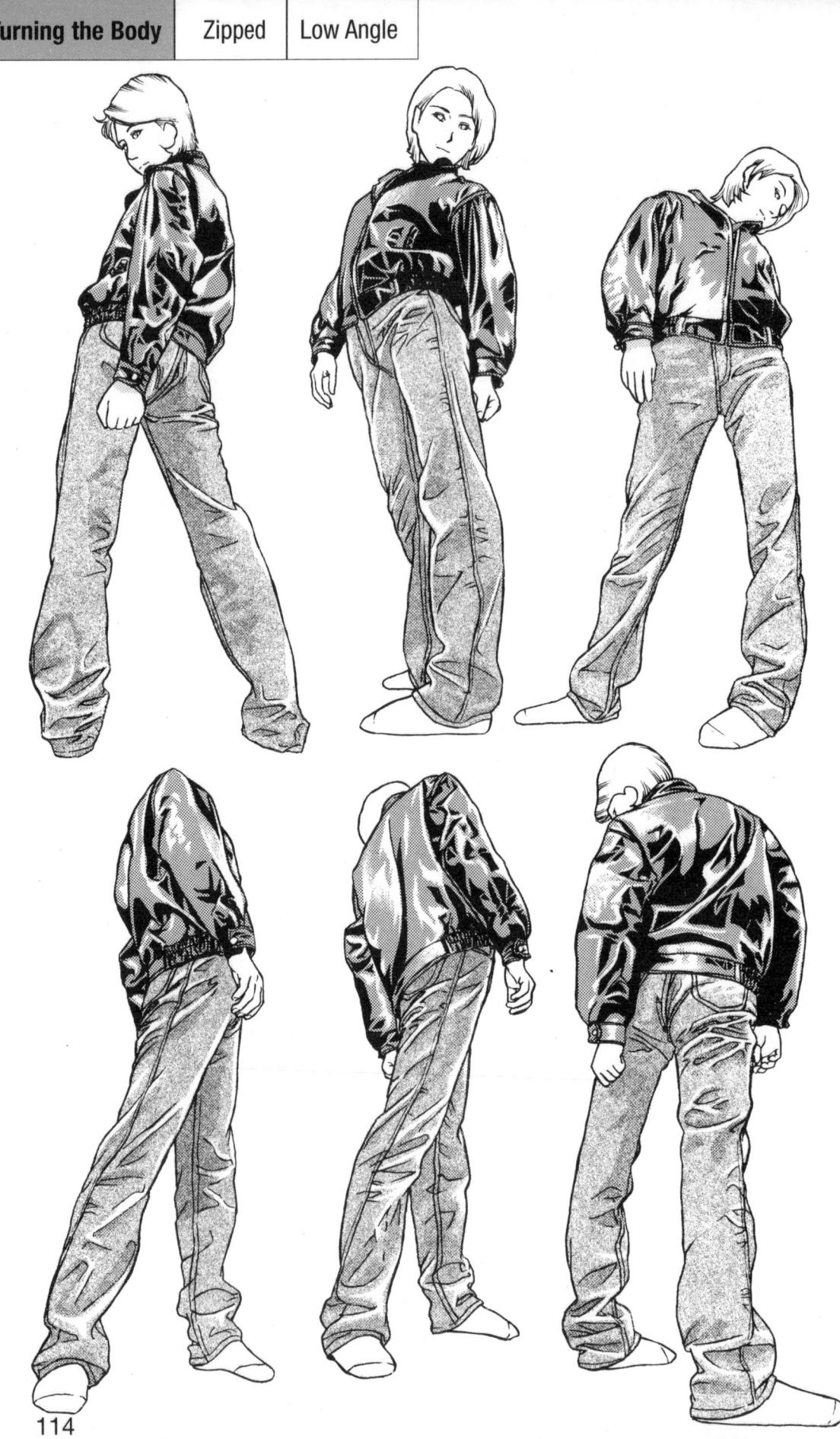

| Turning the Body | Unzipped | Low Angle |

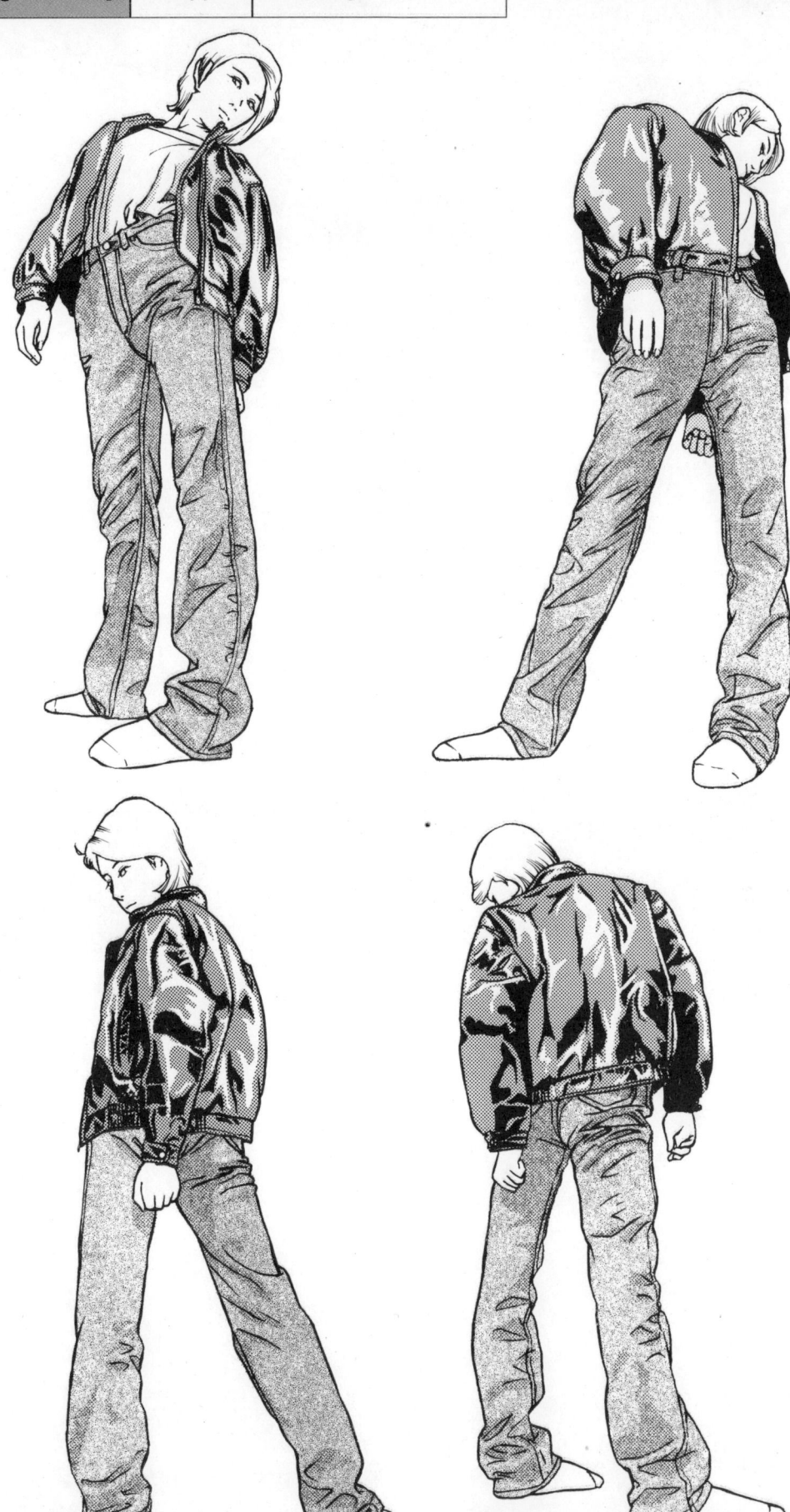

Bending to the Side | Zipped

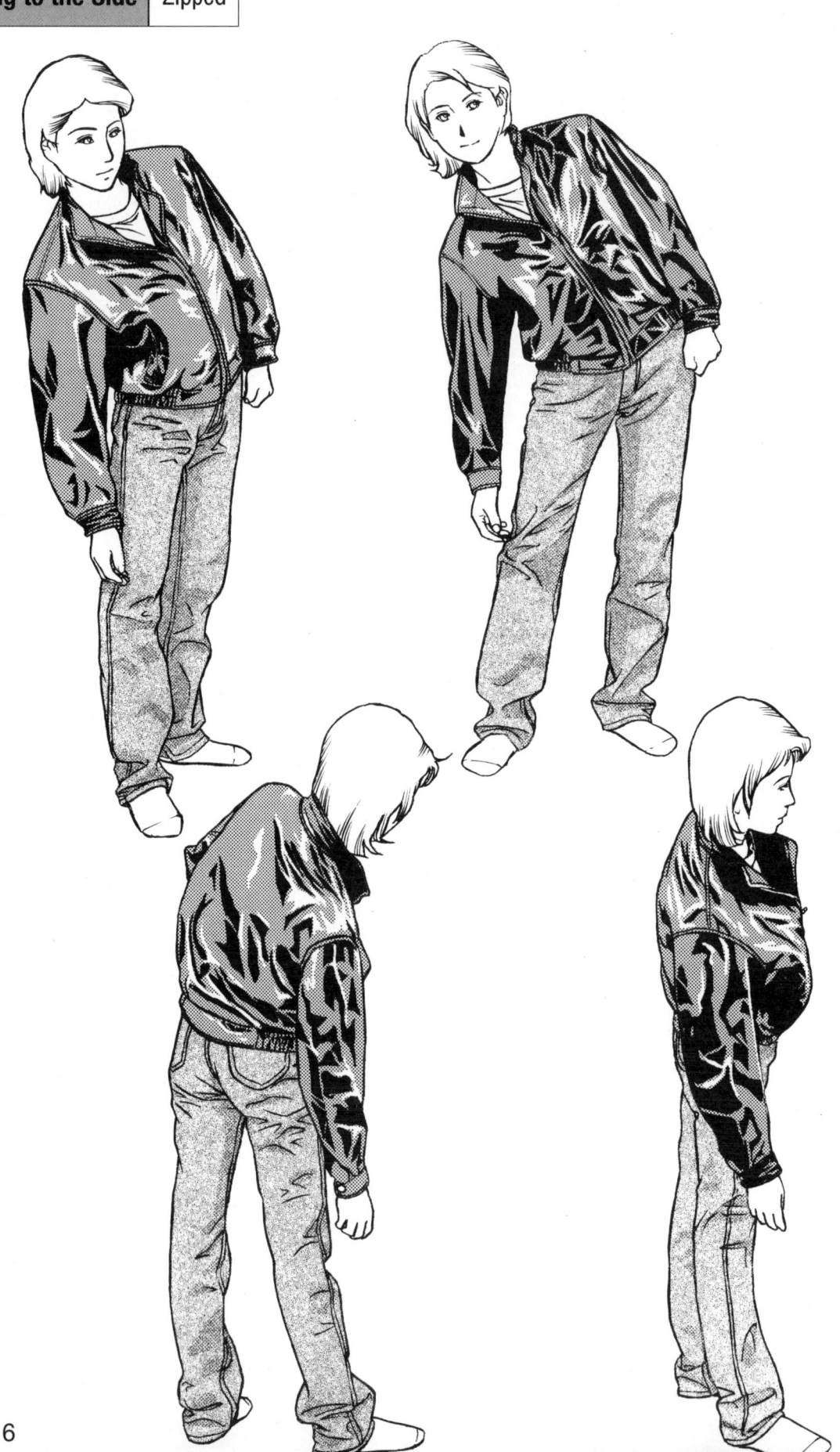

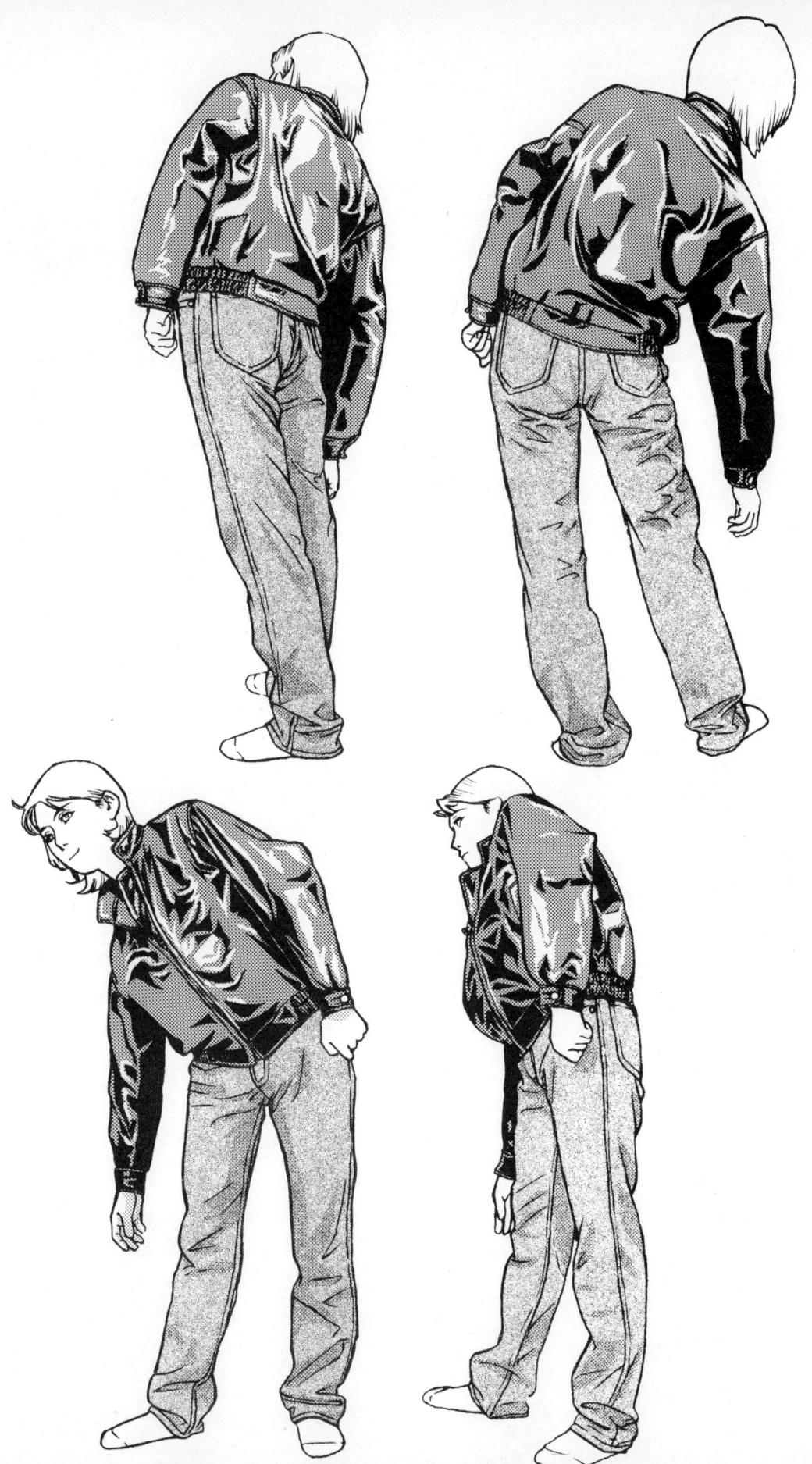

Bending Back | Zipped

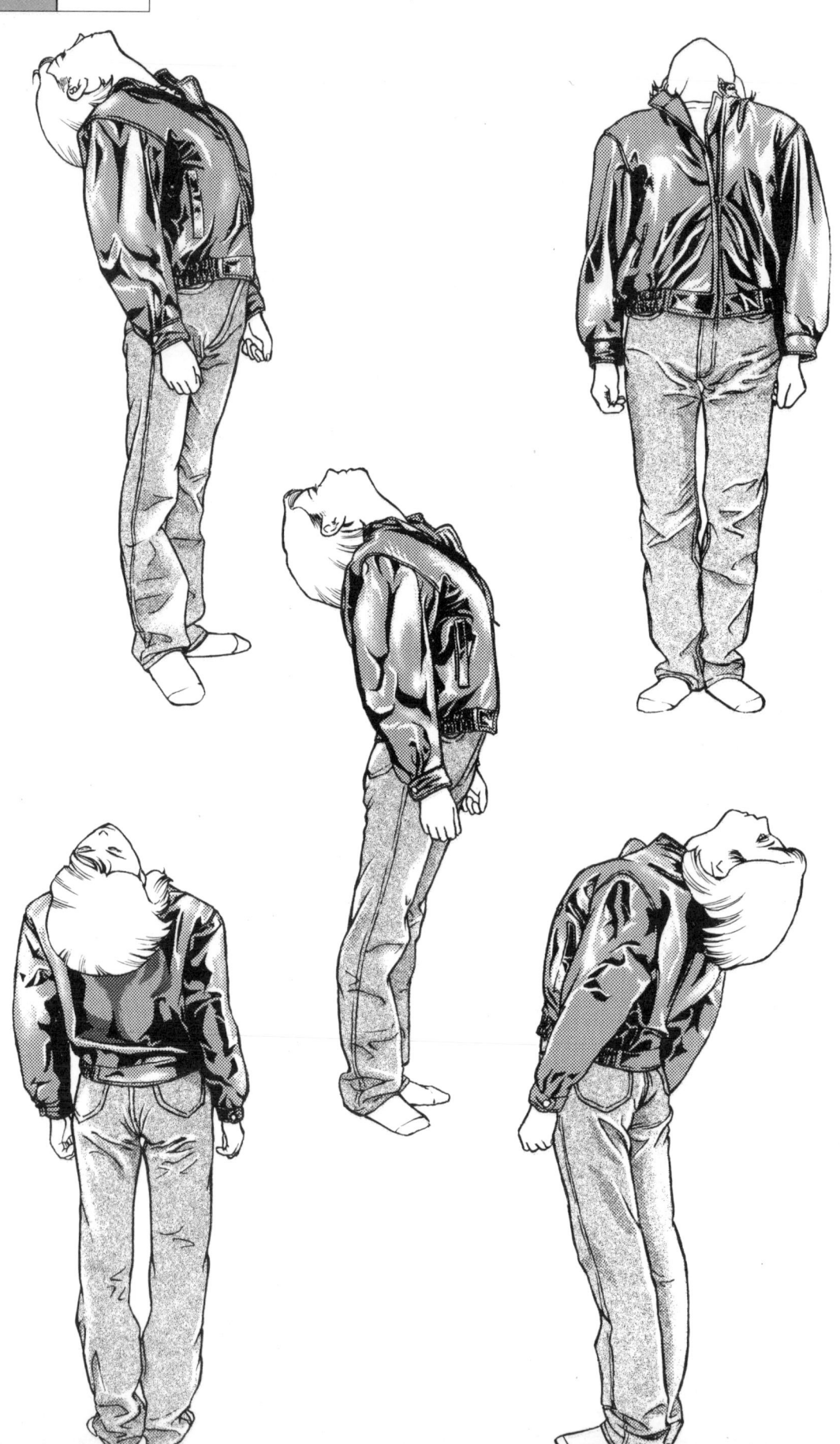

Bending Back | Unzipped

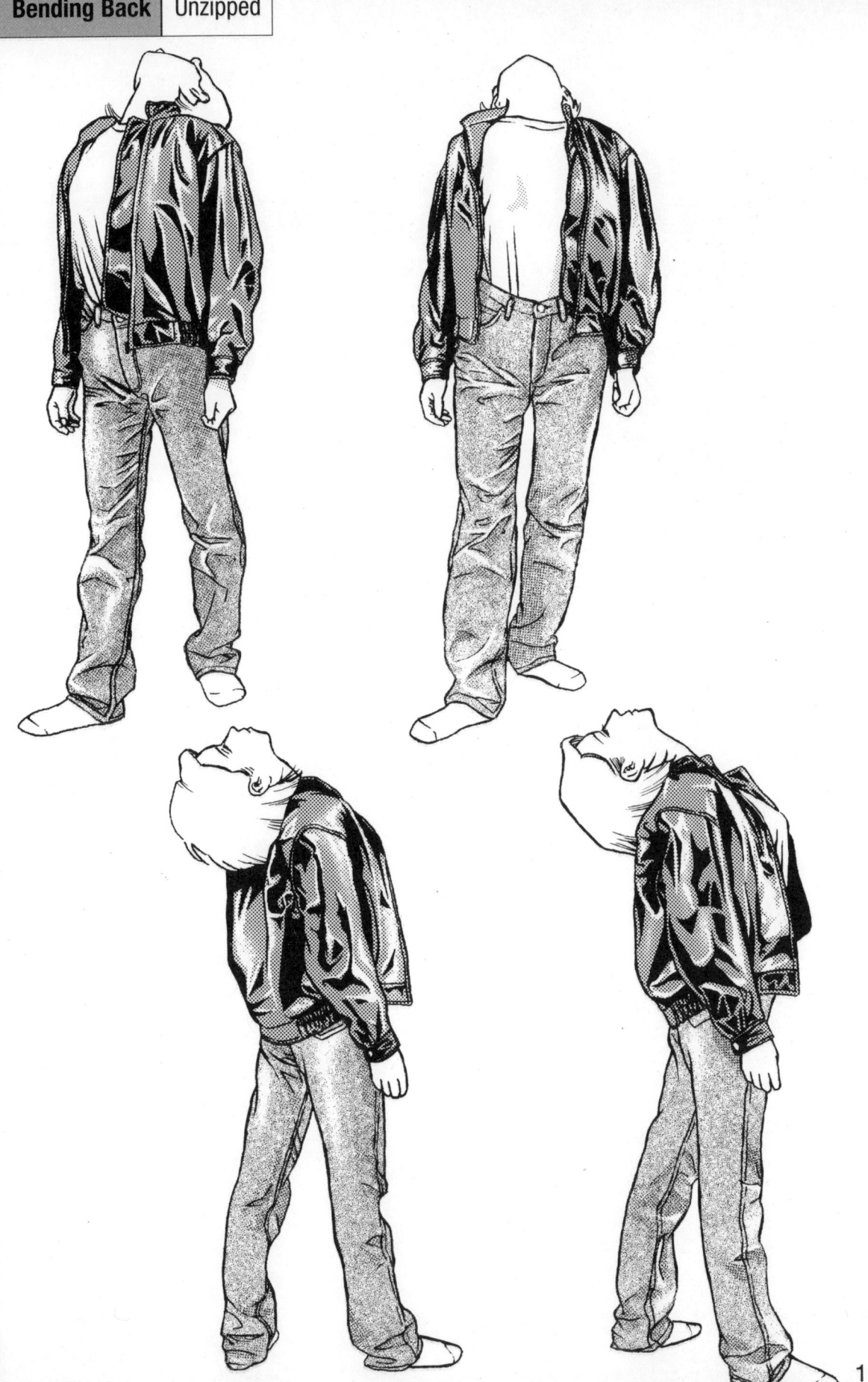

Sitting in a Chair

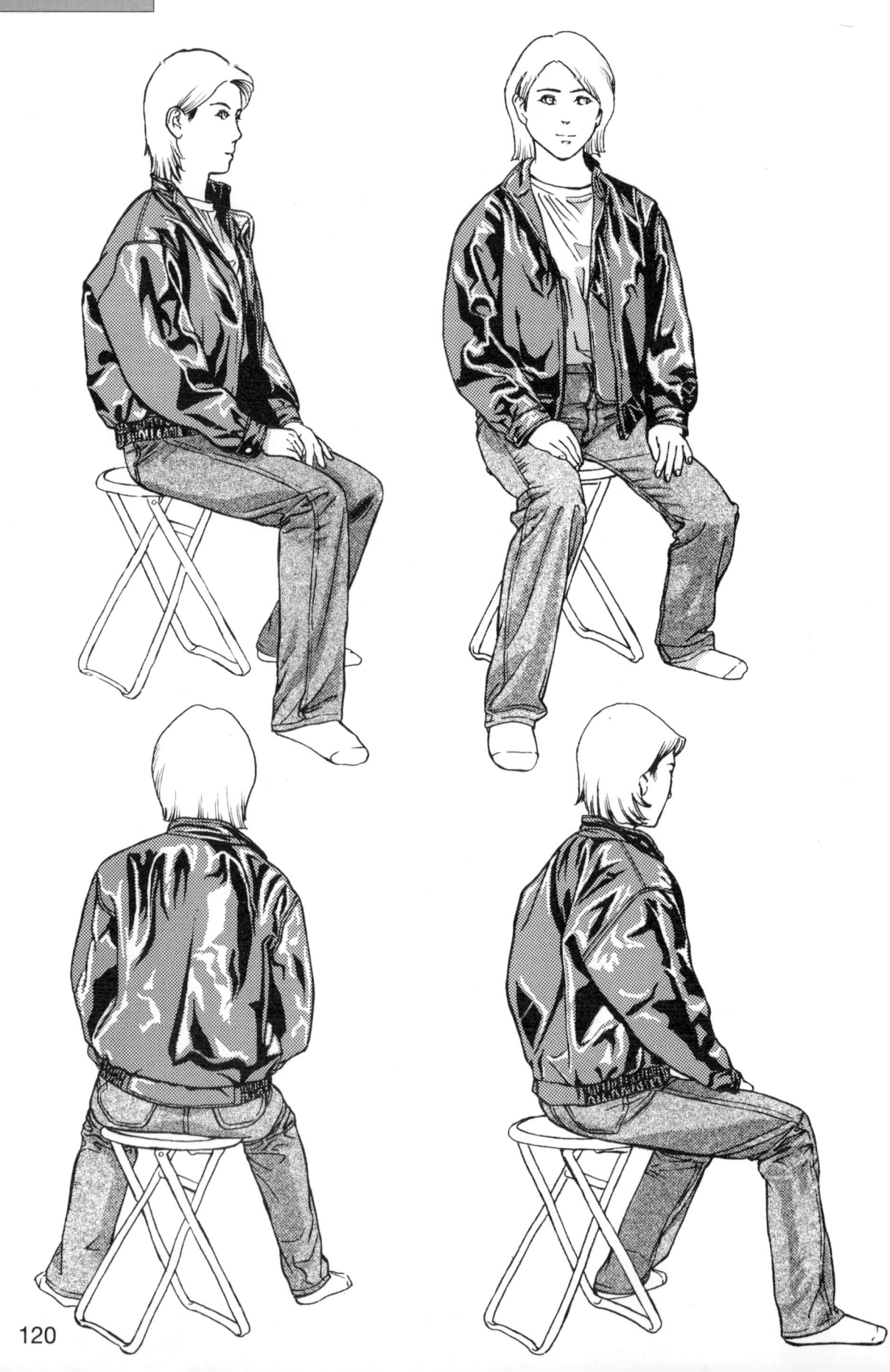

Legs Crossed

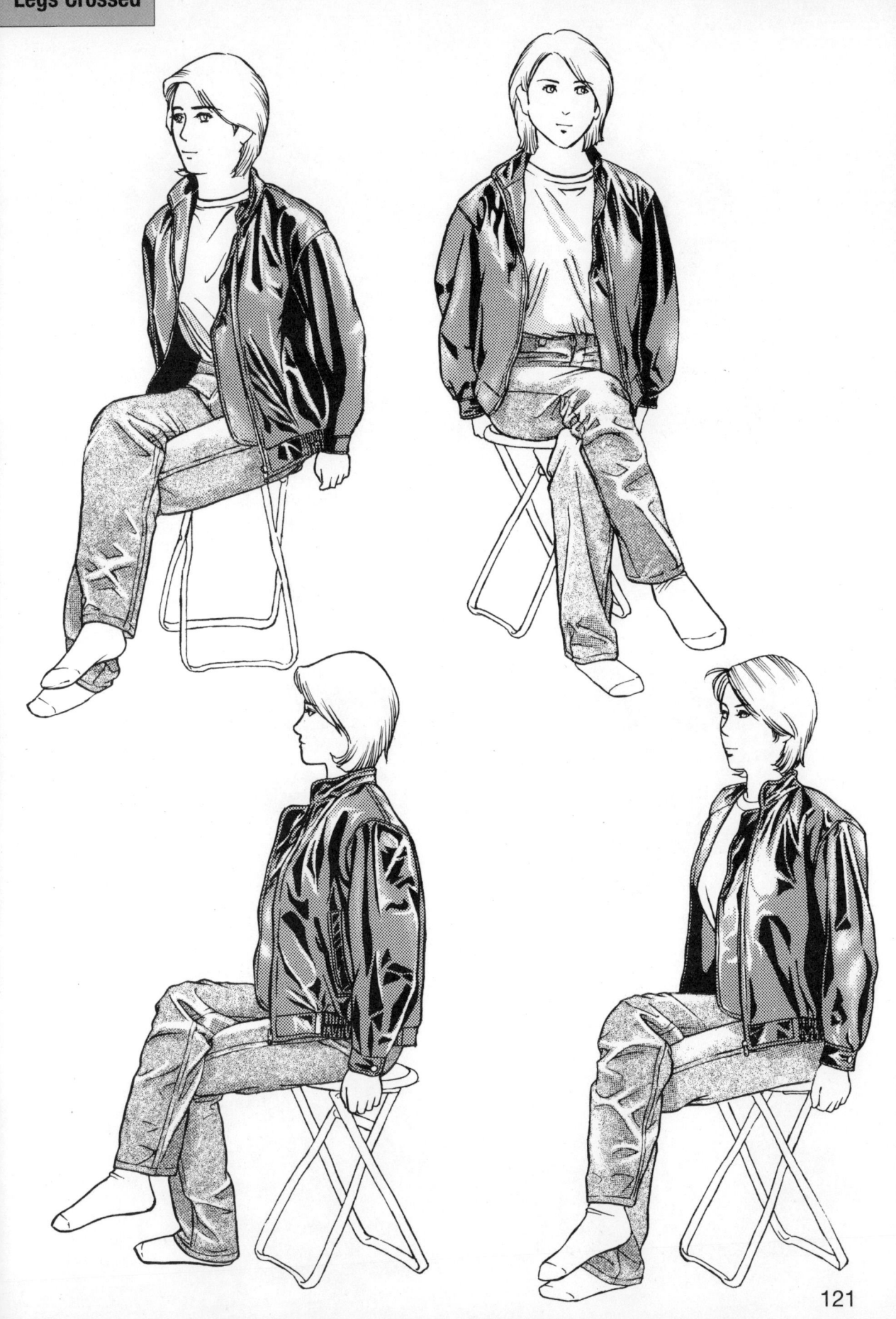

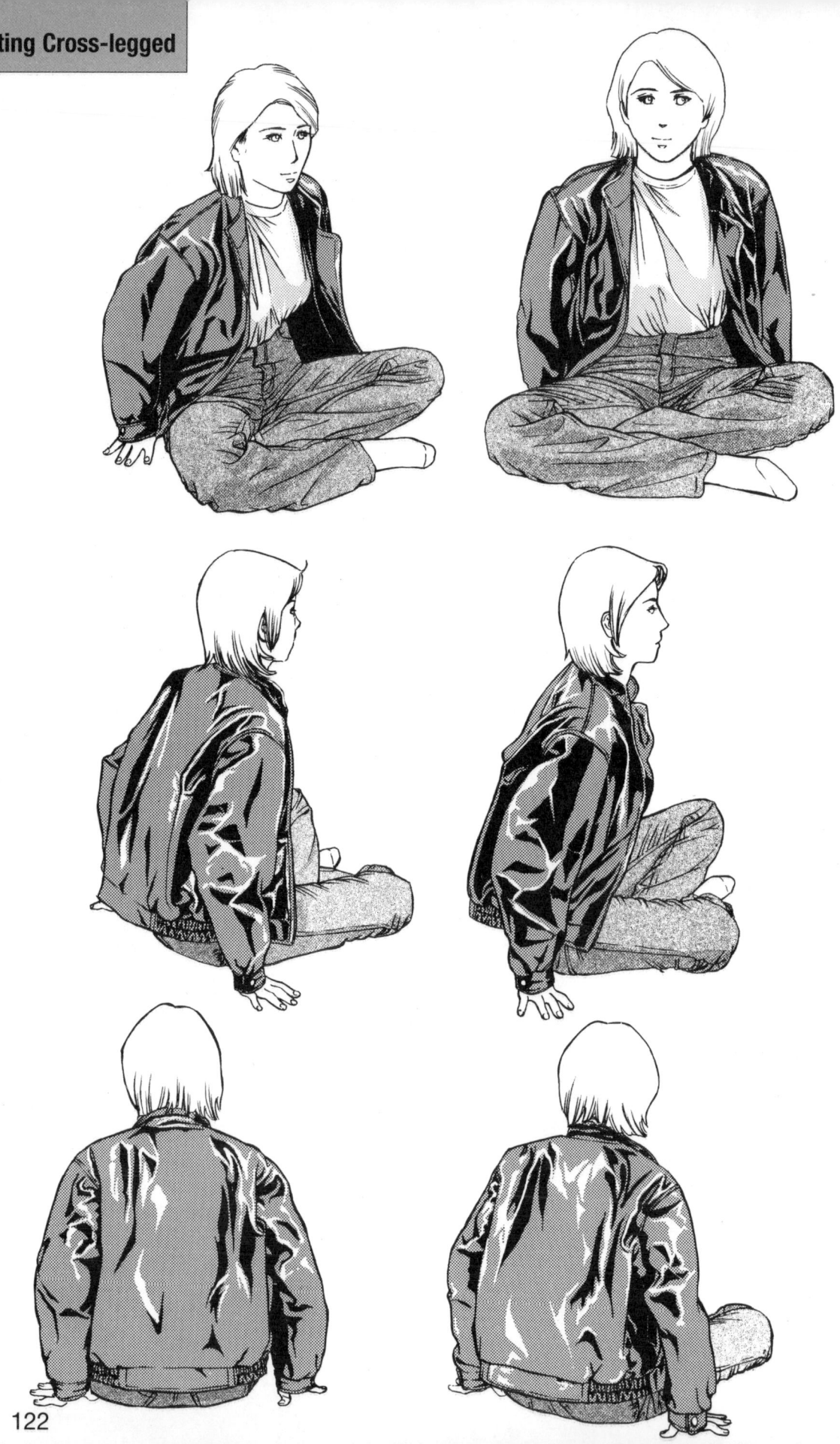

Falling On One's Buttocks

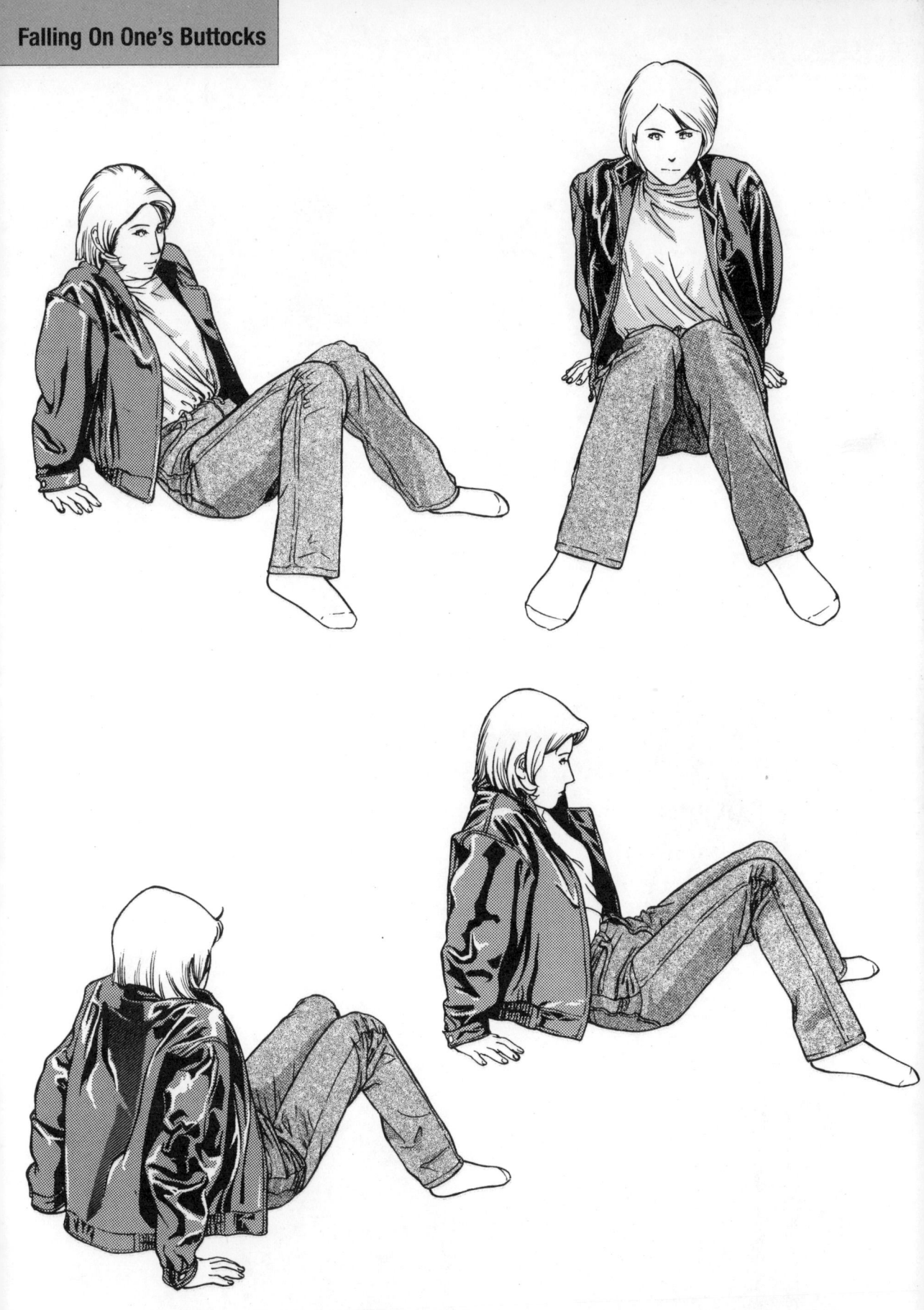

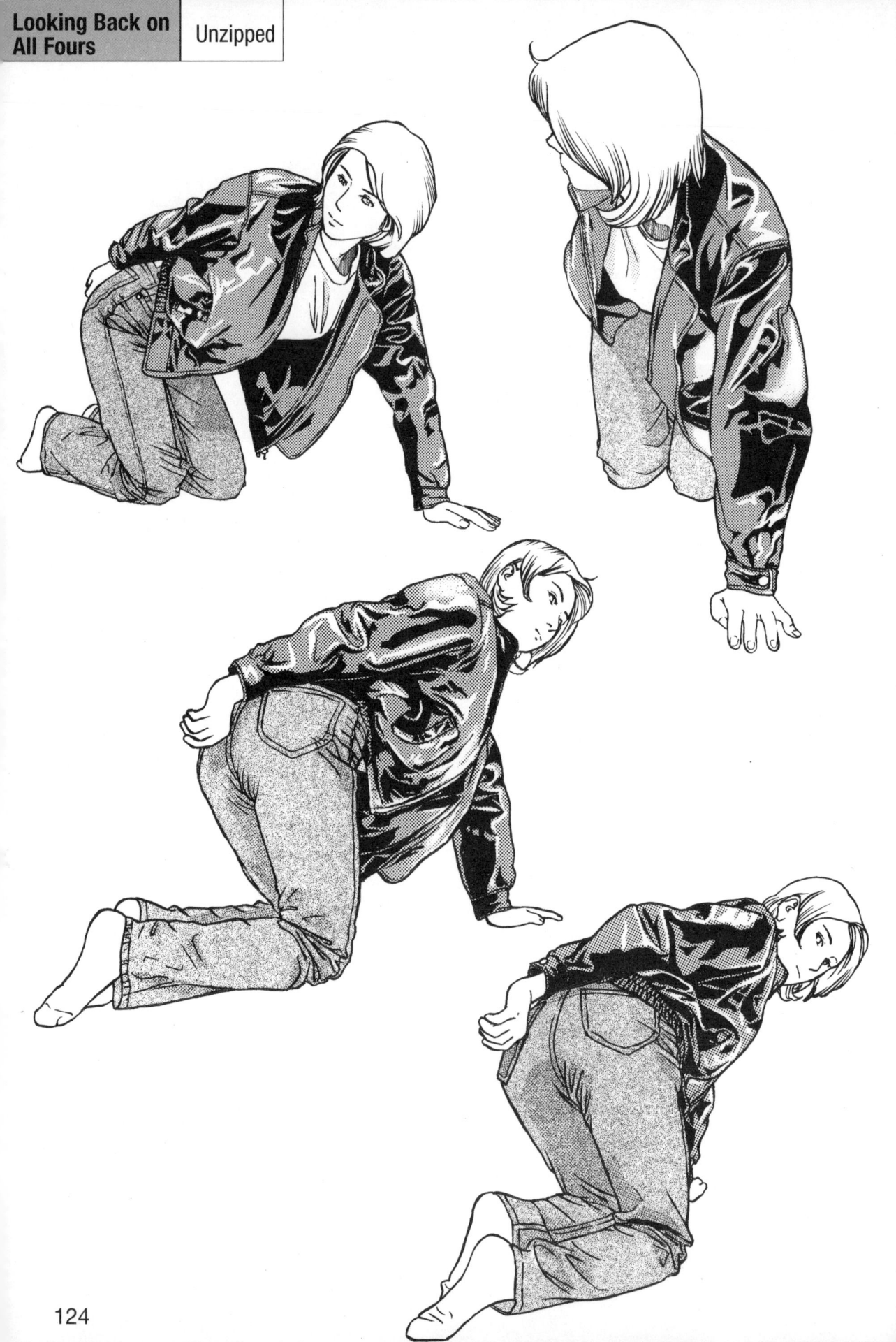

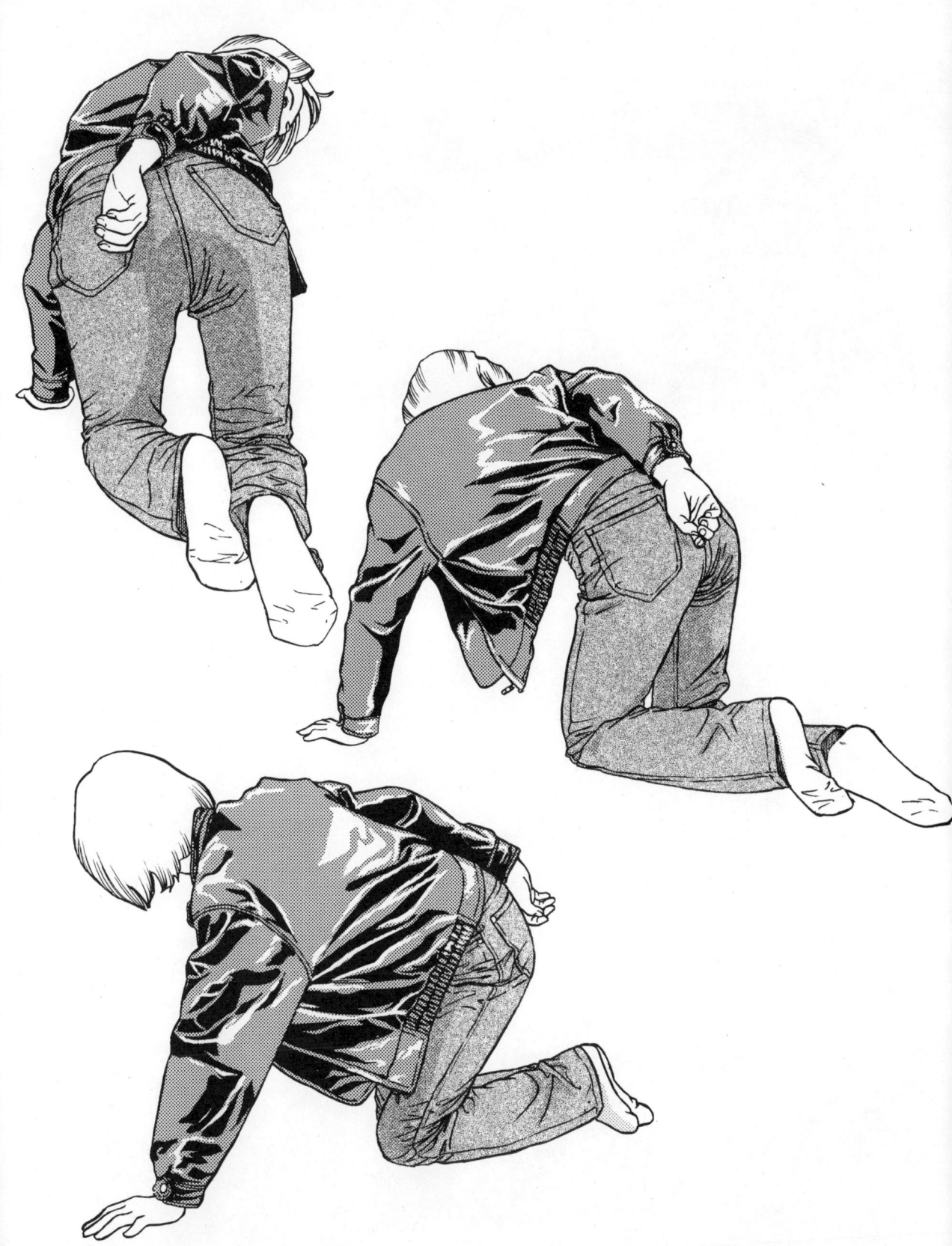

Putting On and Taking Off Jackets – Part 1

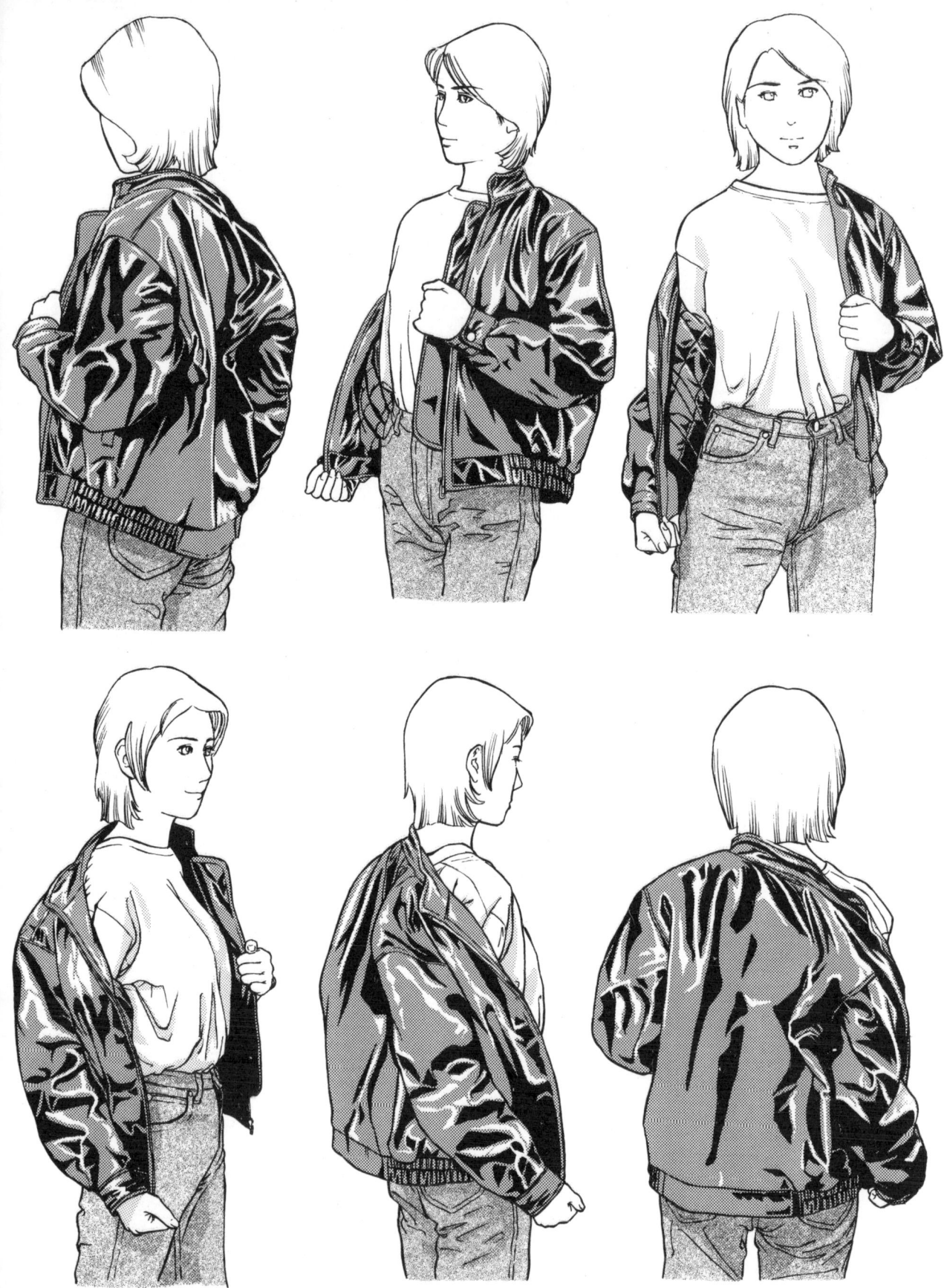

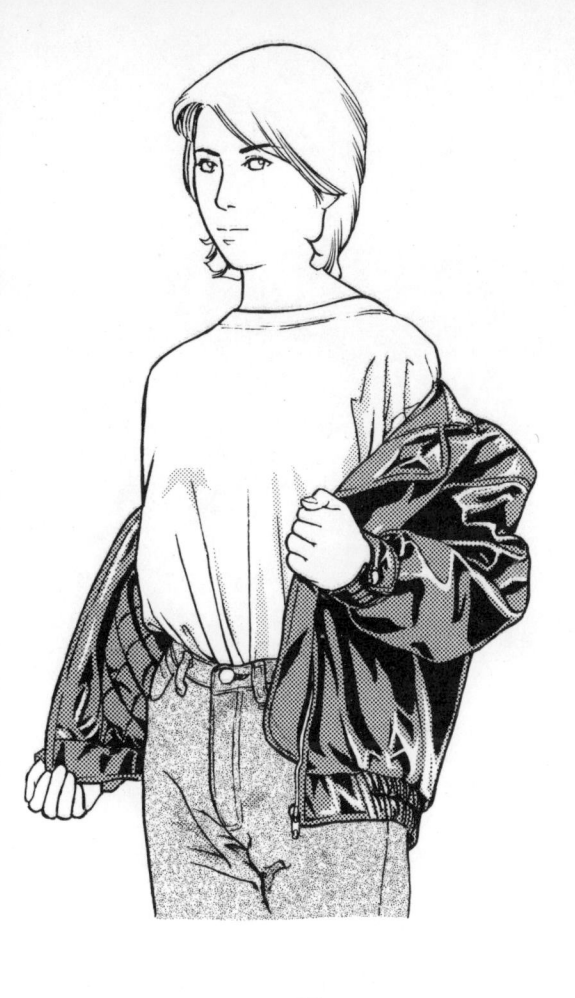
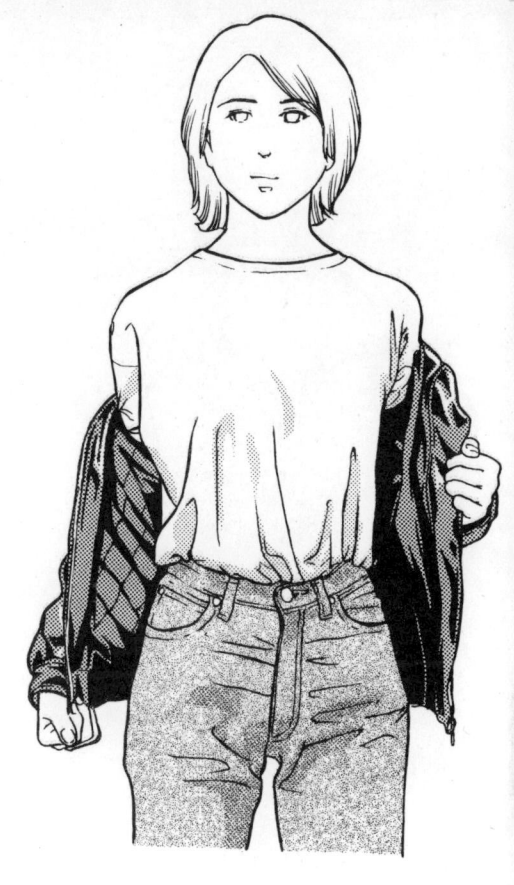
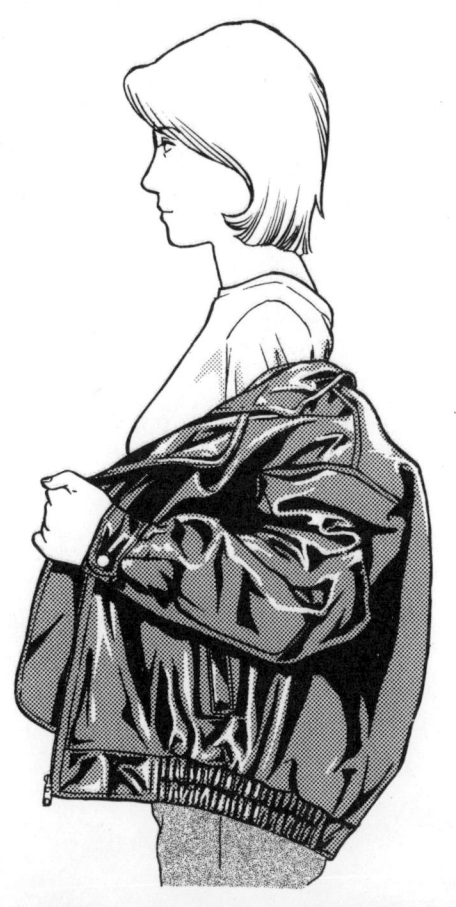
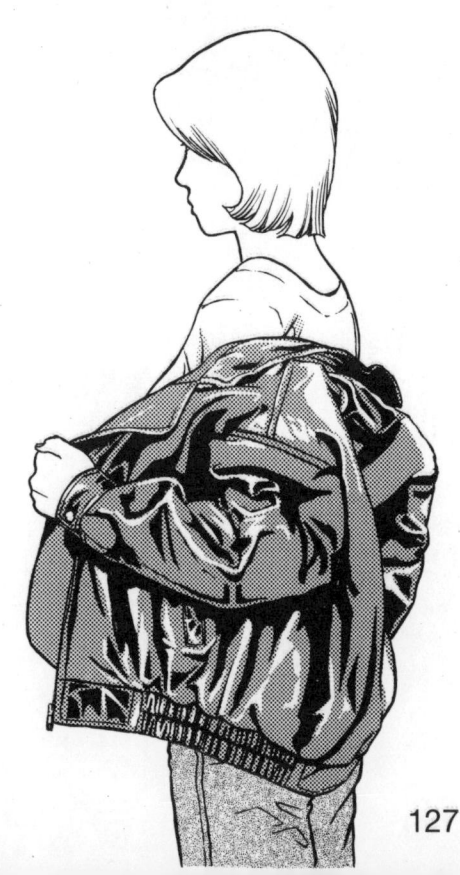

Putting On and Taking Off Jackets – Part 2

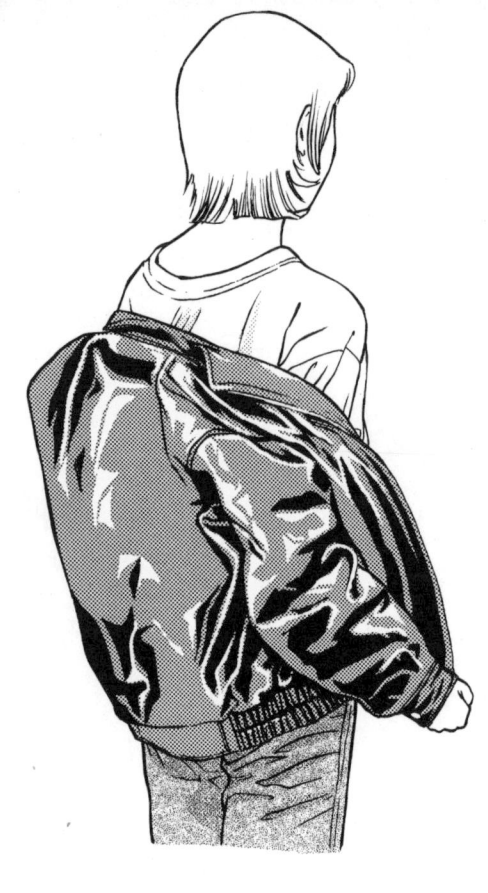
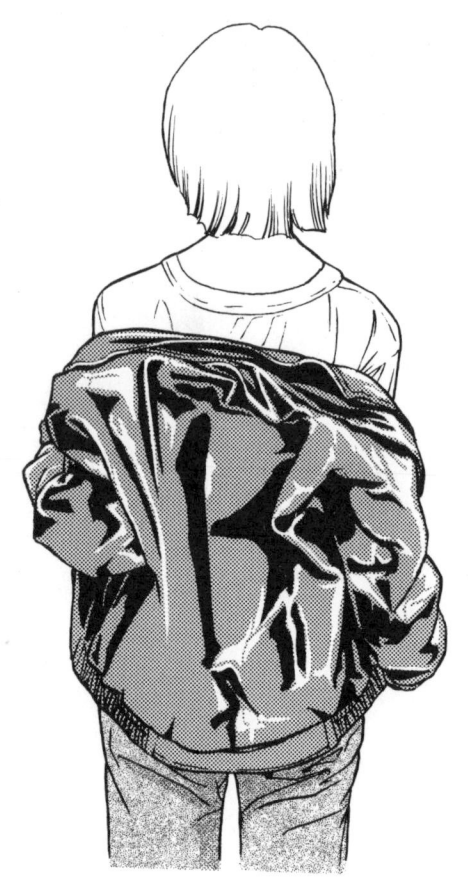
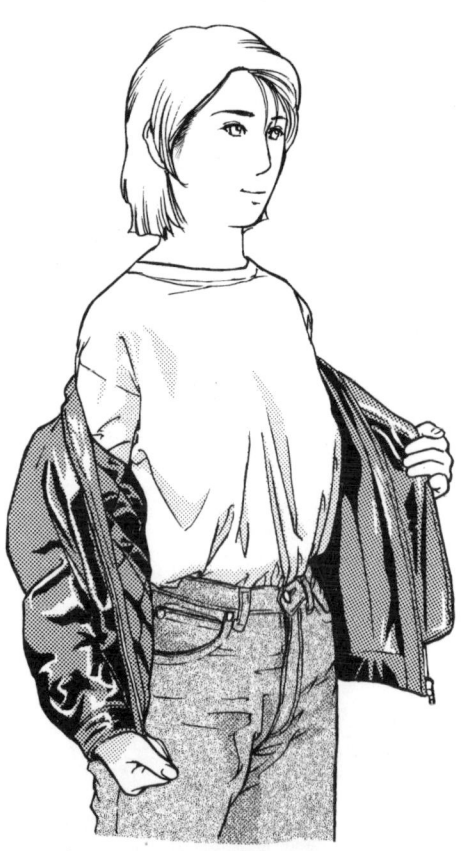
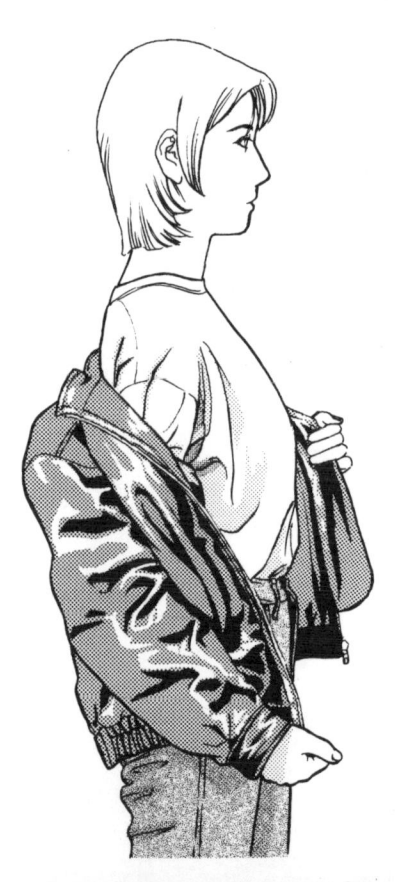